Healthcare Management Strategy, Communication, and Development Challenges and Solutions in Developing Countries

Healthcare Management Strategy, Communication, and Development Challenges and Solutions in Developing Countries

Edited by Emmanuel K. Ngwainmbi

LEXINGTON BOOKS
Lanham • Boulder • New York • Toronto • Plymouth, UK

Published by Lexington Books
A wholly owned subsidiary of Rowman & Littlefield
4501 Forbes Boulevard, Suite 200, Lanham, Maryland 20706
www.rowman.com

10 Thornbury Road, Plymouth PL6 7PP, United Kingdom

British Library Cataloguing in Publication Information Available

Library of Congress Cataloging-in-Publication Data

Healthcare management strategy, communication, and development challenges and solutions in developing countries / edited by Emmanuel K. Ngwainmbi.
p. ; cm.
Includes bibliographical references and index.
ISBN 978-0-7391-8566-7 (cloth : alk. paper) -- ISBN 978-0-7391-8567-4 (electronic)
I. Ngwainmbi, Emmanuel K., 1969- editor of compilation.
[DNLM: 1. Health Communication. 2. Developing Countries. 3. Public Health. WA 590]
RA441.5
362.109172'4--dc23
2013050507

∞™ The paper used in this publication meets the minimum requirements of American National Standard for Information Sciences Permanence of Paper for Printed Library Materials, ANSI/NISO Z39.48-1992.

Printed in the United States of America

Contents

Introduction

Another View of Communication and Healthcare Management in Developing Regions

Emmanuel K. Ngwainmbi

We cannot dissociate the notion of *health* from that of *perception, well-being, ill-being,* or the act of sharing beliefs, practices, and other forms of knowledge. The sharing can be among learned ones, between learned and unlearned ones, or between the care provider and the service receiver. As both science and art, the overall purpose of healthcare practice is to prevent disease, improve human comfort, and promote the policies put together by a community that are designed to extend life. To describe healthcare without taking into account the normative (social, cultural, educational, and economic) systems of a group of people is to live without water—an impossibility. Within the same caveat, understanding the nature of good or poor health requires knowing the thought process of the individual or the values of the community and its socio-economic strengths and frailties. A community living with misconceptions about the nature and function of a disease is likely to deplete its human resources over time.

Much data continues to be recorded on health challenges increasingly being faced by countries with weak economies in Africa, Asia, and the Middle East. For example, according to some reports more than 1.5 million adults and children have died of AIDS in Sub-Saharan Africa, accounting for 76 percent of the world's AIDS deaths in 2013. The number of AIDS-related deaths in that region alone in 2011 was 33 percent. The high numbers are due in part to cultural norms and the absence of a consistent method of collecting data. The practice of polygamy, prostitution, the rampant use of multiple sex partners, early marriages, widespread poverty, and weak judicial systems incapable of bringing rape under control account for the high rate of HIV-infections and deaths. It is difficult to prepare social intervention programs partly because many victims do not have identity cards and do not go to health care centers. However, observers have argued that behavioral change approaches are not likely to stop the HIV/AIDS global pandemic.

Proper healthcare is a recurring challenge in developing countries with the highest percentage of people living and dying from the disease. Ninety-seven percent of the world's population of 7.06 billion (July 2012 estimate) live in developing countries, a growth credited to high birth rates and a young population in these nations. That population is growing at 2.4 percent per year and projected to reach at least 20 billion by 2050. A widely distributed report published by the United Nations Population Division in 2011 states that future population growth will take place largely in developing countries. The greatest increase is expected in the forty-eight poorest countries, which have high economic vulnerability. These countries have poor human development indicators, such as low life expectancy at birth, very low per capita income, and low levels of education. Of the forty-eight countries, thirty-three are in Sub-Saharan Africa (among them, Burundi, Ethiopia, Mozambique, and Zambia), while fourteen are in Asia (including Bangladesh, Cambodia, Nepal, and Yemen), and one is in the Caribbean (Haiti). This calls into question the capacity of those countries to have a steady growth of their population. If they do do not strengthen their economy how are they to sustain population growth?

The sustainability of a population is inextricably tied to the communication of proper health management practices. No country or community can claim to have a strong economy if the majority of its population is permanently ill—certainly not developing countries seeking to develop their resources through industrialization. International agencies, non-

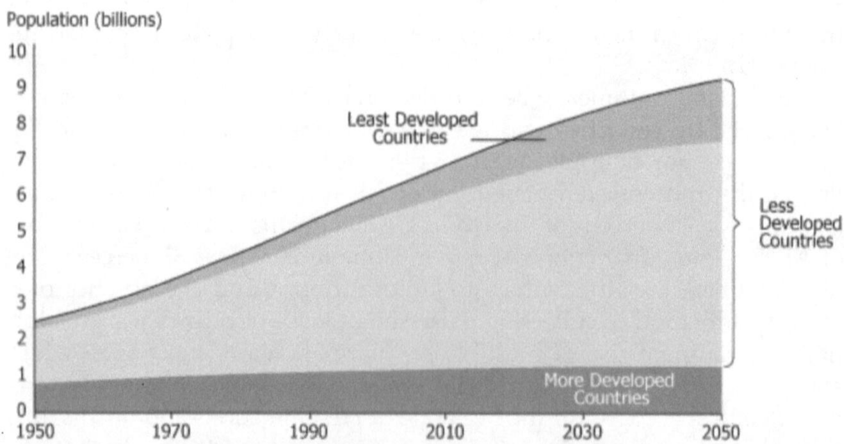

Figure 0.1. The Future of World Population Growth Source: United Nations Population Division, World Population Prospects. The 2010 Revision, medium variant (2011). Available at http://www.prb.org/Publications/Datasheets/2012/world-population-data-sheet/fact-sheet-world-population.aspx. Accessed 6 October 2013.

governmental organizations (NGOs), regional economic communities, and other civic groups have been working round the clock since the turn of the twentieth century, to provide services that allow all citizens to enjoy a free and healthy life in a safe, progressive environment. The fact that those organizations are still serving in the countries dubbed "developing" calls into question their effectiveness and efficiency, the level of accountability, program and project monitoring mechanisms, and the overall rationale for their continued presence. Certainly, however, others may argue that they remain there to promote economic growth and improve the health standards of the "developing country."

The relationship between economic growth and health has also caught the attention of concerned development bodies, such as the World Health Organization and the Commission on Macroeconomics and Health. The Commission posits that malaria and HIV/AIDS and other infectious diseases contribute massively to slowing both economic growth and human development. Economists in the governments of the developing countries and heads of international development governing bodies, including Kofi Annan, former U.S. president George W. Bush, and European Union leaders consider human capital to be the key indicator for sustainable economic growth. Good health is inextricably linked to economic growth through higher labor productivity, demographic growth, and higher educational attainment. In the same way, wellness allows the mind to be more analytical and clairvoyant, explore new ideas, to share knowledge for positive growth, to do good things. The healthier people are, the greater their ability to harness knowledge and make wise decisions about their environment, their people, and the future. Conversely, poor health undermines growth. It is estimated that Africa's per capita growth rate of 0.4 percent from 1990 to 1997 was three times lower than it would have been had HIV/AIDS not existed. Ineffective communication actions, weak advocacy, and limited intervention measures may have contributed to the snail-like growth and information-sharing on the deadly disease.

Specific communication practices in different healthcare settings can affect the success of healthcare management and development. The application of information and communication appliances in support of health programs has its origins in geo-political, historical, and demographic factors, compounded by previous and emerging global and strategic imperatives. This means that the degree of persistence shown by indigenous cultures and the normative systems and corporations can change the existing structures. Emerging political imperatives have brought about a variety of changes in practices across various landscapes in developing regions and new communication patterns. Individuals and groups may not be prepared to manage such information technologies.

Various schools of thought have found that information and communication technologies have more capacity than they have demonstrated to support development in the education and health sectors, build local capacity, and support knowledge sharing and networking. For example, several key organizations have estimated that aid from international health organizations in the developed countries pays for less than 5 percent of the total healthcare costs in the developing world.[1] These organizations include Canada's Foreign Affairs Trade and Development Division, the Carter Center, USAID, UNFPA, WHO, UNICEF, UNESCO, and drug distribution giants such as Merck Pharmaceuticals who conduct research in tropical diseases. Though this does not include the operation costs and programs of national, intergovernmental, and non-governmental agencies in developing countries, it surely points to an additional burden on those countries, which already are suffering the effects of other obstacles. Fifty-two post-colonial countries in Africa struggle with diverse political systems that developed long ago. Changes in the global climate have depleted water/mineral resources and vegetation, displacing farmers and other local residents and causing new health challenges. Even the relocation of foreign companies to fertile and arable ancestral land previously occupied by the locals has affected the ecosystem and raised new health concerns.

POLITICAL AND ENVIRONMENTAL ORIENTATION AND HEALTH COMMUNICATION

The political and mental "wellness" of a country can be detected in the extent to which its people are free to express themselves or to seek economic, social, and educational opportunities. Environmental factors and disasters also prevent the overall good health of the population. Ill health of different sorts can come because the climate is hot or there are floods, hurricanes, drought, or desertification.

Poor countries that do not exploit their own natural resources could be causing great harm to the health and economic well-being of their people. It is easy to find examples of both kinds of disasters: The oil spill in the Niger Basin, the explosion of Lake Nyos in northwest Cameroon, the flooding of the Nile, earthquakes in the Democratic Republic of Congo, the dumping of waste gas products in Chad by Chinese oil companies, and hurricane strikes in the Central American and Caribbean regions. These are among the more recent disasters that have caused huge economic burdens and brought new challenges for local journalists and media management "executives" who must scramble to find financial resources and proper transportation to report and communicate on their impact. Further, those countries lack the financial capital to contain potential problems that can be addressed. Neither can they train the media to properly inform the population of the nature and potential of those mishaps to destroy the environment and human life.

These problems are further worsened by the fact that over 1 billion people—the majority living in developing countries—lack access to electricity and other clean sources of energy. Groundwater remains crucial for the livelihoods and food security of 1.2 to 1.5 billion rural households in the poorer regions of Africa and Asia, and for domestic supplies of a large part of the population elsewhere in the world.[2]

As the population in developing countries grows, water demands are increasing while water levels continue to drop due to global warming, a condition caused by human beings. This situation will mostly likely get worse in the near future if we choose to believe a Gallup World Poll taken seven years ago of a representative sample of people from 132 countries. The report appropriately shows a positive correlation between per capita income in a country and the average self-reported life satisfaction there. The poll data also finds that high-income countries have greater life satisfaction than low-income countries.

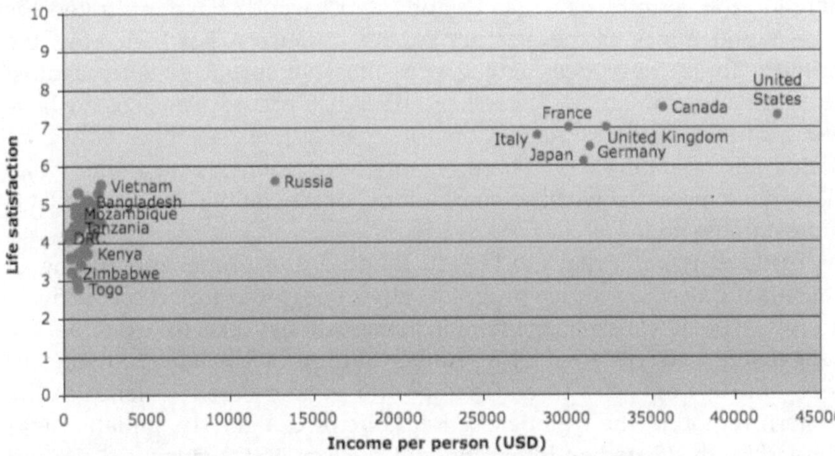

Figure 0.2. Income Distribution, Developing and G8 Countries Source: http://www.givewell.org/international/technical/additional/Standard-of-Living. Accessed 8 October, 2013.

When we recall that the majority of countries popularly described as being in a "developed state" their former colonies of Germany, Spain, Portugal, Belgium, or the Netherlands, we can reach the hasty conclusion that users of information technology in the post-colonized regions keep the same colonial psychology. Since one's skills are based on one's thought processes and thought processes are influenced by political orientation, thinking and interaction are informed by perceptions of self. Hence we might expect a francophone user of an information product to use the tools and channels in communicating mostly with like-minded people.

In a similar way, the governments in developing countries have weak economies and fragile democracies. Corruption is common, particularly in state-run institutions. This would seem to further the rationale for international non-governmental healthcare programs that operate directly with the population.

The rich heritage of natural and ecological resources in Africa, Asia, and some Caribbean countries, with their biodiversity and extensive fresh vegetation, are reportedly gradually being replaced by infrastructures. Trees and other forms of flora are hauled away on heavy machines to make way for electrification, installation of telephone towers, and construction of roads and warehouses. The fresh water reserves in Congo and the Nile and Zambezi basins are damaged as investors seek the gold, uranium, and oil reserves. All of this brings new types of communication situations and health challenges.

Take the case of the Democratic Republic of Congo, which harbors at least 22 percent of Africa's forest resources. Using mostly eye witness accounts, media report that militia from within the country and from neighboring countries such as Uganda and Rwanda have infiltrated the forests and mines as they clamor for the resources. For their part, the military forces have been engaged in massive sexual violence against children and women. More cases of HIV/AIDS occur because of the lawless attitudes of the military. Corrupt legal systems set repeatedly convicted sex offenders free. These horrors and other human rights violations have made the work of international organizations and local NGOs almost untenable.

Another issue is that the lack of funding and proper monitoring of sensitization and advocacy programs have a negative impact on the overall role of healthcare management in some nations. Take, for example, the sensitization activities led by a number of local NGOs, government centers, and UN agencies to end sexual and gender-based violence in the eastern region of the Democratic Republic of Congo. The initiative was funded by the Canadian International Development Agency in 2006, and the project ended in September 2013. Approximately 70,000 people were reached and educated about prevention methods in a population of more than 2 million. Further investigation reveals that the reported results were based on monthly meetings by UN representatives in the territories of North and South Kivu, pamphlets distributed during campaigns, and email exchanges among campaign teams.

HEALTH AND LANDSCAPE IN NATIONAL DEVELOPMENT

Africa's resources, the ecosystem, and political turmoil have contributed to the creation and spread of diseases. Many contradictions and controversies surround HIV/AIDS, such as culture, religion and morality, antiretroviral (ARV) treatment, sex education, funding, social media, and complacency. Indeed, health workers, midwives, and other health professionals are at odds with local religious and traditional leaders over appropriate approaches to providing proper healthcare to the local population. Public sensitization programs and other intervention methods and mechanisms designed and implemented by local NGOs and those sponsored by intergovernmental agencies over the years have not been as efficient as expected in reducing the spread of HIV/AIDS, malaria, and other deadly diseases. There is limited funding, abandonment of the projects by implementing agencies, too many agencies in the same locale duplicating services. Resources are often insufficient to really help areas with a high population. In some instances resources are mismanaged. Funds allocated for specific activities end up in the private bank accounts of local officials. A lot of money is spent reimbursing international staff for unnecessary travel or sponsoring them to meetings and conferences without a plan to implement lessons learned. In some cases, operations managers are pressured to spend all the money in the budget or risk having a smaller budget for the preceding fiscal year.

Different schools of thought blame slow economic progress not on widespread pandemics ravaging the population and depleting human capital but on morality issues. There are plenty of issues to blame, such as corruption, mismanagement, and under-exploitation of natural resources. One factor is the exodus of young men and women and seasoned professionals to developed countries to seek a better life for themselves and their families, both in the adopted country and back home.

This book does not focus on those factors or theories but it will refer to policies and practices based on such theories as the health belief model, planned action, AIDS risk reduction model, and social cognitive theory. Among others, it recognizes the fact that contradictions surround intervention approaches, even polio immunization. Cultural, religious, and moral controversies arising over ARV treatment, sex education, funding, social media, and societal complacency are highlighted in various chapters.

The book covers the provision of health services, public health administration, healthcare policy, advocacy, and intercultural or intergroup communication. It looks at challenges faced by health experts in such intergovernmental institutions as the United Nations Fund for Population (UNFPA), UNICEF, and the governments they serve. Contributors discuss solutions for conveying healthcare messages to affected populations through the government. The book further examines communication strategies in healthcare practices in Somalia, Madagascar, Nigeria, the Democratic Republic of Congo, and India, and provides solutions for the management of malaria, HIV/AIDS, polio, and other infectious diseases. It presents experiences from international health organizations, commissioned in poor countries to assist national governments in improving the wellbeing of their citizens. This volume analyzes the spread of infectious diseases and offers communication strategies for the management of such diseases as malaria, HIV/AIDS, polio, and others.

Issues addressed include challenges experienced by intergovernmental organizations in dealing with partners and stakeholders, and by healthcare practitioners in working with the government legislating women's issues and rights. It also looks at programmatic issues in communication and outreach, ways of increasing investment in reproductive family planning and gender empowerment, and other factors that impede effective monitoring and implementation of laws and policies. The issues regard population and development, reproductive health and rights, women empowerment, gender-based violence (GBV), youth activity, and HIV and AIDS.

The first chapter presents communication as something that can support health programs and bring positive results. Drawing examples from Africa, Andy Alali discusses how communication actions can enhance the programming of health activities and promotion of information sharing among different groups. In chapter 2, Srinivas Melkote reappraises development and community health communication, focusing on disparities in development. He reconstructs the meaning and goal of development within the context of social justice, social mobilization, and participation action. Following this analysis, Mario Azevedo looks at public health in Africa's development agenda within the same theoretico-operational framework of health and social change.

In chapter 4, SubbaRao Gavaravarapu examines the practice of communication and the history of nutrition education in India, and raises the question of whether awareness on proper nutrition led to behavioral change in the latter twentieth century in India. In another chapter, the author provides different perspectives on the changes in food and nutrition priorities in the public health agenda of this populous country.

Still drawing from the Indian experience, Ravindra Kumar Vemula complains of the failure of media campaigns to curb the spread of HIV/AIDS among the marginalized population and blames the government for not being committed. In India, inequalities in income, education, and access to health services are not taken into account when developing or delivering health programs. Regional and gender disparities further undermine efforts of foreign funding groups.

In Sub-Saharan African countries, some political figures outside the ruling party use media platforms to intentionally misinform the public, rather than serve as spokespersons against campaigns designed to prevent communicable diseases. Adebayo Fayoyin and Cosmos Eze tell why persuasion campaign strategies launched in local communities in Nigeria failed to immunize the population against polio. They offer a multitude of reasons for the failure, some linked to unscrupulous politicians, domestic understanding, or cultural taboos. In low-income countries such as Somalia, Niger, and Madagascar, health and population welfare ministers show more interest in seeking personal rewards than in collaborating with international financial sponsors to improve reproductive mother and child health and nutrition programs.

Achu Lordfred revisits loopholes in the agendas of ministries of health and international financing agencies. He offers innovative techniques promoted by the United Nations Population Fund to bridge the gaps. Adebayo Fayoyin presents two case studies, the boycott of polio immunization in northern Nigeria in 2003 and 2008 and the crisis over condom quality, shortage, and promotion in Kenya. Elsewhere, the text explains the impact of public health controversies and reaffirms the significance of the ecological approach to public health communication.

The chapter by Charles Okigbo, Nan Yu, and Angella Napakol seeks to remind readers of the controversies and contradictions in the widely documented story about HIV/Aids in Africa. They contend that knowledge of HIV/AIDS does not gel with expected behavior, and that more knowledge of the disease does not necessarily guarantee lower rates of infection. Certainly, the image of AIDS and its controversies complicates containment and management.

This book is written primarily for communication researchers. It is suitable for graduate courses in communication and healthcare management. It attempts to provide working knowledge to healthcare providers, administrators, policy makers, and practitioners in developing countries. This information can serve as a supplemental undergraduate course resource.

Several chapters discuss using strategies for implementing communication techniques and information among senior government officials, as well as focus groups representing the population, to reduce the spread of infectious diseases and curb infant and maternal mortality rates. It provides answers to educate government officials, healthcare practitioners, and focus groups (NGOs included), to bring about meaningful, sustainable development. Some chapters present case studies on information/knowledge sharing among target groups; and on policy and economics based challenges. Field researchers and staff working with international organizations in various countries share onsite experiences.

The book is divided into five sections:

- Part I: "Theory and Design" provides an overview of healthcare management theories and development communication concepts that address health and social welfare. It looks at the role and practice of communication in developing countries.
- Part II: "Health and Communication Policy" describes different communications strategies that are being used in a number of countries, to manage pressing healthcare issues such as malaria, HIV/AIDS, and polio. It shows the impact of existing national healthcare policies upon the population.

- Part III: "Experiences in the Field: Resources and Practice" analyzes resources, practice and case studies in healthcare management in India, Madagascar, Uganda, Somalia, Nigeria, and other developing regions.
- Part IV: "Implementation of Healthcare Programs: Case Studies and Practitioners' Experiences," examines the interface between focus group heads, experts from international intergovernmental agencies, and senior government authorities.
- Part V: "Cultural Factors and Funding" addresses advocacy and implementation of appropriate measures for sustainable communication enhanced healthcare management. Chapters offer an assessment of health management and communication strategies and provide suggestions for existing and potential donors among international agencies, health workers, advisers, and national governments.

EPILOGUE

Developing countries are still haunted by low capacity, limited capital, and overpopulation. The communication of health information will remain a challenge as long as governments do not invest at least 20 percent of their budget on health communication, monitoring, and evaluation. Cultural taboos also must be properly addressed about the leading causes of death, such as HIV/AIDS, cholera, diarrhea, and tuberculosis.

No amount of financing or increase in the number of healthcare personnel will yield visible results for health-related international organizations in any developing country if local governments remain corrupt. Leaders also must fully understand the import of health communication in the economic development agenda of their own country. International organizations must operate with transparency and collaborate with the authorities in those countries to bring measurable, sustainable results. They must have an exit plan, for extended stay has led to complacency and lukewarm attitude within the ranks of government and among local investors and businesses.

NOTES

1. Available at http://www.imva.org/Pages/orgfrm.htm. Accessed 25 July 2013.
2. "Managing Water Under Uncertainty and Risk," Vol. 1 (2012). UNESCO. For more, visit http://www.unesco.org

I

Theory and Design

ONE

The Role of Communication in Supporting Health Programs

A Researcher's Perspective and Ethical Considerations

Andy O. Alali

INTRODUCTION

In the last few decades, the emergence of health communication as a discipline has ushered in a new era that stimulated scholarly interest regarding the role communication plays in health care, especially in the promotion of healthy lifestyles. As a relatively new discipline, research and theories in the area have convincingly linked communication to health and healing, and in the process scholars in the field have created a marketplace for understanding and sharing health communication strategies that influence health. Clearly, the activities of health communication scholars serve as guide for practitioners by stipulating the appropriate ways the diverse characteristics of audiences and the complex interacting influences on healthy lifestyles can be situated and integrated. Integrated health communication is key to achieving a specified health promotion goal or objective.

Yet, with this new era, health communication is faced with a distinct challenge: How to provide health information in simple and understandable terms so that the public can act on it. This challenge, however, is compounded by some theoretical constraints that impede health promotion objectives. The impact is felt in developing nations where current research activities and health promotion efforts have not developed indigenous health communication theories. Indigenous involvement is necessary if available health knowledge is to serve as the content of persuasive arguments against unhealthy behavior and destructive lifestyles, particularly among the youth. What we are admitting here is that, even though current studies in the field of health communication have produced what Pettegrew (1988) calls "theoretical pluralism," they are not sufficiently embodied in the African contexts of communication. Besides this, they are not aimed at developing effective health promotion and disease control programs in Africa. This is due, in part, to how the African contexts of communication have been relegated to the Western notion of communication process (Nwosu et al. 1995).

The purpose of this chapter is to capture the role health communication plays in health contexts, particularly Africa's. We will try to provide some research direction to facilitate health communication campaigns in this region. In the process, a specific ethical culture for health communication research in Africa will be discussed.

FOCUS ON PUBLIC HEALTH IN AFRICA

Why is there so much focus on public health in Africa? Analysis of the health status of most African countries would indicate that the health of its peoples has become an increasingly critical issue in their developmental agenda. While significant measures of health and wellness may differ from country to country and region to region, epidemiological data, research, and surveillance reports offer a bleak picture and factors that speak to commonalities among the health challenges in Africa. The challenges include barriers to health care access, disparities in access to private health care, a lack of knowledge, and inadequate use of health care services (AfDB 2013; World Bank 2011; Cooke 2009; WHO 2009).

Let's examine some of the major public health issues that have prompted the focus.

The pandemic explosion of communicable diseases such as the human immunodeficiency virus (HIV) that causes acquired immune deficiency syndrome, AIDS, is a case in point. It is estimated that 69 percent (23.8 million) of the roughly 34 million people infected with HIV live in Sub-Saharan Africa (UNAIDS 2012a). Of particular concern is that 91 percent of the world's HIV-positive children live in Africa. The statistics also show that a majority (97 percent) of those living with HIV reside in low- and middle-income countries of Sub-Saharan Africa (UNAIDS 2012b). In Nigeria alone, there are about 3.4 million cases, with adults (3.7 percent) age fifteen to forty-nine and 1.7 million women living with HIV/AIDS (AVERT 2012). By now, it should be obvious that the focus on the HIV/AIDS epidemic in Africa is not misguided. Beyond the human cost, in research the prevalence does provide opportunities for analysis of the role health communication plays in education and disease prevention.

Another area of health concern relates to the rise of substance abuse. In most African countries, alcohol is used to perform important social and cultural functions that have encouraged its abuse. Alcohol abuse is particularly evident during ritual ceremonies, communal planting and harvesting, and spirit media celebrations (Acuda 1995, p. 24). Consequently, a busy health care clinic in Harare reported that "66 percent of the men and 48 percent of the women who drank were getting drunk on each occasion" (Acuda 1995, p. 24).

Because alcohol use is socially sanctioned and culturally accepted in most parts of Africa, the aggressive marketing of this substance seems to legitimize its use in casual settings and social functions, fostering abuse. Clearly, effective health campaigns should be designed to counterbalance the enormous production and social marketing of alcohol that exists in most parts of Africa, thus positioning preventive measures that might help reduce alcohol abuse.

A more troubling concern regarding substance abuse is that most parts of the continent are experiencing an increase in the use of psychoactive substances, such as tranquilizers, cannabis, stimulants, and, more recently, cocaine and heroin. Like alcohol abuse, the use of psychoactive substances may alter the user's state of mind and possibly lead to life-threatening behavior. For example, the sharing of needles by intravenous drug users facilitates the spread of HIV infection (Bergendahl and Hsu 1995). While the intravenous use of drugs has not been directly linked to the increased HIV infections in the continent, United Nations estimates have shown that 37,000 people in Africa die every year from diseases associated with the use of illegal drugs. Given this reality, it would be irresponsible for health promotion and disease prevention curricula to exclude issues related to substance abuse.

Additionally, the growing literature on tobacco research has provided abundant evidence that smoking is a health hazard. Descriptive epidemiological findings on cancer occurrence correlate with levels of exposure to cigarette smoke, which has contributed to the increased incidence of cancer of the lungs, larynx, esophagus, and oral cavity (Page et al. 1995, p. 220). Recent studies show that one in ten heavy smokers is likely to get lung cancer (Perera 1996, p. 54). Similarly, smoking is known to increase the chance that a person will have heart disease, a stroke, or chronic obstructive pulmonary disease.

In spite of the convincing evidence of health risks, cigarette tobacco continues to be one of the most commonly used substances in Africa. In South Africa, one in three adults smoke cigarettes (Alali 1997). Nearly 50 percent of South African males and 18 percent of females are cigarette smokers. Over 25,000 South Africans die each year of smoking-related causes. Cigarette smoking is present in 83.1 percent of South African coronary heart disease patients (McKibbin 1994). Clearly, it appears that aggressive tobacco company advertising in South Africa has not been met with strong anti-smoking campaigns.

As is discussed in other chapters of this book, AIDS, substance abuse, and smoking illnesses are not the only health problems that threaten life in Africa. Malaria, for example, accounts for more than 1 million deaths every year. Recently, the World Health Organization (WHO) announced that 1996 was the worst year on record in Africa for cerebrospinal meningitis, an inflammation of the lining of the brain and spinal cord, with around 150,000 reported cases and 16,000 deaths. These health problems, as well as the outbreak of cholera and Ebola in some regions, have far-reaching implications, not least of which is a shorter life expectancy in the affected countries (Alali and Nwosu 1996).

Most African countries also grapple with such public health issues as cardiovascular maladies, cancer, fake and adulterated pharmaceuticals, the high cost of medicines, vehicular deaths, and the problems of developing good health policies and management efforts. Religious and ethnic challenges also undermine public health efforts. For example, as is described and discussed at length in another chapter, a Center for Strategic and International Studies (CSIS) report on public health in Africa documents how a number of rural imams in northern Nigeria "obstructed the donor-driven polio eradication campaign, leading to a renewed outbreak of the disease over several years, with cases spreading as far as Sudan and Kenya" (Cooke 2009, p. 8).

Such issues have had an impact on the public health status of African countries. Besides the overall decrease in life expectancy, these problems have increased maternal mortality and the prevalence of HIV and brought an alarming increase in tuberculosis and more cases of malaria, all of which also cause developmental challenges. These fundamental issues have influenced public health discussions and prompted health promotion and disease prevention efforts aimed at increasing life expectancy and reducing infant and maternal mortality.

At the center of these discussions are health communication interventions and campaign strategies that can deliver effective health messages to the right audience. Consequently, we have to be reminded of the inseparable connection between communication and health, particularly with the explosion of information and communication technology (ICT) in Africa.

Internet connectivity across the African continent is increasing, as is its potential for useful application in e-Health, particularly in public health promotion and disease prevention. One report notes that broadband penetration has risen rapidly. For example, broadband was used by 0.1 percent of the population in 2000, an estimated 7 percent usage in 2010. It is projected that by 2060, coverage will reach 99 percent of the African population (AfDB 2011). The evolving technology, with its reach, will create a greater opportunity to increase the effectiveness of health systems. And, with its rich research agenda and grounded paradigms and theories, the field of health communication will construct the bridge to public health. We argue that health communication is an effective public health tool, if its strategies are contextually developed and centered within contemporary cultures and evolving public health realities. The health communication efforts that work in Africa for Africans cannot be derived from Western ideology.

Clearly, these public health challenges necessitate effective health communication efforts to educate and help reduce preventable diseases. It is no wonder that, from Algeria to Zimbabwe, country-specific public health efforts are now focused on how to reduce the burden of diseases that result in death among younger generations. This is predicated on the belief that as the prevalence of disease decreases, the development agenda of African countries can be propelled by a capable and healthy workforce to create immense resources that position Africans to be equal participants in world affairs.

RESEARCH CONSTRAINTS IN STUDYING HEALTH COMMUNICATION IN AFRICA

The magnitude of the health problems in Africa has long prompted international donor agencies to address the crises. Agencies such as the WHO, the United Nations Children's Emergency Fund (UNICEF), the United Nations Educational, Scientific and Cultural Organization (UNESCO), the United States Centers for Disease Control and Prevention (CDC), and a number of Europe-based organizations provide funding and technical assistance for research, education and disease prevention efforts. Equally involved in this effort are regional organizations, such as the Economic Community of West African States (ECOWAS), the African Union (AU), and African Development Bank (AfDB).

Yet most of the research aimed at health promotion and disease prevention efforts in Africa appears to be casually linked to the public's health. Communication models developed by those who study health issues have not fully addressed individual and societal factors. Neither do their studies link theory and practice in health promotion and disease control. This is not to suggest that health communication research should be more diagnostic to replace medical experts and those trained in epidemiology. Rather, health communication should be studied as an opportunity to associate health and well-being with culture, values, attitudes, and behavior. It deserves a higher level of commitment from those of us who study the field. Our research findings are expected to stimulate and guide the direction of future health promotion efforts and subsequent research endeavors.

Unfortunately, much of the health communication research coming out of Africa is anecdotal and is yet to help produce campaign programs that bring realistic perspectives to health issues. This, in my view, is attributable to the slow-to-evolving nature of health communication research in Africa. Consequently, it would not be far-fetched to suggest that the dominant paradigms affecting theoretical and methodological issues in health communication research have failed to offer the value of their constructs on health communication practices.

The health communication field has not advanced helpful theories. The social dimension of health care communication seems to fail in the long run, even when the campaign appears successful. Health communicators must learn to collaborate effectively with medical and social sciences. Let's explore this notion further here.

First, the field of health communication, particularly in Africa, has not advanced efficacious theories. It is evident that the current theories of health communication are not sufficient to frame relevantly African health beliefs to explain the elements that shape health campaigns and, in the long run, predetermine health outcomes.

A good example is the AIDS campaigns in Africa, where health communication efforts have resulted in disappointing levels of compliance. African communication research focuses on the end-result or effectiveness of a specific health message. This leaves out a full understanding of the target audience, how they interact with health providers and the sociocultural variables that impede compliance (Alali and Nwosu 1996).

To illustrate this, we will point to the issue of health care provider interaction within the context of public health. Health care providers are crucial instruments of change. They are trained to carry out primary health care, facilitate health education, and execute community intervention programs. In most cases, their encounters with patients create an opportunity for on-the-spot discussion of health issues and counseling for at-risk individuals. They are an important link that can affect patient compliance with health messages. However, current health communication research efforts in Africa have not helped clarify the impact of health providers on patient compliance. This begs an answer to the following question: Is it a benefit, or can it actually reduce compliance?

Some other questions research about communication and health care should seek to answer are: What type of interaction takes place between health professionals and the patients with whom they have contacts? Does the interaction center around the patients' health status and treatment, or does it deal with generalities? How much do we know about the patients' perceptions of health care providers? Does the health care provider-patient relationship provide emotional support beyond being a source of information? Does the patient perceive the care provider to be an authority figure? Do patients believe the care provider cares about them? Do health care providers use go-betweens, such as nurses, community health workers or, in the case of imminent death, the priest? What do the patients want in provider-patient communication? Do patients prefer to delegate decisions to their doctors? Do the ·health provider and patient make health decisions alone or jointly? These questions relate to communicative acts that have an impact on health and patient compliance and must be fully answered by research.

Second, one of the basic philosophical objectives of health communication research is to develop theories and models that foster social health. As health communication scholars, our research efforts are expected to make an impact on disease prevention and control, a socially important issue. Yet, most of the health communication research and the ill-defined sociological expectations that result from it may be ineffective in result or actually have dangerous health consequences. For example, there are questions about the rate at which health campaigns in Africa are declared "successful" and are immediately applied to other health communication contexts and disease prevention efforts. Many health campaigns have been declared successful without the benefit of a constructive evaluation tool that produces the kind of meaningful evaluation that can benefit those planning other health campaigns.

The problem for health communication campaigns is that the totality of tools that have come about through research in this field are insufficient to truly evaluate various African contexts of health. Perhaps even the research methods being used do not fit African contexts of communication. There have long been discussions about the appropriateness of research methods used in African contexts.[1] However, most recent discussions offer a more practical insight into the problems inherent universally applying research methods, especially those developed for Western societies, to African communication. Researchers argue that the African contexts and the Western contexts of communication are distinct and unconnected processes that cannot be evaluated with the same research methodologies (Nwosu et al. 1995). Nwosu et al. suggest that the Western models are not sufficient tools for evaluating African communication phenomena because the Western contexts elevate the individual as the primary source and receiver of information, while community and community values tend to be much more important in African societies (Nwosu et al. 1995, p. 398).

The third constraint deals with the interdisciplinary nature of the field that demands collaborative research effort. Health communication is an interdisciplinary field that draws from biomedical and the social and behavioral sciences. The current environment, in which personal and public health is at jeopardy, requires collaborative efforts to assist professionals in these fields. Interdisciplinary research is required to navigate treacherous waters where patient behavior and recklessness contribute substantially to disabilities and deaths. Understanding human behavior (a difficult variable to measure) is the key to the design of effective campaigns aimed at health promotion and disease prevention. Research efforts in health communication are not collaborative enough, hence their inability to understand the multiplicity of factors that affect human behavior and unhealthy lifestyles in Africa.

The day of the independent researcher is over. Health communication researchers must work with scholars from other fields. For example, biomedical researchers and medical associations in Africa should establish linkages with health communication scholars. Together they can develop ideas to encourage healthy lifestyles and educate people on how to prevent communicable diseases and chronic conditions, such as alcoholism.

The issues articulated here have far-reaching implications on health. A multidisciplinary approach can yield concrete data about the traditional and cultural issues that affect health campaigns, the political and social realities underlying national health policies, and how these policies shape health promotion, disease prevention efforts, and patient compliance. The peculiar nature of the contexts within which health communication research is studied needs to be revisited. Research needs to produce a shift in the paradigm.

The discussions about theoretical and methodological constraints provide the backdrop for developing effective research and, perhaps, identifying some ethical issues that health communication researchers in Africa should consider. To the extent that there are serious challenges for health communication research, the question here is, how do we navigate the so-called treacherous waters of health communication without imposing ineffective models that exacerbate health problems? We need to determine the areas of empirical study on which health communication researchers should focus. The author's desire is that this chapter draws a road map for a health communication research agenda in Africa and some of the ethical considerations for that research. This endeavor can usher in some important directions for health communication research.

NEW AREAS OF RESEARCH CONSIDERATIONS

The crucial role communication plays in health care has forced the exhaustive use of communication constructs that have been in place since before the epidemic diseases in Africa were identified. Communication scholars, especially those who study health, desperately need to understand the variables that render health campaigns ineffectual. We believe that the quality of measurements employed in research should, ultimately, lead to the development of theories and constructs that can facilitate effective health promotion campaigns. There are two areas for research considerations that demand immediate attention: appropriate research methods and health campaign evaluation tools.

For health communication research in Africa to have credibility, an appropriate research methodology for each health context must be employed. The appropriateness of a research method can be determined by evaluating the sources of information, measurement instruments, data collection, and analysis of information.

Health communication researchers are duty bound to clearly describe their sources of information so as to enable interpretations that take sources into consideration. This is not to suggest that confidentiality and anonymity should be compromised. Profiles that violate the confidentiality of sources must meet established guidelines for human subject research.

Another important element researchers must consider is the measurement instruments used for the research. In fact, it is an accepted orthodoxy in research that "the measurement instruments used for the purpose of data gathering must possess relevant psychometric evidences for the particular purposes being used" (Torabi 1993, p. 59). Therefore, it is an appropriate research method for the researcher to produce evidence for the validity and reliability of the instruments used in their research.[2] Selecting and developing the appropriate research tools is crucial to validate research findings.

If the culture of health communication research demands that the sources of information and the instruments used to measure information be clearly articulated, then the researcher must monitor the data collection process. Human error must be minimized or biased interpretations will result. The data generated from any research should be of the highest quality. Health communication research is not exempt from this standard.

The methodological soundness of research is not complete without an appropriate statistical tool to use in the analysis of the quantitative information collected. This is especially crucial when a small sample is used to draw inference on a larger population. If the expertise in statistical analysis is not available within the team of researchers, statistical consultants should be brought in.

EVALUATION TOOLS FOR THE HEALTH CAMPAIGN PROCESS

Ultimately, health communication research efforts should lead to the development of evaluation tools that will be directly useful to people and health promotion programs. The evaluation tools should focus on three areas: planning; program operations; and program outcomes (Pirie 1990).

Planning

During the planning stage, the measurement tools that result from the research effort ought to be able to evaluate key elements of a health program. The effects on the campaign and target audience demographics of existing data about the health problem; the budget available for the specific health campaign; and political realities, institutional constraints, and religious and ethnic concerns must be understood.

The target audience is one of the most important elements in public health campaigns. A target audience defines the ways a public health educator should design, conduct, and implement a campaign. The challenges posed by differences in audiences, as well as the different approaches and perspectives in health communication, require that appropriate evaluation tools be available to measure areas crucial to campaign success. For example: Who is the target audience? Does the proposed campaign identify the relevant categories of at-risk populations for the health problem? What personal characteristics, values, and ideological beliefs are likely to increase or impede the target audience's chances of compliance? What are the target audience's previous experiences? Most important, is the campaign culturally appropriate and sensitive to the target audience's sensibilities? These questions are aimed at impressing on public health educators that the target audience is at the center of health promotion and disease prevention and that notion should drive the design, nature, and fears of health campaigns.

An evaluation tool that carefully assesses these elements at the beginning of the campaign can illuminate the dark alleys that public health educators occasionally stumble into. Without understanding, they attempt to inoculate the public with messages that are aimed at changing their attitudes, beliefs, and behavior toward a health issue.

Program Operations

Research efforts may assist public health educators with the tools to best define objectives of their programs, particularly those that relate to the design, message objective, medium of communication, and channel selection.

The contents of a health campaign are a measure of their impact on learning and behavior. To determine whether the contents of a health campaign can produce the desired impact on learning and behavior, an evaluation tool should be capable of:

1. assessing the accuracy, relevance and currency of health information in the campaign;
2. determining the appropriateness of the information for the target audience;
3. assessing the readability level of the health message;

4. determining its objectivity, or lack of bias;
5. determining whether the health information is authoritative and supported by scientific evidence;
6. determining whether the health information is free of all controversial religious, political or ideological views; and
7. determining whether the health promotion objectives can be accomplished through the specified campaign.

Program Outcomes

Lastly, the health communication research that may result from these considerations is expected to focus on the development of an evaluation instrument for assessing health campaign effectiveness. Such an evaluation tool should ask the right questions about the effectiveness of the program: Will it continue/discontinue or expand/reduce? What shifts in behavior affect the campaign and will affect the policy initiative resulting from the campaign? The aim here is to develop evaluation measures that document short-term results of the campaign to determine whether the program objectives have been met and how well each stage of the campaign process are handled.

ETHICAL CONSIDERATIONS THAT SHOULD GUIDE HEALTH COMMUNICATIONS

Responsible research on health communication in Africa must be governed by specific ethical standards that are couched as six climate types: *professional; caring; role oriented; instrumental; efficient;* and *independent* (Victor and Cullen 1990). The generally accepted belief that ethics govern the moral acceptability of behavior in different contexts will have no value if those within a social context have no shared perception of how issues in their environment should be addressed and, to some extent, what is ethically acceptable behavior. Health communication research should not be made exempt from such precepts.

In health communication research, issues of ethics should revolve around specific objectives, such as the use of information to promote health and prevent the spread of diseases. Because health communication depends on information, it should not be value laden. In other words, ethical standards in health communication research should be governed by the six climate types articulated above (Victor and Cullen 1990). There is no doubt that the research tasks can be complicated by the ethical issues that confront researchers. However, not knowing about ethical systems and ethical principles may inhibit the success of the research.

Additionally, as health communication researchers, we must position ourselves as equal participants in the development of an appropriate framework for health promotion and disease prevention programs in Africa. Consequently, we must adopt ethical standards to guide our research agenda. The following are a few ethical issues that health communication researchers should consider.

Ethical Obligations of the Researchers

In developing an appropriate agenda for health communication research, it is important to define ethical obligations for researchers, especially in relation to their motivation for pursuing the research. Some scholars in the medical community accused communication researchers of being attracted to health communication research because there is money to be made through extramural funding (Burgoon 1995). To answer such criticisms, it is imperative that we establish ethical standards for researchers. We must validate the findings of those who are committed to the objectives of health communication. This is to say that researchers in this field are ethically bound to do the right thing by developing information that is not value laden but is valuable to health promotion and disease prevention. Anticipation of ethical problems in our research is the starting point for delineating ways to handle those ethical issues when they confront researchers.

Goal Orientation

Health communication research efforts should be goal oriented and realistic enough to offer effective solutions to problems as well as to anticipate the course of health campaigns. They must know the premise for a coordinated effort to promote healthy lifestyles for individuals and prevent the spread of diseases to the larger population. Again, such efforts must not be value laden.

Examination of Cultural and Religious Contexts

Health communication researchers in Africa must recognize and respect the cultural and religious sensibilities that surround the health issue being studied. Elements of culture and religion are not easily divorced from other aspects of life in Africa. Therefore, health communication researchers should examine carefully the cultural and religious backdrop for each health issue. Ethically appropriate ways must be found to recognize such issues, while still preserving the public's health.

Research and Policy Papers

Ethical research culture demands disclosure to enable readers to distinguish between research and a policy paper that is aimed at advancing a particular perspective. It is acceptable for a researcher to identify the sponsors of their research and the interest being represented in their paper. It is possible that the sources of research funding have a stake in the outcome of the studies they fund. We must declare our position and identify those who sponsor our research to eliminate any suspicion that may be associated with our findings or suggest that our research is motivated by financial gains from extramural fundings (Burgoon 1995).

Explicit and Open Communication

While research on health matters should encourage explicit and open communication about health, we must also exercise restraint over the extent to which researchers talk to patients about a potential disease. We are not physicians and, as such, should not be involved in epidemiological or clinical/diagnostic aspects of the disease or patient. If not well-managed, our lack of training in the pathology of diseases may create situations that panic the public into adopting unhealthy therapy.

Vulnerable Groups

Health communicators have the ethical obligation to design campaigns that aim at vulnerable groups who are most affected by preventable diseases. These campaigns should place heavy emphasis on *proximal interventions* that directly target individual perceptions and behaviors, as well as *contextual interventions* that focus on the larger contexts within which perceptions and behaviors are shaped.

Accuracy and Truth

Responsible and effective health communication depends upon accurate and unbiased research. Accuracy and truth in information gathering, analysis, and reporting provides decision makers with necessary information, and reduce misunderstanding by the public.

Timeliness

Health communication researchers must share their findings with the appropriate sources in a timely manner. Because of the nature of the subjects being studied, delaying the release of any findings may cost lives and, in the long run, diminish the importance of the findings.

CONCLUSION

Health communication is a real and inescapable global need. As customs of the world spread across cultures, so do health issues. There is a consensus among epidemiologists that no country is immune from disease. Research efforts aimed at health promotion and disease prevention in Africa must be articulated with a perspective that also recognizes diseases as a global issue with local implications. At the same time, health communication researchers must work within the political realities and institutional influences that determine the research agenda, directions, contexts, and outcome.

Health communication researchers should spearhead efforts to understand variables that interact with health promotion and disease prevention campaigns. Also, because the findings that result from such research have immediate and important impact on people's lives, health communication research requires a measure of variables which would be included in theoretical models for health promotion and disease prevention in Africa.

The challenge here is for health communication researchers to find ways to work collaboratively with allied fields to develop and disseminate accurate, up-to-date health information to the public so as to serve as persuasive injunctions that influence behavioral and lifestyle changes. There is a role in health communication research for all disciplines, particularly medicine, health education, communication, sociology, psychology, political science, philosophy, and anthropology. The fusion of these disciplines allows researchers to provide the public with health information in simple and understandable terms so they can act on it and, in return, reduce the probability of infection or contracting disease.

It is fitting to cite Becker (1995, pp. 19–20), who sums up the role of health communication scholars well:

> We can do our society a tremendous amount of good by bringing our special expertise to bear on getting people to lead healthier lifestyles. In the process we will also help the public and the institutional perception of our field quite considerably when they see us and other colleagues helping to solve problems that they recognize as important, especially if our efforts are successful.

Even though African health communication research potentially can make great contributions to the continent, its success depends on the collaboration that exists between stakeholders. For example, we must recognize the important roles interpersonal networks and the mass media must play in strengthening individual and community commitment to healthy lifestyles. That means our research must empower the media to provide adequate information about health and help interpersonal networks to be more sincere about their discussion of health issues. Collectively, the contributions of health communication researchers, allied fields, and institutional networks can create an environment sufficient to the task of effective health communication in Africa.

BIBLIOGRAPHY

African Development Bank (2013). *Health in African over the Next 50 Years.* Tunis: African Development Bank Group.

——— (2011). *Africa in 50 Years' Time: The Road Toward Inclusive Growth.* Tunis: African Development Bank Group.

Alali, A.O. (1997). "Health Warnings and Contents Disclosures in Cigarette Advertisements: The Case of South Africa," unpublished research report.

Alali, A.O., and Nwosu, P. (1996). "Social and Cultural Considerations in Planning AIDS Education and Campaigns in Africa." Paper presented at the 10th Biennial African Council for Communication Education Conference, Cape Town, South Africa, 15–22 November 1996.

AVERT (2012). "Africa HIV and AIDS Statistics." Avert.org Website. Available at http:www.avert.org/Africa-hiv-aids-statistics.htm.

Becker, T.L. (1995). "Improving the Nation's Health: The Role of Communication Scholars," *SCA Summer Conference Proceedings and Prepared Remarks, Washington, D.C., 19–23 July, 1995.* Annandale, VA: Speech Communication Association.

Bergendahl, P., and Hsu, L. (1995). "Women and Substance Abuse," *World Health,* 4 (July–August 1995).

Boafo, T., and George, N., eds. (1992). *Communication Research in Africa: Issues and Perspective.* Nairobi: African Council on Communication Education.

Burgoon, M. (1995). "Navigating the Treacherous Waters of Health Communication: Dawning of the Age of Aquarius or Rule of Proteus?" *SCA Summer Conference Proceedings and Prepared Remarks, Washington, D.C., 19–23 July, 1995.* Annandale, VA: Speech Communication Association.

Cooke, J.G. (2009). *Public Health in Africa: A Report of the CSIS Global Health Policy Center.* Washington, DC: Center for Strategic and International Studies.

McKibbin, E.C. (1994). "An Analysis of the Risk Factors for Coronary Heart Diseases in Patients Aged 55 and Younger with Proven Heart Disease," *South African Journal of Nursing,* 17 (3): pp. 51–56.

M'Bayo, R. (1996). "Methodological Considerations in the Study of Communications and Information Policies in Africa," *Journal of Research Methodology and Africa Studies,* 1 (1): pp. 1–33.

Mukasa, T., and Becker, L. (1992). "Toward an Indigenized Philosophy of Communication: An Analysis of African Communication Educational Resources and Needs," *Africa Media Review,* 6 (3).

Nwosu, P. (1990). "Communication and Agricultural Development in Swaziland: Toward a Need-Based Integrative Model. Ph.D. dissertation, Howard University, Washington, D.C.

Nwosu, P., Taylor, D., and Onwumechili, C. (1995). "Search for Appropriate Research Methods in the African Context." In P. Nwosu, C. Onwumechili, and R. M'Bayo, eds., *Communication and the Transformation of Society: A Developing Region's Perspectives.* Lanham, MD: University Press of America, 397–426.

Okigbo, C. (1985). "Is Development Communication a Dead Issue?" *Media Development* 4 (23): p. 5.

Page, R.M., Cole, G.E., and Timmreck, T.C. (1995). *Basic Epidemiological Methods and Biostatistics: A Practical Guidebook.* Boston, MA: Jones and Bartlett.

Perera, F.P. (1996). "Uncovering New Clues to Cancer Risk," *Scientific American,* May 1996: pp. 54–62.

Pettegrew, L.S. (1988). "Theoretical Plurality in Health Communication." In J.A. Anderson, ed., *Communication Yearbook 11.* Newbury Park, CA: Sage, pp. 298–308.

Pirie, P.L. (1990). "Evaluating Health Promotion Programs: Basic Questions and Approaches." In N. Bracht, ed., *Health Promotion at the Community Level.* Newbury Park, CA: Sage, pp. 201–208.

Taylor, D.S. (1991). "Application of the Uses and Dependency Model of Mass Communication to Development Communication in the Western Area of Sierra Leone." PhD dissertation, Kent (Ohio) State University.

Torabi, M.R. (1993). "General Standards for Educational Evaluations," *Health Values,* 17 (4): pp. 57–59.

Ugboajah, F.O. (1985). "Oramedia in Africa." In F.O. Ugboajah, ed., *Mass Communication, Culture and Society in West Africa*. London: Hans Zell.

UNAIDS (2012a). "Global Report: UNAIDS Report on the Global AIDS Epidemic 2012." Available at http://www.unaids.org/en/resouces/c/globalreport/.

——— (2012b). "Regional Fact Sheet 2012: Sub-Saharan Africa." Available at http://www.unaids.org/en/media/unaids/contentass/globalreport/.

Victor, B., and Cullen, J.B. (1990). "A Theory and Measure of Ethical Climate in Organizations." In W.C. Frederick and L.E. Preston, eds., *Business Ethics: Research Issues and Empirical Studies*. Greenwich, CT: JAI Press.

World Bank (2011). *Healthy Partnerships: How Governments Can Engage the Private Sector to Improve Health in Africa*. Washington, DC: World Bank.

World Health Organization (2009). "Women and Health: Today's Evidence, Tomorrow's Agenda." WHO.

NOTES

1. See Boafo and George 1992; Mukasa and Becker 1992; Taylor 1991; Nwosu 1990; Okigbo 1985; Ugboajah 1985.

2. For further discussions of measures of validity and reliability within African communication contexts, see M'Bayo 1996; Nwosu et al. 1995.

TWO

Social Structural Contexts in Health and Healthcare

Reappraisal of the Roles of Development and Health Communication

Srinivas R. Melkote

Over the last several decades, psychosocial theories have been invoked to deal with a plethora of health-related challenges. In the 1960s and the 1970s, family planning communication research was predominant, especially in the developing countries. In the 1980s, the issue of teenage pregnancies was the prime focus in many research studies and interventions. Since the 1990s, the challenge of HIV/AIDS has been the target. Psychosocial theories have been invoked in most cases to deal with the challenges of HIV/AIDS prevention. Various scholars have cited a combination of theories within their typologies. For example, Freimuth (1992) identified the Health Belief Model (HBM), cognitive social learning theory, the diffusion of innovations, social marketing, and media advocacy as having been applied in AIDS campaigns. Other scholars have cited HBM, the theory of reasoned action, problem behavior theory and social learning theory as being frequently used in research on knowledge, behavior, and attitude in the AIDS context. In this chapter we will review some of the core psychosocial theories and models that have frequently been used in AIDS/HIV prevention campaigns.

HBM is a value-expectancy theory. Behavior is seen as a function of a subjective value, the desire to avoid illness, and as an outcome of the subjective probability or the expectation for remedial or preventive action. These basic components are expanded to form the framework of the model. The Theory of Reasoned Action (Ajzen and Fishbein 1980) is based on the idea that the most immediate determinant of a person's behavior is his or her behavioral intention—what the person intends to do. Influencing behavior is to be accomplished through influencing the person's intentions. Intention in turn is seen as a joint function of one's positive or negative feeling toward performing the behavior, and one's perception of social pressure to perform or not perform that behavior.

The Social Cognitive Theory is based on self-efficacy and social marketing, two elements of Bandura's (1994) theory that have been widely used in AIDS campaigns because of their holistic approach to providing knowledge, skill, and the confidence to undertake preventive measures against HIV/AIDS. Self-efficacy refers to a belief in personal efficacy, while social modeling is based on the principle that people learn vicariously by observing the actions of others.

Health communication scholars have tried to understand how individuals process information and have identified factors that contribute to appropriate behavior change. These approaches are concerned with individual behavior change. The exclusive emphasis on psychologically oriented models does not account for social structural and cultural processes that mediate the impact of AIDS or other health challenges. More attention needs to be paid to the manner in which political, economic, and social contexts have constrained or enabled individual behaviors. This chapter aims to fill that gap. While cutting edge work in psychosocial variables is necessary to deal with health challenges, structural issues in societies and systemic challenges, such as poverty, inequality, and marginalization of individuals and communities are core reasons why people are unable to live healthy lives and communities are unable to function harmoniously.

Development and health communication as an area of scholarship and practice is looking for its niche in the efforts to tackle unequal development, healthcare, and marginalization of people and communities through directed social change. What should be the mission of this field in the face of contemporary realities and challenges? What are the ways in which we can visualize and reconstruct the mission and role of media and communication in directed change, including health-related changes?

As we entered the twenty-first century, the challenge of unequal development continued to be intractable. The Millennium Development Goals (MDGs), approved by the United Nations (UN) and adopted by most countries in 2000, present us with a blueprint of the pressing priorities in development through the next decade. The MDGs constitute the centerpiece of the Millennium Declaration of the United Nations and serve as an important milestone in the history of the development agenda for most countries. They also remind us of the formidable development-related challenges that lie ahead. MDGs, which provide basic guidelines on eight development goals to be achieved by 2015, address and highlight the needs of the poorest and the most marginalized individuals and groups. The eight goals are (1) eradicating extreme poverty; (2) achieving universal primary education; (3) promoting gender equality and empowering women and girls; (4) reducing child mortality; (5) improving maternal health; (6) combating HIV/AIDS, malaria, and other major diseases; (7) ensuring environmental sustainability; and, (8) developing a global partnership (UNDP, 2010).[1] The MDGs constitute the benchmark and serve as signposts for decision makers in national governments, civil society, NGOs, and other significant groups concerned with unequal development.

HEALTH-RELATED CHALLENGES

The problems of development dealing with health and healthcare are important. MDGs 4, 5, and 6 focus on specific health-related challenges. Millennium goal 6 turns the spotlight on the pandemics of malaria, HIV/AIDS, and tuberculosis. According to the World Health Organization (WHO), at the end of 2009, 33.3 million people around the world were living with HIV (WHO 2010). That year about 3 million people were newly infected, and about 2 million died of AIDS, including 260,000 children. The problem is endemic in Sub-Saharan Africa, where 68 percent of people living with AIDS are concentrated. Here, an estimated 10.6 million people need antiretroviral therapy.

The WHO reports that malaria has made a comeback in many parts of the Third World, especially in Africa, South Asia, and Southeast Asia. Malaria kills nearly 1 million people a year. A majority are children below five years of age in Africa. On average, a child succumbs to malaria every thirty seconds. Meanwhile, tuberculosis (TB) has been rampant in many parts of the world, especially the Third World countries. There were approximately 9.4 million new cases of TB in 2009 and an estimated 1.7 million deaths, making TB a deadly infectious disease.[2] It is not a coincidence that these deadly diseases are especially spreading in the poorer parts of the world and affect the most poor and vulnerable populations.

What is the extent of deprivation and marginalization of millions of the poorest individuals and communities in the world today? Here are a few sobering highlights of the health-related challenges:

- More people exist in extreme poverty. Millions, especially in the developing countries, earn less than $1.25 US per day.
- In the developing countries, one out of four children under five years of age is underweight.

- Thousands of children do not live to see their fifth birthday. The child mortality rate in much of Africa is more than 100 per 1000. Nearly 30,000 children under five years old die each day in developing countries from preventable causes.
- Communicable diseases strike 30 million children a year, often resulting in blindness or deafness and killing more than 600,000.
- Ninety-nine percent of maternal deaths occur in developing countries. In many poor African countries, one mother dies for every 100 children born.
- Tuberculosis kills about 1.8 million people per year.
- Nearly 1 billion people lack access to reliable source of clean water and nearly 2.5 billion need improved sanitation services.[3]

Other formidable challenges include the lack of food security, affecting millions of people, including children, and environmental and habitat destruction or unsustainability.

DEVELOPMENT/HEALTH COMMUNICATION SCHOLARSHIP AND CONTEMPORARY REALITIES

Today, the challenge is not just to achieve a certain level of development. It is important to identify the reasons for its unequal spread and to suggest theories, models, programs, and strategies to eradicate—or at least minimize—the ravages of unequal development in societies. Many today would prefer to reconstruct the challenge of directed social change; it is unconscionable to justify the present inequality among people on issues so basic as food security, clean drinking water, basic education, and healthcare. The foci of development communication should go beyond facilitating development. We also must to look at the state of unequal development among global communities, document its negative consequences on people and communities, and identify reasons for such an unequal spread of development benefits. Out of this exercise in deconstruction, the scholarship in development communication should be better able to reconceptualize and re-operationalize the real meaning and goal of development. This in turn would provide a better understanding of the real constraints to achieving development, thus providing scholars with opportunities to incorporate models and theories germane to the task of achieving equitable development.

The articulation of the MDGs is itself a testament to the stark differences among individuals and global communities regarding issues basic to human survival.[4] Over the last seventy years, since development was adopted as a goal by the UN, it has become increasingly evident development did occur in many countries, but its spread has often left individuals and communities behind. Some suggest that it is the nature and process of development (as it has been conceptualized and operationalized), which is associated with increasing inequality among global communities. They believe this is true regarding such indicators of basic needs for human survival and growth as adequate food and nutrition, clean drinking water, basic education, and basic healthcare. True, individuals and communities have benefitted from the development process; their health, standards of living, and consumption have improved. However, for millions, the outcomes have been continued incapacity. People are unable to lead effective lives. The relative state of countries today and stratification of people within them on basic human development indicators indicate that the process of development has failed a very large section of people and communities around the world (Berger 1974).[5] It is the poor, the marginalized, and the vulnerable who are worst affected by inadequacies in healthcare and the ravages of killer diseases. The WHO reports that malaria disproportionately affects poor people, who are not in a position to pay for the treatment or have limited access to health care. Families and communities are trapped in a downward spiral of poverty. As the same report states:

> Poverty is associated with the undermining of a range of key human attributes, including health. The poor are exposed to greater personal and environmental health risks, are less well nourished, have less information and are less able to access health care; they thus have a higher risk of illness and disability. Conversely, illness can reduce household savings, lower learning ability, reduce productivity, and lead to a diminished quality of life, thereby perpetuating or even increasing poverty.[6]

In a scathing report, the WHO states that the poorest of the poor suffer from the worst health conditions. Within many countries, the data indicate that, in general, the lower an individual's socioeconomic position, the poorer is his/her health. "There is a social gradient in health that runs from top to bottom of the socioeconomic spectrum. This is a global phenomenon, seen in low, middle and high income countries."[7]

RECONCEPTUALIZATION OF DEVELOPMENT

Increasingly, the idea of establishing social justice is finding common ground among development scholars. I agree with this view and conceive development as a process of directed social change that has the ultimate goal of establishing social justice. The achievement of social justice should serve as an anchor for development communication theory and propel social transformations in global communities. The concept of social justice creates a common platform for scholars, adminstrators, and practitioners from different disciplines and professions that seek development communication. While the term *social justice* connotes a common understanding in the conceptual domain, its operationalization has been a challenge. The main reason why unequal development prevails around the world is that the operationalization of development has not captured all facets of social justice.

What is social justice in directed social change and what are the ways in which it may be operationalized? In table 2.1, I present a tabular model in which the achievement of social justice (or the elimination of injustice) is the ultimate goal of directed social change (in level 1).

The model operationalizes the indicators of social justice through the outcomes desired at national and community levels (in level 2); it then presents the outcome desired by development support communication (in level 3), which would constitute the means by which outcomes articulated at national and community levels may be achieved. In turn, the model lists the principal communicative actions by which the outcome desired by development support communication may be achieved (in level 4). All through the model, the interactivity among the different

Table 2.1. Reappraisal of the Role of Development Support Communication in Developmen.t

1. Ultimate goal	• Establish social justice and eliminate injustice.
2. Desired societal outcomes toward achieving social justice	• Eliminate social-political-economic-cultural policies, laws, or arrangements that foster or sustain inequity.
3. Outcomes to be achieved by developing support communication	• Create, expand, and sustain claims and access to resources and rights of all, including those at the margin. • Create, expand, and sustain choices, opportunities, capacity, and capability for people to lead effective, meaningful lives. • Create, expand, and sustain individual and group agency. • Increase countervailing power of victims of unequal development.
4. Development support communication actions	• Empowerment of individuals and communities through • Social mobilization: expand and sustain public participation and discussion. • Participatory action and communication. • Empowered organizations and communities.

Source: Melkote, 2012.

levels and among national and community contexts is stressed. The role and place of development support communication is highlighted as it addresses the challenges in both the national and community contexts.

In table 2.1, the elimination of injustice is the ultimate goal of directed social change. Achieving social justice would eliminate persistent and endemic deprivation of individuals and communities in health and other areas basic to human survival. It would enhance the capacity and ability of people to live effective lives. There would be sustained access to such resources as adequate food and basic health care, basic education so that one can live effectively in society, access to land or income generating employment, access to clean drinking water and sanitary living conditions, political participation, and basic civil rights. This list is not exhaustive, but it is a good beginning.

Since elimination of social injustice is central to the process of directed social change, media and communication processes and actors attempting to bring about social change must be committed to this goal. Therefore, the contribution of development and health communication must be assessed according to its success in eradicating the egregious injustice. The model in table 2.1 also suggests that elimination of injustice (in level 1) could help achieve outcomes desired at level 2 and vice versa. This interrelationship is evident and empirically verifiable among the different levels in table 2.1. They feed each other through symbiotic relationships.

OUTCOMES AT NATIONAL AND COMMUNITY LEVELS

At the national level, the state and the civil society are the main agencies or avenues. Therefore, should share the primary responsibility of protecting and strengthening the welfare of their citizens. Specifically, these agencies would include government from the federal to the local levels; such public institutions as schools, hospitals, and courts; political parties; market structures; media systems; legal systems; professional associations; and NGOs, social service organizations, cooperatives and other organizations. Together, these entities in a society influence the social, political, economic and cultural laws. They shape policies, arrangements and conventions that have a bearing on individual opportunities, capabilities, capacities, and welfare.

What should be the primary normative concerns in a society that is sensitive to the ravages of inequality in directed social change? What are the facets of social justice that all people in a society must be guaranteed? At the most elementary level, all should have access to basic education, to basic health care, and to land or sustainable and gainful employment opportunities. Individuals must have claims to social safety nets, such as social security and unemployment benefits, during times of distress and guarantees of individual safety at all times. In addition, there should be opportunities for people to participate in a market system that is monitored by the state to provide avenues for production, exchange, and consumption (Sen, 2000). All citizens should have claims and access to civil rights, which include free expression of speech, an autonomous mass media, and transparency in all public transactions in that they are open to public and media scrutiny. Society must establish and sustain social, political, economic, and media structures and policies that foster equity.

This includes health and gender equity. Inequities in healthcare or inadequate health behaviors and skills are not just due to poor understanding or attitudes of individuals. They are largely due to oppressive structural obstacles. As Campbell and Scott (2012) emphasize, what is needed are enabling social environments. Writing about the evaluation of social change communication for HIV/AIDS, Byrne and Vincent (2012) posit that the challenge of effective multilevel programming may be traced to structural issues, leading to an examination of the social determinants of HIV. These authors present challenges at the macro, intermediate, and micro levels. At the macro level are social characteristics that affect people's lives, such as racism, sexism, and discrimination. At the intermediate level are infrastructure and service availability, neighborhood characteristics, and local resources. Then there are individual micro-level factors. Hess, Meekers, and Storey (2012), on the other hand, posit that individuals and households become health-competent when they can successfully access or mobilize the resources they require to make health decisions and achieve positive health outcomes. These resources come in the areas of information, social factors, and empowerment-related factors.

Table 2.1 highlights the interconnections among levels. For example, the elimination of injustice (in level 1) could be instrumental in helping achieve desired outcomes at the institutional and local levels. The elimination of inequities in society (in level 2) could facilitate social justice. In addition, there are linkages among the factors within the expected outcomes. The learning of literacy and numeracy skills through education helps improve a person's economic participation and productivity. Access to adequate health care will have a positive impact on individual productivity, which in turn helps economic growth. While a free and robust market is the engine of development, its beneficial effects on the entire society is contingent upon equitable social and political policies, laws, and arrangements. It has also been demonstrated that access to education for females has had a positive impact on fertility rates and the empowerment of women (Sen 2000). These and other interconnections have been empirically verified and further reinforce the idea that practical advantages would accrue from the eradication of major sources of injustice in a society.

OUTCOMES EXPECTED BY DEVELOPMENT AND HEALTH COMMUNICATION

At level 2 in table 2.1, we see the different roles and responsibilities of the state and civil society in protecting and strengthening individuals and communities from the ravages of social injustice. This perspective, however, does not see communities or individuals as passive recipients who wait for social institutions to be benefactors and protectors. Individuals and the groups they belong to, or the communities of which they are members, should actively make social, political, and economic structures and policies in a society that are appropriate and effective in establishing social justice through directed social change. The outcome desired by development support communication, then, should be to create, expand, and sustain the agency of communities, organizations, and individuals in directed change.

This means a move from being a passive "patient" to an active "agent" of change. The new avatar of development support communication should be one that encourages and pursues an agent-oriented view for individuals and communities engaged in directed social change. Individuals and communities must have the capacity and opportunity to articulate and shape the change they desire. This could be aided by communicative actions at the larger societal level. These would be encouraged by creating or strengthening a vibrant public sphere, active public discussion and debate, empowered communities and coalitions, and a supportive public mass media. At the community level, communicative actions should strengthen social norms that are compatible with the notion of equity in the distribution of resources and rights. These include rights to health and gender equity, democratic participation of all local stakeholders, building of social capital, and the countervailing power of the community and its constituents. Again, there is an active link between levels 2 and 3.

While the outcomes in level 2 help in strengthening the capacities and abilities of individuals and communities to craft the kinds of change they desire, the active agency of individuals and groups outlined in level 3 aids in the quest to create a more just society. This agency helps create a more equitable spread of the benefits of directed change.

However, the task of creating active agency at the societal, community, or individual levels will not succeed until the lack of economic, political, and social power among individuals or communities is addressed. Any meaningful discussion of unequal development must address issues of the inequitable spread of power in a society. The reality of the social and political situations in most societies is that the urban and rural poor and other oppressed people at the grassroots are trapped in a dependency relationship. This dependency comes through highly stratified and unequal socioeconomic structures that are punctuated with sharp inequities in countervailing power. Therefore, power inequities in societies are major impediments to creating active agency in marginalized people and communities.

The WHO's Commission on Social Determinants of Health (CSDH) report for 2008 warns that the social determinants of health are crucial for the poor, oppressed, and marginalized populations.

> The social determinants of health are the conditions in which people are born, grow, live, work and age, including the health system. These circumstances are shaped by the distribution of money, power and resources at global, national and local levels, which are themselves influenced by policy choices. The social determinants of health are mostly responsible for health inequities—the unfair and avoidable differences in health status seen within and between countries.[8]

In 2005, in response to the persistent and wide inequities, the WHO set up the CSDH to provide guidelines for meeting the growing health inequity between the haves and the have-nots. The 2008 report contained important recommendations for improving daily living conditions and tackling the inequitable distribution of power, money, and resources.

PRINCIPAL MEANS OF DEVELOPMENT SUPPORT COMMUNICATION

Social Mobilization

If directed social change is to have any relevance to the communities and people who need it most, it must start where the real needs and problems exist, the rural areas, urban slums, and other depressed sectors in society. People and communities living in such peripheries must perceive their real needs and identify their real problems. Identification of needs and constraints are, to a great extent, influenced by public participation and dialogue. To a large extent, these people and communities have lacked agency because they have not had genuine participation in the change strategies ostensibly set up to ameliorate their problems.

Alternatively, bottom-up communication strategies have often turned out to be mere clichés, lacking in substance. The bottom line is that people lack a voice in making the social change they need to live the life they desire. Therefore, the new task of development support communicators should be directly linked to the building and exercise of social power of individuals and communities. These are not mere targets of change agencies in directed social change programs (Speer and Hughey 1995). Individuals and communities affected by societal injustice should be able to craft what they want and can accept. This civil right should not be the prerogative of political, economic/business or religious leaders alone. Public participation and discussion are necessary for transparency and for making responsible social choices, which are fundamental to policy-making in the social arena. Besides, public participation can create shared norms, especially on social and cultural issues. Public policies, arrangements, and conventions relating to social change and concerns can benefit (Sen 2000). Other communicative actions include the mobilization of public media to influence public opinion, raise awareness, and win public support for projects and debate of issues that challenge systemic social injustice.

Social movements have always played an important role during times of great change in societies. Many observers are now visualizing a new post-development phase in which social movements can serve as radical alternatives that work on behalf of the marginalized and against dominant knowledge structures and ideology (Wilkins 2008; Escobar 1995). In the post-industrial societies of today, social movements are seen as vehicles to craft political identities, challenge dominant social norms, and develop channels of resistance (Atkinson 2010; Steeves 2003). Examples of social movements include stands against environmental destruction, against global capitalism or big government, and for greater human rights (Wilkins, 2003). While social movements may produce desired outcomes, what should interest scholars in development support communication are movements that sensitize people and the media to unequal and unjust development, and counter power structures that maintain the status quo. This may be done in many ways, by collecting and sharing pertinent information, framing issues, building coalitions, targeting media attention, and acting as vehicles of social mobilization community, national, or transnational environments. Recent events in Egypt, Tunisia, Syria, China, the United States, and other places have also shown that using mobile communication technologies can be effective in "crowd sourcing" and bringing pressure to bear on authorities. These technologies can raise global media awareness of structures and polices that sustain systemic injustice.

Advocacy communication has been regarded by some as separate from the work of development support communication (Mefalopulos 2008). However, the new avatar of development communication must include advocacy communication to win the support of constituencies and influence policy debates, especially on matters relating to unequal distribution of development's benefits in a society. The WHO recommends making health equity a marker of a government's performance. They further recommend enabling public sector leadership to provide essential health-related goods and services, controlling health damaging commodities. Civil society should be encouraged to organize and act to promote political and social rights affecting health equity and base healthcare systems on principles of equity, disease prevention, and health promotion with universal coverage, focusing on primary health care.[9]

Grassroots Participation

A number of scholars and practitioners (Greiner 2012; Campbell and Scott 2012; Sengupta and Elias 2012; Byrne and Vincent 2012) have favored active participation of the people at the grassroots level in community health, women's health and healing, HIV/AIDS, and participatory communication research. On the surface, this has seemed to signal a positive departure from the predominantly top-down and prescriptive change approaches. However, the structure of elite domination may not be disturbed in participative approaches. Diaz-Bordenave (1980) noted that in these approaches the expected participation is often directed by the sources and change agents. Thus, the people participate in change efforts but the agenda and solutions to alleged problems are controlled and selected by the external change agencies. People at the grassroots can be co-opted in so-called participatory activities that are directed and controlled by agencies outside the community. Participation becomes a means to greater dependence of the local people on national or international external agencies. This is the case in many traditional social marketing projects.

True participation should go beyond such tactics to involving the people and communities in social and political action. The participatory model that I envision would incorporate the framework of critical social change and involve social mobilization at the community level. The goal should be to facilitate conscientization of marginalized people and communities to the unequal social, political, economic, and spatial structures in their societies. It is through conscientization and collective action that people can perceive their needs, identify constraints to addressing the needs, and plan on overcoming problems and constraints.

Paulo Freire (1970) introduced the concept of conscientization. He was disappointed with the educational systems in Brazil and Chile and advocated their replacement with a type of pedagogy that would be more receiver-centered, involving the people, especially in their existential situations, reflection, and dialogue. Armed with the knowledge of their existential situation, the people could then come up with action plans to liberate themselves from their dependent and exploited status. This was truly empowerment pedagogy and contrasted sharply with the "banking education" practiced by the authorities wherein exogenous prescriptive information was deposited into the heads of passive recipients. Especially among the marginalized victims of societal injustice, the process of action/experience and reflection of their unequal power situation led to a critical consciousness on pertinent situations. They were set on a path to social change where they could be risk-taking agents and not merely targets (Cadiz 2005; Tufte 2005).

The participatory communication model provides a heuristic role for development support communication. It is a clean break from the role it played in the earlier modernization paradigm of transmitting and disseminating exogenous messages. Instead, development support communicators in the participatory model serve as facilitators of empowered local communities, strengthening local knowledge, experiences, and narratives and encouraging active agency at the grassroots in the process of social change. As enunciated by Campbell and Scott (2012), individuals need to engage in critical reflection and dialog, understand the debilitating consequences of unequal social relations, which limit their health and other opportunities. Development support communicators need to work with these individuals and communities so that they can enter the social, economic, and political arenas as active agents of change.

Participatory Action Research

The Participatory Action Research (PAR) model has been influenced by Freire. It has emerged as a forceful methodology cum action approach, principally in reaction to the degradation of economic and social conditions of poor and marginalized groups. It is dedicated to resuscitating both the power and knowledge of marginalized people. The knowledge that PAR attempts to generate is specific, local, non-Western, and non-positivist. It initiates collaborative social action to empower local knowledge and wrest the social power that is inherent in knowledge away from the privileged (Friesen 1999).

The idea of PAR is that endogenous efforts and local leaders play the leading role in social transformation, using their own praxis. It encompasses an experiential methodology. In this process, the people on their own develop methods of consciousness-raising or critical awareness of their situation. The knowledge is generated or resuscitated by collective and democratic means. This is followed by reflection and critical self-evaluation, leading to participatory action. This in essence forms the praxis (Rahman 1991). PAR takes place in a local context, uses local material and other inputs, and is dominated by local people and their organizations. PAR displaces the external agents of change with internal agency. Successful PAR efforts will lead to the acquisition of countervailing power by the people's groups. In Latin American and Asia, where land and other resources have been keenly contested and where class and ethnic divisions have been sharp, marginalized groups and their organizations have used PAR for macro-level empowerment.

CO-EQUAL KNOWLEDGE SHARING MODEL

The symmetric (subject to subject) relationship of community participation models allows for exchange of information between equals. Asymmetric (subject-to-object) communication does not. The emphasis is on symmetric knowledge-sharing rather than top-down teaching (Ascroft et al. 1987; Ascroft and Masilela 1989). The co-equal knowledge sharing model is interactive. It is decentralized, less dependent on professionals and institutions. The roles of senders and receivers are interchangeable. This orientation, contrary to the oligarchic communication models of the past, is fundamentally two-way, interactive, and participatory. The pluralistic nature of this model fits well with the "multiplicity in one world" idea (Servaes 1985). It implies a more dialectic social mobilization, thus complementing the Freirian approach.

Communication on a co-equal basis is ethically preferable and practically more relevant and useful. By promising a more democratic forum for communication, it supports the basic human right to communicate that is recognized by the UN charter. Access to communication channels are afforded to all people at all levels. Communication at the grassroots is active and relevant. Co-equal knowledge sharing provides access to the storehouse of information and ideas of people and communities.

In communication models and practices of the modernization paradigm, the experts and policy makers have often neglected to listen, understand, and incorporate the innate wisdom and knowledge of the rural and urban poor concerning their environment. The diffusion of innovations model and research reinforced the stereotype that people in the margins have little useful knowledge or skills to contribute to directed social change. Newer approaches, such as the positive deviance model (Singhal and Dura 2012) question the assumption of the superiority of ideas introduced from outside over local knowledge. Often, local knowledge and practices have proved very useful in solving health and development problems. Sengupta and Elias (2012) provide an instructive example of local knowledge and wisdom related to an understanding of a healthful life. Working among Amazonians, they questioned the local stakeholders about their ideas of a healthy lifestyle. They found that these ideas were not as constrictive as the biomedical idea of being free of illness. A holistic and grounded version of reality looked at other environmental factors, such as good interpersonal relationships and a life free from damaging forces like domestic violence, disharmony with nature, and discrimination. People's ideas of good health are related to how they perceive themselves, their experiences, and membership in their communities. Tapping their local knowledge enriches our understanding of a healthy life. Knowledge-sharing on a co-equal basis will mobilize the large knowledge base that exists in local communities, whether rural or urban, First World or Third World. The elevation of the knowledge of local communities could provide relevance and utility and also contribute to active agency and strengthen their ability to question the presumed superiority of outsiders' knowledge in directed social change processes.

COMMUNICATION FOR EMPOWERMENT

While the radical variants in participatory communication models have advocated empowerment and social action on the part of the downtrodden and marginalized individuals and communities, other communication models, especially in the modernization paradigm, have ignored the barriers that permit or perpetuate inequality. Elimination of social injustice in directed social change is not possible unless the crucial problems in society are confronted, namely the lack of economic, political, and social power among individuals at the grassroots in marginalized groups (Steeves 2000). Individuals are impoverished or sick or often slow to adopt useful practices that improve their lives, not because they lack knowledge or reason, but because they do not have reasonable access to beneficial, sustainable opportunities. This is an issue of unequal power.

The focus on unequal power dynamics has a direct consequence for development support communication. The objective of development support communication professionals should be to work with individuals and communities at the periphery of a society so that they eventually can enter and participate meaningfully in political and economic activities and processes. This calls for grassroots organizing and communicative social action on the part of women and others who have been marginalized in the process of social change. Greater importance will need to be directed to the use of communication in empowering citizens. The new focus in development support communication then should be to assist in the process of empowerment.

Therefore, I support a social system change model, as opposed to the social equilibrium model of the modernization paradigm. This is not an easy task. It requires dealing with enclaves of power and influence that are deeply anchored in global and national structures. It also involves the active participation of individuals and communities in intervention efforts affecting their welfare. However, it is the right thing to do if we are truly interested in the elimination of injustice through directed social change.

The concept of empowerment is heuristic in understanding the complex constraints in directed social change. The empowerment-oriented outcomes include increased access of all citizens to social, economic, political, cultural resources through social mobilization, social movements, and other types of communicative social action. Empowerment-oriented outcomes hone individual and group competence, leadership skills, life and communication skills, and critical awareness skills. Empowered local organizations and communities provide a useful niche for development/health communication.

While the construct of empowerment has been mentioned quite often in the social change literature, the terms, best practices, levels of analyses and outcomes have not been thoroughly explained. Table 2.2 attempts to

Table 2.2. Development Support Communication in an Empowerment Paradigm

Phenomenon of Interest/Goal:	Empowerment of people, social justice, building capacity and equity
Belief:	Underdevelopment due to a lack of access to economic, political and cultural resources. Underdevelopment and unequal development due to lack of power and control on the part of the people and communities; diversity of standards
Bias:	Cultural proximity, diversity, and ecological
Context:	Local, community, national, and global settings
Level of Analysis:	Individual, group or organization; community
Role of Change Agent:	Collaborator, facilitator, participant, advocate for individuals and communities, risk-taker, and activist
Communication Model:	Non-linear, participatory, and reflexive. Used to convey information as well as empower communities and organizations
Type of Research:	Quantitative and qualitative; longitudinal studies; labor intensive participatory action research; communication for empowerment
Exemplars:	Activate and sustain social support systems, social networks, mutual help and self-help activities. Encourage participation of all actors. Empower community narratives. Facilitate critical awareness and community and organizational power. Communicate to strengthen interpersonal relationships.
Outcomes Desired:	Increased access of all people to material, psychological, cultural and informational resources; honing of individual and group competence, leadership skills, useful life and communication skills; honing of critical awareness skills; empowered local organizations and communities; a vibrant public sphere; active public discussion and debate; building of social capital

Source: Melkote and Steeves, 2001.

articulate elements for a conceptual framework of development support communication. The table reveals that the phenomena of interest in the empowerment communication model are vastly different from the modernization paradigm, and so are the underlying beliefs about underdevelopment. The bias in the modernization paradigm was to favor exogenous ideas and innovations over the local. In the absence of local people participation, such introduced ideas most often resulted in social engineering by the government or the elite.

The differences between the two frameworks are stark when it comes to the communication models used. An examination of the communication model in the empowerment framework brings into sharp relief its differences from the modernization paradigm. Communication models in the modernization paradigm looked at communication as a process of moving a message through some channel with the hope that it would reach the receiver and have an impact. The process was usually linear, top-down, prescriptive, preachy, and quite often technical. The transmission approach or the delivery of technical information (as in the modernization paradigm) will be insufficient for the task because empowerment requires more than just information delivery and diffusion of technical innovations.

CONCLUSION

If the ultimate goal in directed social change is the achievement of social justice for all, the objective of media and communication processes goes beyond serving as vehicles for information delivery. Rather, communication works with individuals and communities, especially those at the peripheries of a society, so that they eventually have a voice and agency in political, economic, and ideological processes in their societies. This creates a useful niche for development and health communication professionals. Some authors have alluded to this as "bridging social capital" by communication professionals acting as liaisons between local stakeholders and the power holders (Campbell and Scott 2012). In table 2.2, we can see that the new role of a development/health communication practitioner is to serve as a collaborator, facilitator, participant, advocate, risk-taker, and even an activist.

Social change is inherently non-linear and quite often chaotic. This understanding cautions us against putting all our faith in models of communication and evaluation that are essentially linear and deterministic. Lessons learned from participatory approaches and complexity science (Lacayo 2012), applied to the strategies of directed social change, will provide us with more open-ended and non-deterministic models to work with. In terms of an overarching theory, the communitarian theory emphasizes preservation of community and emancipation from oppression at all levels (Tehranian 1994). Liberation, feminist, environmental, subaltern, and some Third World social movements have made arguments consistent with communitarian theory. It appears that communitarian theory offers potential as a general framework that could ground participatory and empowerment-oriented perspectives in directed social change.

BIBLIOGRAPHY

Ajzen, I., and Fishbein, M. (1980). *Understanding attitudes and predicting social behavior.* Englewoods Cliffs, NJ: Prentice Hall.

Ascroft, J. (1987). "Communication in Support of Development: Lessons from Theory and Practice." Paper presented at "Communication and Change" seminar, University of Hawaii and the East-West Center, Honolulu, Hawaii.

Ascroft, J., and Masilela, S. (1989). "From Top-Down to Co-Equal Communication: Popular Participation in Development Decision-Making." Paper presented at "Participation: A Key Concept in Communication and Change" SEMINAR, University of Poona, Pune, India.

Atkinson, J. (2010). *Alternate Media and Politics of Resistance.* New York: Peter Lang.

Bandura, A. (1994). "Social Cognitive Theory and Exercise of Control over HIV Infection." In R. DiClemente and J. Peterson, eds. *In Preventing AIDS: Theories and Methods of Behavioral Interventions*. New York: Plenum, pp. 25–60.

Berger, P.L. (1974). *Pyramids of Sacrifice.* New York: Basic Books.

Byrne, A., and Vincent, R. (2012). Innovations in the Evaluation of Social Change Communication for HIV and AIDS." In R. Obregon and S. Waisbord, eds., *The Handbook of Global Health Communication.* Malden, MA: Wiley-Blackwell, pp. 288–308.

Cadiz, M. (2005). "Communication for Empowerment." In O. Hemer and T. Tufte, eds., *Media and Glocal Change.* Nordicom.

Campbell, C., and Scott, K. (2012). "Community Health and Social Mobilization." In A. Sengupta and E. Elias, "Women's Health and Healing in the Peruvian Amazon: Minga Peru's Participatory Communication Project."

Diaz-Bordenave, J. (1980). "Participation in Communication Systems for Development." Unpublished paper.

Escobar, A. (1995). *Encountering Development: The Making and Unmaking of the Third World.* Princeton, NJ: Princeton University Press.

Freimuth, V. (1992). "Theoretical Foundations of AIDS: Media Campaigns." In T. Edgar, M. Fitzpatrick, and V. Freimuth, eds., *AIDS: A Communication Perspective*. New Jersey: Lawrence Erlbaum Associates, pp. 91–110.

Freire, P. (1970). *Pedagogy of the Oppressed.* New York: Seabury Press.

Friesen, E. (1999). "Exploring the Links Between Structuration Theory and Participatory Action Research." In T. Jacobson and J. Servaes, eds., *Theoretical Approaches to Participatory Communication.* Creskill, NJ: Hampton Press, pp. 281–308.

Greiner, K. (2012). "Participatory Health Communication Research: Four Tools to Complement the Interview." In R. Obregon and S. Waisbord, eds., *The Handbook of Global Health Communication.* Malden, MA: Wiley-Blackwell, pp. 348–373.

Hess, R.; Meekers, D.; and Storey, D. (2012). "Egypt's *Mabrouk!* Initiative: A Communication Strategy for Maternal/Child Health and Family Planning Integration." In R. Obregon and S. Waisbord, eds., *The Handbook of Global Health Communication.* Malden, MA: Wiley-Blackwell, pp. 374–407.

Lacayo, V. (2012). "Using Complexity-Informed Communication Strategies to Address Complex Health Issues: The Case of Puntos de Encuentro, Nicaragua." In R. Obregon and S. Waisbord, eds., *The Handbook of Global Health Communication.* Malden, MA: Wiley-Blackwell, pp. 215–232.

Mefalopulos, P. (2008). *Development Communication Sourcebook.* Washington, DC: World Bank.

Melkote, S. (2012). "Development support communication for social justice: An analysis of the role of media and communication in directed social change." In S. Melkote (ed.). *Development Communication in Directed Social Change: A Reappraisal of Theory & Practice*. Singapore: Asian Media and Information Center (AMIC).

Melkote, S., and L. Steeves (2001). *Communication for Development in the Third World: Theory and Practice for Empowerment.* New Delhi/Newbury Park/London: Sage Publishers.

Rahman, M.A. (1991). "The Theoretical Standpoint of PAR." In O. Fals-Borda and M.A. Rahman, eds., *Action and Knowledge: Breaking the Monopoly with Participatory Action-Research.* New York: Apex Press, pp. 13–23.

Sen, A. (2000). *Development as Freedom.* New York: Oxford University Press.

Servaes, J. (1985). "Toward an Alternative Concept of Communication and Development," *Media Development*, 32 (4, 1985).

Singhal, A., and Dura, L. (2012). "Positive Deviance, Good for Global Health." In R. Obregon and S. Waisbord, eds., *The Handbook of Global Health Communication.* Malden, MA: Wiley-Blackwell, pp. 507–521.

Speer, P. W., and Hughey, J. (1995). "Community Organizing: An Ecological Route to Empowerment and Power," *American Journal of Community Psychology*, 23 (5): pp. 729–748.

Steeves, H.L. (2000). "Gendered Agendas: Dialogue and Impasse in Creating Social Change." In K. Wilkins, ed., *Redeveloping Communication for Social Change: Theory, Practice and Power*. Boulder, CO: Rowman & Littlefield, pp. 7–25.

Steeves, H.L. (2003). "Development Communication as Marketing, Collective Resistance, and Spiritual Awakening: A Feminist Critique." In B. Mody, ed., *International and Development Communication*, Sage Publications, pp. 227–244.

Tehranian, M. (1994). "Communication and Development." In D. Crowley and D. Mitchell, eds., *Communication Theory Today.* Stanford, CA: Stanford University Press, pp. 274–306.

Tufte, T. (2005). "Entertainment-Education in Development Communication." In O. Hemer and T. Tufte, eds., *Media and Glocal Change.* Nordicom.

United Nations Development Programme (2010). "Basic Facts about the Millennium Development Goals." UNDP. Available at http://www.undp.org/mdg/basics.shtml.

Wilkins, K. (2003). "International Development Communication: Proposing a Research Agenda for a New Era." In B. Mody, ed., *International and Development Communication.* San Francisco: Sage, p. 245–257.

Wilkins, K. (2008). "Development Communication." In W. Donsbach, ed., *The International Encyclopedia of Communication*. Blackwell Publishing, pp. 1229–1238.

World Health Organization (2010). "*World Malaria Report.*" Rome: WHO.

NOTES

1. See http://www.undp.org/mdg/basics.shtml.
2. See these and other statistics related to disease and the MDGs at http://www.who.int/topics/millennium_development_goals/diseases/en/index.html.
3. Statistical analysis from "The Online Atlas of the Millennium Development Goals." Available at http://devdata.worldbank.org/atlas-mdg/.
4. Ibid.
5. Ibid.
6. The complete report is available at http://www.who.int/social_determinants/en/
.
7. Ibid.

8. The WHO's Commission on Social Determinants of Health (CSDH) report for 2008 can be found at http://www.who.int/social_determinants/en/.

9. See the WHO recommendations at http://www.who.int/social_determinants/thecommission/finalreport/closethegap_how/en/index2.html.

THREE

Understanding the Factors Associated with Ill-Health and the Role of Public Health in Africa

Mario J. Azevedo, Francis M. Bwambale, and Tom S. Kiiza

Two or three concepts stand out as critical when we speak of health and public health in Africa, particularly Sub-Saharan Africa. One is *health* and the others are *public health* and *double burden of disease*. Public health is a relatively new field of socio-behavioral disciplines, whose relevance emerged from the shadows during the late 1950s. As a result, its proponents still struggle to see public health recognized as critical to society and needed to protect the health of the globe's population.

This new field of study and practice has had to contend with contradictory research findings, clinical conclusions leading to ambiguous conclusions from the studies undertaken over the years. The ambiguity damaged the credibility of the public health movement as health advocates gave advice about the nature, etiology, or association of certain disease and risk factors, claiming that this advice came from the use of scientific methods. Internally, this new field has also had its share of disagreements among its own proponents and defenders. The disagreements related to the field's definition and unique function. Public health has developed relatively recently as scientific field, since its emancipation from the controversies over its nature, purpose, and scientific claims. Quack doctors' practices, such as bloodletting, were abandoned only at the end of the nineteenth century.

Controversies notwithstanding, the consensus on a definition for the concept of *public* is slowly emerging. Yale public health epidemiologist professor Charles-Edward Winslow once defined *public health* as

> the science and the art of preventing disease, prolonging life, and promoting physical health and efficiency through organized community efforts for the sanitation of the environment, the concept of community infections, the education of the individual in principles of personal hygiene, the organization of medical and nursing services for the early diagnosis and preventive treatment of disease, and the development of the social machinery, which will ensure to every individual in the community a standard of living adequate for the maintenance of health. (Gostin 2002)

This all-encompassing definition drew the criticism of many socio-behavioral science colleagues. The well-known sociologist Paul Starr called it simply "provocative" and "downright subversive," as it encroached upon the fields of medicine and created more confusion by trying to cover all disciplines remotely related to the immediate and precise focus of public health (Starr 1982, p. 180). For the purpose of this discussion of the "double disease burden" in Africa, and summarizing the most recent trend in the field, we appropriate the definition presented by the Institute of Medicine. This definition sees public health as aiming to fulfill "society's interest in assuring conditions in which people can be

Public health has expanded over the years to include such disciplines as epidemiology, biostatistics, behavioral and environmental health, health policy and management, maternal and child health, nutrition, and, more recently, global health. In contrast to the role of physicians and their individual patients, which is public health's primary focus, the emphasis may target the prevailing disease environment and prevention of disease through surveillance and monitoring of outbreaks. This effort looks at populations rather than isolated individuals. It employs scientific measures, raises disease awareness and modifies behaviors as immediate responses to threats to people's health. In the long run such campaigns reduce the need for costly treatment and frees societys wealth for other purposes.

It is generally agreed, therefore, that

> ...public health diagnoses the health state of a population; finds illnesses' causes, risk factors, and associations that disturb the equilibrium of a population's health at a certain point in time. Unlike a physician, on the level of one patient, public health collects, analyses, and applies morbidity and mortality data on a population scale, making its findings available to the public and helps develop policies that safeguard the health of a state, the nation, and the globe, with the ultimate goal of ensuring that access to basic health services is fairly distributed within the community, regardless of ethnicity, race, religion, national origin, sexual orientation, and socio-economic status. (Azevedo 2013)

In sum, while medical practice focuses on the individual, public health looks at the health of population segments in nations, across continents, or around the globe.

AFRICA AND ENVIRONMENTAL CHANGES

One of the problems facing those who would implement the Millennium Development Goals (MDGs) is climate change, the implications of which have been made much clearer by new scientific tools, such as geographic information systems and meteorological advances. These tools have clarified the changes the globe is undergoing and identified disease "transmission dynamics" that Africans are bound to face within the next decades (Thomson 2013, p. 1). The dynamics include inconsequential policies the leaders allow to exist in the face of real health threats. Policies are linked to environmental factors, such as land use, often motivated by the desire for instant profit on the part of multinational corporations and greedy citizens.

Regrettably, environmental policies are barely enforced, whether these policies or realistic and effective or just "in the books." Not all is negative on the continent. For example, as one expert put it, "Africa is moving into a new phase that could see the continent become a major player in the transition to a global inclusive green economy, but to do that it needs a healthy population with guaranteed access to well-managed natural resources" (WNN 2013).

The pathways of many infectious diseases in Africa are fairly well understood and can be linked to "seasonal, inter-annual, and decadal fluctuations" of weather patterns. The knowledge we have should warn leaders to think both retrospectively and prospectively as they craft health care systems that protect the health of citizens and preserve resources. This requires robust surveillance and monitoring systems that track current and potential disease outbreaks resulting from changing environmental factors. Even when the factors are at the mercy of nature in many cases, they are also a result of unwise and selfish policies.

To illustrate the impact of climatic changes on diseases, Madeleine Thomson points to the examples of meningitis and malaria. We know that these population illnesses can be prevented or mitigated, even in Africa.

Meningitis is seasonal but devastating in causing deaths in certain regions of the continent. Outbreaks in the so-called "meningitis belt" have been predicted to hit the Sahel every five to ten years, at times at the rate of 400 to 500 cases per 100,000 population. Its death toll has ranged from 5 to 10 percent of the cases, especially among young adults and children (Thomson 2013). Thomson's reference is to the area stretching from Senegal to Ethiopia, affecting some fifteen countries, a population of more than 300 million people.

Malaria is known to infect 2.7 million people worldwide, 90 percent in Sub-Saharan Africa, striking children the hardest. The disease belt also stretches from Senegal to Djibouti, to East Africa, including parts of southern Africa, and specific areas of southwest Africa. A disease said to hit the poor more frequently, malaria largely affects non-immune populations living on the fringes of malaria transmission.

The malarial area and the sources of outbreaks, as well as the impact of frequent natural and man-caused floods and droughts, are well documented. Leaders' unscrupulous neglect of their own environmental policies, if they have any, are frequently to blame for much of the spread. Cultural practices also play a role. On one hand, the WHO estimates that environmental factors account for 28–30 percent of ill health in Africa today. Floods, for example, create the breeding conditions beneficial for mosquitoes that cause yellow fever and malaria, flies that cause onchocerciasis or river blindness and trypanosomiasis or sleeping sickness, parasites that result in schistosomiasis or bilharzia; and rodents that carry such diseases as the plague. Extreme weather variability is on the rise, with floods almost seven times more likely now than in the 1980s.

Along with the immediate mortality and injury from extreme weather, indirect problems can contribute to a rise in water-borne diseases, the migration of pathogens, and food shortages from crop damage and livestock death" (*Guardian* 2013, p. 3). According to the WHO, environmental health risks in Africa are mainly from "agrochemicals, persistent organic pollutants (POPs), chemical stockpiles, e-waste, and petroleum waste."

Drought is recurrent in the Sahel belt and in parts of north central, central, and southern Africa. Drought causes hunger, famine, and kwashiorkor, stunting children's growth and damaging health. This is especially true in rural areas that make up at least two-thirds of the continent.

Air pollution is a major hazard in Africa's cities and towns, although many countries have begun to pay more attention to its devastating impact. In most of Africa, except in parts of certain cities, environmentally-associated diseases can be classified as *vector-borne* (e.g., malaria, trypanosomiasis, and onchocerciasis); *vessel-borne* (e.g., diarrhea, dysentery, and cholera), transmitted through water, drinking cups, food, milk, and blood; *airborne* (e.g., common cold, TB, measles, and respiratory ailments). Pollution contributes to cancer, heart ailments, and lung diseases, known as emerging chronic or non-communicable diseases.

The emerging non-communicable diseases have become what is called the "second disease burden" on the continent, infectious diseases being the "first burden." Thus it is said that Africa now suffers from a "double disease burden." Over 80 percent of these second burden diseases can be prevented with the appropriate vaccines, hygiene, and environmental control.

Ground and air pollution in Africa came to world attention in 2006, when a Dutch charter ship Trafigura illegally dumped 500 tons of toxic waste in the ports of Abidjan. About 30,000 people fell sick as a result of water contamination. The same has happened in Guinea-Bissau, where Westerners have been allowed to dump their toxic waste, and in Nigeria, where people of the Niger Delta have been fighting for over two decades to control soil degradation and deforestation resulting from oil companies' activities. Overall, it is claimed that human insensitivity and environmental neglect of the oil companies have resulted in numerous illnesses, deadly explosions, extortion, and hostage taking. Much of this has come as people tried to stop the exploitation or else sought to benefit from the oil by forcibly and carelessness trying to harness the flowing pipeline to power vehicles and meet house energy needs. Areas that were almost pristine forty years ago are becoming sources of pollution, ill-health, and death.

The harmful impact of human and corporate activity is illustrated vividly by a description of what has happened to Lake Malawi:

> Twaling in Lake Malawi . . . has led to a decline in snail-eating fish populations and a related increase in schistosomiasis, a parasitic disease hosted by snails. Though common in tropical regions, schistosomiasis was absent around Lake Malawi until recently. Pressure from population growth and agricultural conversions are also destroying coral and forest habitants, creating conditions favorable to disease transmission. (*The Guardian*, March 25, 2013)

Since 2002, the United Nations has made a concerted effort to convince African governments to think seriously about the environment and the potential disaster awaiting policies that are oblivious to the changing climate and its impact on survival and health. The international body has been exerting pressure on appropriate ministries to focus on air quality, biodiversity, chemicals and waste, climate change and variability, coastal and marine resources, fresh-water and sanitation, and land. Indoor pollution is another major health hazard plaguing the African continent, whose magnitude is said to be thirty times higher than the limits suggested by the World Health Organization.

AFRICA'S GEOGRAPHIC BARRIERS TO HEALTH

Inhabited by about 1.7 billion people, Africa is the second largest continent in the world and is comprised of fifty-four independent countries, occupying a surface area of 11,650,000 square miles. The continent is 5,000 miles from north to south and 4,600 miles from east to west. Africa is a continent of geographical and demographic diversity.

Yet, life has not been easy on the continent. Even at the dawn of the third millennium, about 70 percent of the African population engage in subsistence agriculture, producing primarily to feed their families, rather than to sell products in the marketplace. Some have characterized the soil of Africa as a "chunk of iron ore," although of low grade. Such soil renders agricultural activity more difficult and less productive. Given that only about 6 percent of the land is arable, most of the farming is still agriculture intensive, rather than extensive. Farming is characterized by shifting and slash-and-burn practices, in which the tools are still simple, and resources, such as fertilizers, are often non-existent. In the arable areas, parts of the savannah and highlands of East Africa, a pastoral life, often nomadic, characterizes the culture. A tiny percentage of people in Central Africa (as among the Bambuti and the Twa) and in the Namib and the Kalahari deserts live essentially by hunting.

As a result of the harsh reality of life in the farms of the countryside and the lure of urban lifestyle brought on by Western colonization, African cities are bursting. Waves of rural migrants make life even more miserable in these urban enclaves. There is overcrowding, poverty, slums, and violent crime in such cities as Cairo (Africa's largest city), Johannesburg, Lagos, Kinshasa, Lusaka, and Abidjan. In Zambia urbanization has occurred so rapidly that over half of the country's population lives in the urban areas.

The continent has been described by geographers as a high plateau, with 90 percent of its land mass located 500 feet above sea level (compared to Europe's 50 percent). Eighty percent of it lies within the tropics of Cancer and Capricorn, and the land mass is divided almost in half by the Equator. Major geographical features include the Great Rift Valley, which extends from the Red Sea through the Ethiopian mountains to East Africa's lakes and out of to the Indian Ocean in Mozambique. Parts of its plateau are made of isolated mountains or mountain chains, including Kilimanjaro (19,340 feet), Rwenzori (16,000 feet), Kenya (17,000 feet), Cameroon (13,000 feet), the Drakensberg of South Africa (11,000 feet), the Atlas Mountains of Northwest Africa (13,000 feet), and the Manica Plateau of Mozambique and Zimbabwe.

Africa's long rivers (Nile, 4,000 miles; Niger, 2,600 miles; Zambezi, 1,600 miles) and the largest freshwater lakes (Victoria, Tanganyka, Rudolf, and Chad) have formed within several internal basins, such as the Djouf Basin of the Middle Upper Niger River; the Chad Basin around Lake Chad; the Sudan Basin of the Upper Nile; the Congo Basin, mainly in Congo-Kinshasa; and the Kalahari Basin of Southern Africa. Although Africa's rivers range in length from 4,000 miles, as is the case with the Nile, to over 1,600 miles for the Zambezi, they are not entirely navigable. Still, they constitute an important means of communication, transportation, and trading activities. Both rivers and lakes provide fishing opportunities for their surrounding populations and offer great hydroelectric potential for the entire continent. Unfortunately, except for the Aswan Dam in Egypt, the Cahora Bassa Dam in Mozambique, and the Upper

Volta Dam in Northern Ghana, Africa has been unable to effectively harness the tremendous resources its waters offer. Some years ago, geographer W. Hance wrote:

> The water power resources of Africa are tremendous and are estimated at about 40 percent of the world's total (275 of 688 million horsepower). It is somewhat ironic that this continent, plagued with aridity over such great areas, should at the same time have such a magnificent hydroelectric potential. The high rainfall in the rainforest and savanna areas, and their high average elevation, combine to explain this wealth. About 18 percent of the world total and 45 percent of the African potential are in the Congo Basin. The 217-mile stretch of the Lower Congo River from Leopoldville to Matadi has an estimated potential of 85 million horsepower. (Hance 1969, p. 19)

The problem is, of course, related to topography, which forces rivers to meander through flat regions. Dams also are very costly and rarely efficient. The unpredictability of heavy rain and the absence of or short duration of rain in many parts of the continent makes life difficult. Grove expressed this complexity:

> In January inflows of unstable moist air from the South Atlantic brings rain to the Congo [former Zaire] basin while the Indian Ocean is the source of rain for the countries stretching from Natal to Tanzania. As the sun moves north, so the inter-tropical convergence zone (ITCZ) follows. By March the rainy season is over in Botswana and Zimbabwe and is beginning in a zone stretching across the continent from Kenya to Sierra Leone. By July/August, the ITCZ has reached furthest north and Atlantic air occupies much of the continent between a few degrees north of the equator and the tropic of Cancer; rain falls over most of West Africa and Ethiopia with occasional showers even on the Tibesti mountains in the Sahara. In September and October the rain belt moves rapidly south again, bringing a second rainy season to the equatorial zone. Then the cycle starts again. (Grove 1989, p. 18)

The laymen can best understand the geographical complexity of Africa by examining its four or five almost distinct climatic and vegetation zones.

One of these climate zones is the tropical rainforest (with the highest population density in Africa, up to 500 people per square kilometer, which straddles the Equator from the Atlantic Ocean to the start of the East African highlands. Here temperatures never fall below sixty-eight degrees F. This region is characterized by heavy and constant rainfall, receiving over fifty inches (127 mm) of rain per year. Therefore, it has no dry season. Because the constant heavy clouds reflect the sunlight, average temperatures remain between eighty-four and ninety degrees F in this zone.

Tropical rainforest vegetation is made up of thick, heavy trees, at times becoming a jungle that covers 15 percent of Africa. There are brushes, ferns as tall as 10 feet, palm trees, wood climbers or lianas that may reach a height of 60 feet, and a canopy of broadleaved evergreens up to 150 feet tall. Soils of the tropical rainforest are not the best because they lack humus and are low in organic nutrients and essential minerals, but they can sustain enough agricultural activity to feed millions of people. Rainforest crops include cassava; yams; sweet potatoes; such grains as rice and corn; fruits, including plantains and bananas; coffee; cotton; palm oil; sesame; squash; melon; peanuts; peas; beans; onions; tomatoes; tobacco; mushrooms; edible leaves; snails; and termites.

Mahogany and ebony trees are abundant in the rainforest region and constitute important export items in the form of wood and timber. Rubber trees produce sap, and quinine is extracted from certain trees. Livestock and poultry include goats, sheep, pigs, and chickens. Mineral resources consist of iron, uranium, copper, gold, petroleum, diamonds, gold, zinc, bauxite, and titanium, among others.

Here, one finds almost all of the tropical diseases, including yellow fever, malaria, chagas, dengue fever, cholera, sleeping sickness, and even ebola virus, which make the environment a threat if one is not protected.

The savanna vegetation zone covers most of Africa's land mass and lies just above and below the equatorial rainforest. Life in the savanna is pleasant, and most of the large game (elephants, lions, rhinoceros, giraffes, and hippopotami) are found here, some of which live in national parks. Here the rainy season, called the high sun, is long and is followed by a short dry season, called the low sun. Even in this coolest period of the year, temperatures never drop below sixty-five degrees F. The soils are capable of high agricultural yields, producing sorghum, wheat, cotton, bananas, and cashew nuts. Livestock production produces cattle and sheep, which are sources of milk, butter, and blood and are high in protein content. Minerals range from phosphates and chromite to diamonds, tin, gold, coal, zinc, copper, manganese, iron, and petroleum, some of which is exported. Vegetation in the savanna is varied, but the essential features are shrubs, grasses, scattered thorn trees, and acacias in the dry areas.

Diseases here are virtually the same as in most rainforest, including malaria, onchorcerciasis, trypanosomiais, and livestock rinderpest. All of the parasitic diseases common to the Tropics and the Equator are a danger. Many areas of the savanna are infested with mosquitoes, flies, and other insects that cause such diseases as malaria (the greatest killer of African children), yellow fever, river blindness, and sleeping sickness.

The desert or low-lying zone contains the Sahara Desert (about 3 million square miles) in the north. The Namib and the Kalahari deserts are located in southern Africa and form part of the countries of Namibia, Botswana, Zimbabwe, and South Africa. The desert, especially the Sahara, is hot during the day, reaching over 120 degrees F, but can be as cool as fifty degrees F at night. In the Sahara, oil, gas, uranium, and phosphate have been found, while the Kalahari and the Namib deserts are rich in diamonds, copper, coal, nickel, asbestos, kijamite, manganese, gold, barite, limestone, and chrome. The few meager crops that can be produced include sorghum, millet, beans, cowpea peanuts, and sunflowers in the Namib and Kalari deserts, and dates in the Sahara Desert. Sheep and goats can be raised in the Sahara.

The fringes of the Sahara Desert are less barren, and receive between 8 and 80 inches of rain yearly, but recurring droughts affect Senegal, Mali, Niger, Mauritania, Chad, Burkina Faso, Kenya, Somalia, and Sudan.

The Sahel constitutes a transition zone between the desert and the savanna, located between zero degrees and 150 degrees north latitude and extending from the east to the west coasts. Sahelian soils lack humus and are much less productive than elsewhere, except when irrigated. Crops include peanuts, millet, corn, sesame, tobacco, barley, wheat, and cotton. The Sahel hosts many nomadic groups, such as the Tuareg and the Tubu, who raise camels, cattle, sheep, and goats along the sparse oases. Phosphate, iron, and salt, as well as oil, have been found in several areas of this zone. The disease problem is caused by drought, which may result in hunger and starvation, malnutrition, and outbreaks of meningitis. There are fewer cases of malaria. In 1968 to 1974, about 100,000 people of the Sahel died from starvation.

The Mediterranean climate zone is found on both extremities of Africa. In the north are Morocco, Algeria, Libya, Tunisia, and part of northern Egypt, and the southern tip of South Africa. The major climatic feature of the Mediterranean zone is that there are two distinct seasons, a dry summer and a cold, rainy winter. Rainfall can exceed twenty inches a year. Citrus fruits, grapes, apples, peaches, wheat, olives, cotton, rice, and onions are grown in both northern and southern Africa's Mediterranean zones. Cattle and sheep flourish, although desert winds from the southern interior, called sirocco, khamigin, or ghibili, have been devastating economically. Oil, natural gas, manganese, cobalt, lead, and mercury are found in the northern zone, whereas in South Africa gold and diamonds are abundant. Given the Mediterranean zone's mild climate most of the year, with a cold winter, most diseases of the rainforest and savanna are not found in this region. Cardiovascular diseases are not common either, and studies have shown that the Mediterranean diet may have something to do with good cardiovascular health. Peculiar to the area is Thalasemia, an inherited disorder manifest through the reduction or absence of sufficient hemoglobin, the oxygen-carrying protein inside the red blood cells. Thalasemia causes several types of anemia. Other diseases include familial Mediterranean fever, brucellosis, west Nile virus, and viral hepatitis.

The East African highlands found in Ethiopia, Uganda, Kenya, Tanzania, Rwanda, and Burundi constitute the best climatic zone for human habitat in Africa, with moderate to very cool temperatures. The land here is generally fertile. A wide variety of crops include millet, sorghum, corn or maize, cassava, bananas, potatoes, yams, beans, sugar-cane, tobacco, coffee, tea, sisal, coconuts, sesame, mangoes, and cashew nuts. The soil is known to contain diamonds, copper, gold, tin, beryl, soda, ash, tungsten, phosphate, iron, coal, and uranium. Cattle, sheep, goats, and poultry also supplement the diet of the people who are fortunate to live in these areas. Compared to rest of the continent, the most important feature of the soil is its high organic content.

For a long time, the European colonizers preferred the highlands because they were fertile, cooler, and had few mosquitoes that could cause malaria and yellow fever or parasitic diseases. Over the past sixty years, however, mosquitoes have migrated to these areas and are causing as much havoc as in the rainforest and the savanna, as exemplified by Kenya, Tanzania, and Uganda.

Obviously, one can argue about whether the continent's geographical conditions are a hindrance or a facilitator to health and economic development. Griffiths notes:

> Africa is a continent of wide horizons of broad, flat plateau surfaces. . . . The plateau consists of a number of vast, swallow basins separated often by barely discernible watersheds, occasionally by mountainous tracts of considerable height in the Tibesti [Chad], Air and Hoggan mountains of the Sahara. In Southern Africa the Kalahari basin presents an outward-facing scarped rim, the Great Escarpment, which in places rises to 10,000 feet (300m) proving a formidable obstacle to transport development. (Griffiths 1984, pp. 5–6)

Over the centuries, people have tried to tame the geography of Africa, but the struggle has been difficult. Soil erosion, deforestation, intermittent fires, desertification, and the apparent rise in temperatures constitute perhaps the most serious problems Africans face regarding their continent and their health and survival. In this context, the many rivers and lakes notwithstanding, long distances from these waters present a major challenge for at least fifteen landlocked countries that share a common legacy of colonial neglect and continue to be very poor and underdeveloped. Some development is taking place in these countries, but per capita income still averages less than $400 a year, except in Botswana, Mauritius, Ghana, Lesotho, Swaziland, Uganda, Gabon, and Nigeria (Stock 1995, p. 16). The geography of a continent determines not only the economic activity and wealth of its people but also the course of their history, their health, and their health care system.

AFRICA'S POVERTY AND ITS ILL HEALTH

Significant to the discussion of the causes or risk factors associated with health and disease in Africa is the issue of poverty, which quite often is absolute. The association between poverty and ill health has been established by numerous studies over the past decade, prompting a WHO report to characterize it as a "vicious circle," in which poverty breeds ill-health and ill-health maintains poverty. (Wagstaff 2002). Such is the cycle as long as socio-economic inequalities and disparities, most often based on race and ethnicity, remain in society. As McCally and colleagues noted in 1998:

> A growing body of research confirms the existence of a powerful connection between socio-economic status and health. . . . Absolute poverty, which implies a lack of resources deemed necessary for survival, is self-evidently associated with poor health, particularly in less developed countries. . . . Strong evidence now indicates that relative poverty, which is defined in relation to the average resources available in a society, is also a major determinant of health in industrialized countries. (McCally et al. 1998, p. 726)

Several statements from the U.S. Centers for Disease Control and Prevention (CDC), based on CDC studies, make it quite clear that the association is strong, particularly in reference to HIV/AIDS (CDC Public Health Reports 2008, p. 9). The CDC noted in 2010 that "Heterosexuals living below the poverty line in [Western] cities are five times as likely as the nation's general population to be HIV-positive, regardless of their race or ethnicity" (see Maugh 2010, p. 1).

In Africa, where poverty is rampant, as in most villages and slums of the continent's cities and towns, its nefarious impact on health cannot be underestimated. Thomson emphatically stresses that "poverty is at the root of environmental diseases."

> Poverty means isolation from clinics and doctors; lack of money to pay for treatment; the use of inexpensive and sometimes less effective free treatments by governments. Poverty also means that people are malnourished or undernourished—this makes them easier targets for all kinds of environmental diseases, from which they either find it hard to recover or die. (United Nations 2013, p. 1)

Despite disease and ill health, made worse by the environment, Africa is still the fastest growing continent. This population exerts maximum pressure on the land, making it difficult to provide safe water and sanitation. Currently, about half of Africans do not have these two requisites for good health. Many cities and towns simply do not have sewages systems. In many parts of the country, those responsible are overwhelmed by ineffective sewage systems that ooze fecal matter and chemicals harmful to people, a condition that is made the worse by ingrained centuries-old cultural practices. Indeed, as the UN notes:

> In rural areas with no modern sewage systems, water points can be easily contaminated if the water is used for more than one purpose, for example, when drinking water is also used for washing clothes or the body. Feces and chemicals in the water cause diseases such as diarrhea.

> In poor and isolated communities, this is often fatal as there is little or no access to hospitals, clinics and medicines to cure them. Disease such as malaria and sleeping sickness are also diseases of rurality mainly, as the insects that cause them live in agricultural areas. (United Nations 2013, p. 1)

Determinants of poverty and ill-health include, among other things, low income, unemployment, lack of adequate education, absence of clean drinking water; inadequate health insurance coverage; unsanitary conditions; long travel time or distance to local primary health care facilities, and absence of essential drugs. The WHO concludes that household income is a major culprit of health disparities, "probably a larger cause of impoverishment than out-of-pocket payments for health services" (WHO 2002, p. 98). Income ultimately affects a person's ability to afford shelter, food, clothing, and health care." The poor "frequently face a higher price at the point of use because they are less likely to have insurance coverage, whether private or public" (North et al. 2000). Unfortunately, the disparity gap in health is wide and "the net effect has been to remove from view—and from policy discourse—the pervasive patterning health disparities by a socio-economic position within and across racial/ethnic groups, as well as to retard understanding of the contribution of economic and non-economic aspects of racial discrimination or racial/ethnic disparities" (Krieg and Faber 2005, p. 312). It is worth noting that poverty is a relative term associated with country and class, but the United Nations and the World Bank define a poor person in the developing world as someone who makes less than $2 (U.S.) a day. That includes at least one-third of the population of Africa.

THE CRITICAL IMPORTANCE OF HYGIENE IN AFRICA

Public health studies have established the fact that many infectious diseases (ID) are still around or emerging due partly to the lack of home and community hygiene both in the developed and developing worlds. Scientific evidence has proven that habits such as a simple hand washing can stop the spread of a plethora of infections, halt the development of diseases, and curtail the number of untimely deaths. Says the International Scientific Forum for Home Hygiene (IFH), "Indications are that a significant proportion of the global infectious disease burden is caused by diseases which are hygiene-related (i.e., transmitted via food, water, fecal and other waste material, hands and other surfaces, and via the air)." Indeed, the IFH continues, within the home and family settings, standards of hygiene, "in relation to hand washing, handling of food and water, disposal of feces and other waste materials, care of at risk groups and people who are infected, are key factors which determine the ID burden within and between communities" (IFG 2009, p. 1). One medical assumption is that simply washing hands could reduce the incidence of diarrheal infections by 47 percent and that respiratory infections (common colds, and the flu and its complications, such as pneumonia), could be reduced by over 23 percent by hand hygiene alone.

In a 2003 report, the World Health Organization (WHO) noted that food borne illness is almost always preventable. Studies carried out in one of the most developed countries of the world, the United Kingdom, between 1993 and 1996, reported that "for every one reported case of Campylobacter, Salmonella, rotavirus and norovirus, another 7.6, 3.2, 35 and 1,562 cases, respectively, occur in the community." We know that non-food borne gastrointestinal infections are transmitted from person to person through contaminated hands and surfaces or by inhalation of particles produced when an infected person vomits. A number of pathogenic infections and antibiotic resistance microbes, such as methicillin resistant Staphylococcus aureus (MRSA), could be eliminated or greatly decreased if everyone would adopt hygienic practices.

The spread of infections through non-hygienic handling of pets, such as dogs and cats, which can carry infectious organisms causing salmonella, campylobacter, staph. aureus, and clostridium difficile, is common in American homes. Most American pet owners never imagine the risk they live with. In the United States, 39 percent of dogs may carry campylobacter and between 10 percent and 27 percent may carry salmonella. Asthma and wheezing in children may be triggered by easily avoidable respiratory infections. Even among such diseases as HIV/AIDS, malaria, diarrhea, and tuberculosis, scientists note, good hygiene is the most cost-effective means of prevention. One of the leading causes of blindness in the developing world is completely preventable with face washing. A children's hygiene study in one residential area in England found that

> Child carers washed hands with soap after changing a dirty nappy [diaper] on 42 percent of occasions, and . . . one in five toilet users did not wash hands with soap afterwards. Microbiological samples were taken from household surfaces at sites thought likely to be involved in the transfer of fecal material. . . . Fifteen percent of bathroom samples showed contamination with polio vaccine virus. Nappy [diaper] changing took place mainly in living rooms. Contact with living room surfaces and objects during nappy [diaper] changing was frequent and evidence of fecal contamination was found in 12 percent of living room samples. Evidence of fecal contamination was also found in kitchens, again on surfaces thought likely to be involved in the transmission of feces (taps and soap dispensers). (Curtis et al. 2003)

Several studies have studied the rapid spread of MRSA, especially in such crowded conditions as homes and prisons. A lack of personal hygiene has been one of the major risk factors. The CDC has thus quoted one interesting study conducted by Calfee: In a community-based study, Calfee et al. demonstrated that close contact with a person colonized or infected with MRSA resulted in a 7.5-fold greater risk of becoming colonized with MRSA. Persons colonized with MRSA also have an increased risk for MRSA infection. Improved personal hygiene may provide protection for inmates living and working in such contaminated environments.

The CDC also cites a Nguyen et al. study, which found that, after taking other risk factors into account, being African-American had no bearing on contracting MRSA. Sharing soap was associated with recurring MRSA infections in a football team and with sharing personal hygiene items. Personal hygiene is so important, that it remains a prime objective of health care in the United States.

With little clean water to spare in most of Africa, it is difficult for many families and communities to maintain acceptable hygienic practices in homes, families, and schools, particularly among children, the elderly, and the sick. Preserving one's health is virtually a matter of chance on a continent where people live in underdeveloped rural areas and there is a close interface between nature, the animal kingdom, and insect and parasitic micro-organisms. The nature of housing also presents a perennial obstacle to good health where the distance to health centers and hospitals makes transportation challenging. Children play in open ponds and in the mud after rains or floods in water infected by snails and other disease vectors. In such situations, hygiene and good health become almost an insurmountable problem. Also, lower literacy rates in the countryside through almost all Sub-Saharan Africa impede populist understanding of disease and other infection transmission. It is even harder to build awareness of prevention regarding non-communicable illnesses that are silent and asymptomatic.

GLOBALIZATION

We cannot address the issue of health in Africa without looking carefully at the phenomenon we have come to call globalization. Globalization comprises "multiple, interacting policy dynamics, or processes the effects of which may be difficult if not impossible to separate." Pathways from globalization to changes in social determinants of health are not always linear, do not operate in isolation from one another, and may involve multiple stages and feedback loops. "Similarities exist with the task of analyzing causal links between environmental changes and human health which are complex because often they are indirect, displaced in space and time, and dependent on a number of modifying forces" (Labonte et al. 2007). Studies have shown that globalization has resulted in higher inequalities, both within and among nations. Indeed, in countries with higher income disparities, "the greater the inequality, the harder it becomes for the economic growth presumed to follow trade liberalization actually to lift people out of poverty."

It is well known that poor groups in societies with higher income disparities are more likely to contract non-communicable diseases (NCDs) and have less access to treatment, resulting in NCDs epidemics. In developing countries, greater disparities in income, living conditions in urban slums and the lack of regulation of food markets have led to an increase in NCDs. This is certainly tragic for Africa, which also suffers from infectious disease on a massive scale. It has become clearer that integration into the international economy or economic globalization usually does not help people pay for the services they require. Instead, there is an increase in cost to receive such services, thus negating any beneficial income that results from alleviating poverty. Yet access to health services is claimed to be one of the ultimate aims of the Structural Adjustment Programs by proponents of the International Monetary Fund and the World Bank. Okasha writes on globalization:

> The global village allegedly created by globalization is not global after all. If we assume that 100 people are living on earth, 57 of them are Asians, 21 are Europeans, 8 are Africans, 6 are Americans; 48 are men and 52 are women; 30 are white and 70 are non-white; 30 are Christians and 70 are non-Christians. On the other hand, 6 people own 59 percent of the community wealth and they are all North-Americans. Eighty live in poverty, 70 cannot read, 50 die in famine, 1 has higher education and 1 has a computer. It is obvious that power and resources do not seem to follow the majority/minority pattern of the world population, i.e., globalization has failed until now to democratically represent the world it has claimed to globalize (Okasha 2005).

Globalization plus unregulated urbanization has made physical activity less desirable and has promoted unhealthy habits. It has encouraged international competition and overproduction of unhealthy consumer items—especially fatty foods, tobacco, and alcohol. In spite of the now obvious adverse effects of these dietary factors on health, the economic incentive for their production remains huge. Furthermore, "with poverty and socioeconomic inequalities comes increased exposure and vulnerability to these risks" (Consultancy Africa Intelligence 2012, p. 2). Other analysts of globalization have stressed the erosion of government authority because "the domains that affect the double disease burden beyond health care applies to the food industry, agricultural production, alcohol, urban planning, pharmaceutical industries, water and sanitation, among others" (Consultancy 2012, p. 3). Lobbying by private industry also has stalled the ability of the World Trade Organization to regulate food, tobacco, and alcohol in the developed and developing world.

INFECTIOUS VERSUS CHRONIC OR NON-COMMUNICABLE DISEASES

Infectious Diseases

How is the dichotomy between infectious and chronic or non-communicable diseases affecting Africa? In such developed countries as the United States, we like to think that infectious diseases are largely a thing of the past. Having reached the stage called the epidemiologic transition, our efforts must be redirected to dealing with chronic illnesses. This is evident in remarks made by the U.S. Surgeon General as early as 1967. He declared that it was "time to close the book on infectious disease, declare the war against pestilence won, and shift national resources to such chronic problems as cancer and heart disease" (Nelson 2003). While such a statement is not completely misguided, as there have, indeed, been laudable improvements, the fight against infectious diseases is far from over. More than four decades after this pronouncement, the U.S. is still dealing with various old and emerging infectious diseases. The resurgence in tuberculosis infections and the increase in the number of HIV/AIDS infections among the elderly in the United States justify the continued need to maintain robust surveillance systems focusing on infectious diseases.

Indeed, compared to the rest of the world, most developed countries have either eradicated or significantly reduced the prevalence of such infectious diseases as smallpox and polio. These seem to have been replaced by chronic illnesses. In spite of the more successful strides against infectious diseases in the West, the 1996 comments made by the director-general of the WHO, the world's most powerful and respected public health body, underscore the ubiquitous nature of infectious diseases, even if they are most prevalent in the developing world. Director-General Nakajima said, "We are standing on the brink of a global crisis in infectious diseases. No country is safe from them. No country can any longer afford to ignore their threat" (Nakajima 1996). What must be understood is not how many infectious diseases are ravaging the global community, but rather how virulent they are when they strike. A review of the global prevalence of infectious diseases shows that six—pneumonia, tuberculosis, diarrhea, malaria, measles, and, more recently, HIV/AIDS—account for half of all premature deaths. These diseases predominantly kill children and young adults (WHO 2011). In the United States, for example, pneumonia-influenza was the eighth leading cause of death in 2009.

Thus, the global community has refined strategies to address the health needs that arise from the scourge of infectious diseases. The strategies are encapsulated in the Millennium Development Goals, signed by all 193 UN member states and twenty-three international organizations at the Millennium Summit in 2000. The goals, to be achieved by 2015, include

- eradicating extreme poverty and hunger;
- achieving universal primary education;
- promoting gender equality and empowering women;
- reducing child mortality rates;
- improving maternal health;
- combating HIV/AIDS, malaria, and other diseases;
- ensuring environmental sustainability; and
- developing global partnerships.

To assist the heavily indebted poor countries, in 2005 the G8 finance ministers agreed to provide sufficient funding to the World Bank, the International Monetary Fund (IMF), and the African Development Fund (ADB) by cancelling some $40 billion to $50 billion (U.S.) in debt, on the condition that the amount forgiven would be used to improve education and health and alleviate poverty. Unfortunately, Africa is far from achieving these goals.

The WHO characterizes Africa as the continent that is experiencing a double burden of disease, consisting of massive new infections and infectious diseases and emerging chronic non-communicable ailments that have shortened life expectancy at birth. The shorter life expectancies have arisen despite the great infusion of domestic, international, philanthropic, and non-governmental organization resources. Worthy of note is PEPFAR, which undoubtedly has slowed the spread of the HIV/AIDS epidemic in Africa and treated those infected and lucky enough to receive AZT treatment. Unfortunately only 30 percent of the HIV/AIDS infected Sub-Saharan Africans receive this treatment, even though this experienced a major improvement over the past decades. Estimates are that, by 2012, the number of people receiving anti-retroviral treatment jumped to 7 million from one million in 2005, a seven-fold increase in eight years. In 2012, one million new patients received treatment (UNAIDS 2013). However, as Jennifer Cooke notes, "Some evidence also indicates that the massive inflow of resources to fight the continent's 'big three' infectious diseases (HIV/AIDS, tuberculosis, and malaria) has led to some distortions within Africa's health systems and in policy priorities and drawn resources and attention away from some of the continent's most important and looming health challenges." As a result, she said, maternal health, bacterial and parasitic diseases, and non-communicable illnesses have been neglected. Mental health remains grossly unreported because of its complexity, cost, and associated stigma.

It was noted above that, despite the most recent advances in medicine and public health, Sub-Saharan Africa represents only 13 percent of the world's population, yet experiences 24 percent of the global burden of disease. This is partially caused and exacerbated by poverty, underdevelopment, political conflict, and weak or ill-managed institutions (see CSIS 2009). The history of infectious diseases is such that, all other things being equal, many infections should by now have been relegated to the past.

Infectious diseases can be chronic or acute. Some begin as acute illnesses before they become chronic problems. Acute diseases are relatively severe disorders with sudden onset and a short duration of symptoms. Acute illnesses spread from one case to another and may cause an outbreak and epidemic, endemic, and pandemic conditions. They are caused by microbial agents, such as bacteria, viruses, fungi, protozoa, helminthes, and arthropods. These diseases are called vector-borne. Transmission follows the epidemiologic triangle of vector, host, and environment through a fly, a mosquito, lice, fleas, or ticks into the human host. Even though vector-borne protozoan and bacterial infections are often less virulent than HIV, TB, and malaria, they affect an estimated one billion people worldwide (most in Africa). Some are fatal; others leave their victims blind or with physical deformities, stunted in intellectual and physical growth. Productivity and pregnancy are affected (Cooke 2012, 6). Infectious diseases are also known as communicable or transmissible diseases as they are transmitted from the infectious agents to the host through several mechanisms.

Chronic Diseases

Non-communicable diseases (NCDs), chronic diseases, or degenerative illnesses, on the other hand, are usually less severe but lasting for a long time. They may go on for a lifetime, even if they do not cause relatively immediate death. They generally include conditions related to prolonged exposure to an agent or unhealthful behaviors and socio-environmental factors. In many cases, there is a genetic predisposition.

For NCDs, the risk factors can be independent and or synergetic (Bhuiyan et al. 2013). They are most often characterized by uncertain etiology, multiple risk factors, a long latency period, prolonged illness, and functional impairment or disability. They are non-contagious and incurable. As noted, the causes of many chronic diseases remain unclear, but some risk factors have been identified. These include tobacco and alcohol use, high cholesterol, inadequate diet, physical inactivity, obesity, stress, occupation, pollution, and low socio-economic status (Brownson, Remington, and Davis 1998). Such chronic illnesses as heart disease, cancer, and diabetes are still the leading causes of deaths in most developed countries and are taking their toll among the developing nations.

Seven of the top ten causes of death can be attributed to chronic conditions. They are major causes of disability and contributors to exponential increases in health care costs. Yet, despite their frightening impact, according to the Centers for Disease Control and Prevention (2009), chronic diseases such as cancer and diabetes are among the most preventable of all health problems. Indeed, the most cost-effective measure of lowering chronic morbidity and mortality lies mainly in the reduction of modifiable risk factors as obesity, tobacco use, and physical inactivity. The incidence of non-communicable diseases has been growing alarmingly over the past twenty years, turning chronic degenerating ailments into major causes of disease and death in middle income countries, especially in Sub-Saharan Africa.

This has been predicted in the field and has become a major challenge for governments and health systems in the sub-continent, precisely where infectious diseases have hit Africa the hardest when compared to the rest of the globe. Such diseases as obesity and diabetes mellitus, hypertension, stroke, and asthma contribute to 63 percent of deaths globally and 70 percent of deaths in developing countries. It is also estimated that by 2030 NCDs will be the leading cause of death in Sub-Saharan Africa. As one commentator put it, "We are in a risk transition from our 'modern risks,' which include smoking, physical inactivity, alcohol abuse, and unhealthy diets." Consequently, with the increase in life span and modern risks, NCDs are predominantly an issue in older segments of the population. Nevertheless, this still partially accounts for only the increased burden of NCDs. It is also predicted that, by 2025, the number of diabetics in Africa will reach 20 million from the prevalence of 10 million in 2006.

The 1978 International Conference on Primary Health Care at Alma-Atta, Kazakhstan, declared that health is a right of all and not a privilege of a few. The Alma-Ata Declaration stressed the paramount role that primary health care should play. Africa and its donors have focused attention on the eradication of infectious diseases, with special emphasis on HIV/AIDS, tuberculosis, and malaria. Globally, 33 million people live with HIV/AIDS today, 330 million suffer from malaria every year, and 8.8 million are infected with TB. Ninety percent of malaria deaths occur in Africa, the most responsible agent being the mosquito plasmodium falciparum, source of the most severe and life-threatening malaria infections on the continent (Cooke 2012, p. 5).

The WHO reports that 68 percent of those living with HIV/AIDS are in Africa and affect people's most productive years of life. Seventy percent of new HIV infections are estimated to occur in Africa, while 90 percent of new infections among children are on the continent. It is also known that 75 percent of the global infections from HIV/AIDS, equivalent to 1.9 million annually, occur in Africa.

The regional distribution of HIV/AIDS infections in Africa is uneven. North Africa, which comprises six countries, has always had the lowest prevalence rates on the continent. In 2011 the rate was 0.1 percent among fifteen to forty-nine year olds. The Horn of Africa experiences low rates, between 0.6 percent and 1.4 percent in 2011. In Central Africa, made up of nine countries, the prevalence is moderate to high, at 1 percent in the island nation of Sao Tome e Principe and 5 percent in Gabon. In East Africa, with twelve countries, the prevalence is moderately high, ranging from 0.3 to a high of 7.2 percent in Uganda. West Africa's seventeen countries, with two types of HIV—HIV 1 and the less virulent HIV 2—has a moderate prevalence. The highest prevalence rate in West Africa is 3.7 percent in Nigeria.

Research findings in West Africa identifies commercial sex as the culprit for HIV, which is very common among the young. In Accra, Ghana, for example, it is estimated that 80 percent of the HIV infections in young men result from commercial sex encounters with inflected women. The study also found that, in Nigeria, whereas the overall prevalence rate of infections is only 0.8 percent, commercial sex among the young accounts for 36 percent of those that occur.

In southern Africa, where there are nine countries, the rates tend to be much higher, according to UNAIDS. There is an average prevalence rate of 10 percent in Botswana, Lesotho, Malawi, Mozambique, Namibia, South Africa, Zambia, and Zimbabwe. South Africa has the highest prevalence (17 percent). Despite these alarming numbers, it must be noted that the rate of HIV infections in Africa decreased by 25 percent from 2005 to 2012.

The heavy reallocation of resources by African governments and bilateral assistance has brought progress in the battle against HIV/AIDS. President George W. Bush committed $48 billion dollars to prevention and treatment in 2003. There have been grants from the Bill and Linda Gates Foundation, the Global Fund, and the Global Alliance for Vaccines and Immunization. At this writing, East Africa has reached a plateau in incidence and prevalence of this curse. According to Eran Bendavid and Jayanta Bhattacharya, writing in the *Annals of Internal Medicine*, George Bush's Emergency Plan for AIDS Relief or PEPFAR, in combination with greater investments in health systems by African governments, resulted in 12 million lives being saved in Africa. Death rates in twelve African countries declined by 10.5 percent during the five-year period of the funding. However, there have been setbacks in vaccine and microbicide trials in east and southern Africa. Cultural and health systems have undermined effective outreach. The decline has come in such areas as testing, behavioral change messages, condom availability (where governments allow it), and programs that empower women to take more control over sexual contact (Cooke 2012, p. 4). One cannot overemphasize the role women play in creating a healthy society. On the issue of women's contribution to reduction of ill health in a society, studies have shown that "An increase of 1 percent in income per capita [for women] would lower infant mortality by one death per thousand in countries averaging 100/100,000 [MR (infant mortality)]. If that 1 percent gain in income were used to promote basic education, literacy rates would rise by 20 percent (Pannenborg 1995, p. 51).

The "Big Three" diseases have received so much attention that other infectious illnesses, such as dengue fever and chagas, have taken back stage, particularly following the eradication of smallpox in 1977 and the virtually total victory over polio during the past five years. It is disappointing that certain diseases, beside polio and smallpox, have been eradicated all over the world except in Africa. These include leprosy, elephantiasis, and trachoma (Mirabadi 2011).

Tuberculosis is most prevalent in Southeast Asia, but Sub-Saharan Africa has a TB incidence rate double that of Southeast Asia, and has the highest number of TB-related deaths and the highest per capita TB mortality in the world (Cooke 2012, p. 4), South Africa and Nigeria being the hardest hit in Africa. South Africa also has the highest prevalence, incidence and death rates per capita worldwide, followed by Zimbabwe and Mozambique. On TB, WHO notes that "HIV is the single most important factor behind Africa's TB resurgence," accounting for the continent's largest number of people known to be co-infected with HIV and TB" in the world (Cooke 2012, p. 5). Overall, Sub-Saharan Africa has the highest HIV/AIDS/TB co-infections, with the following absolute numbers in 2011: a total of 874,000, distributed as follows: 330,000 in South Africa; 83,000 in Mozambique; 50,000 in Nigeria; 47,000 in Kenya; and 46,000 in Zimbabwe. The region experienced a 20 percent co-infection rate increase from 2000 to 2001, which is extremely alarming. However, Swaziland had the higher rate per 100,000 population, namely, 1,010/100,000 population (WHO 2012).

The work of eradicating TB is complicated by the fact that some of its strains show multi-drug-resistance. Thus, there has been a setback to the UN much touted Direct Observation Treatment (DOT). Where things were improving, as in Uganda, a relapse seems to be occurring, especially among the youth (Mulekya 2013). The tragic impact of NCDs is that they cause premature death and disability on a delayed but massive scale. NCDs affect family livelihood and society's health as a whole due to their long latency, protracted duration and debilitating consequences. Solutions to infectious diseases are well known, but they are hard to eradicate because they involve personal and group behavior, even when awareness is present. Even though knowledge is power, awareness does not necessarily cause one to change behavior.

The spread of the automobile and other powered means of transportation have been a blessing to Africa but also a source of frequent and unnecessary injuries and deaths. Vehicular mortality, currently ranked tenth among Africa's public health threats and projected to rise to the top three in 2019, is virtually absent on the national and international health agendas (Cooke 2009, p. 3). The WHO estimates that, by 2020, road injuries will represent the third leading cause of disability in Africa, as the per capita ratio of vehicles increases.

There is some progress towards reducing the impact of malaria through the Roll Back Malaria Campaign, despite the failure of the various vaccine clinical trials. Indeed, whenever governments have adopted the campaign against malaria as a priority, the results have been almost immediate and dramatic. In Eritrea, malaria cases dropped by 80 percent, and death was reduced by 85 percent in 2000. In Rwanda, Sao Tome e Principe, and Tanzania, especially in Zanzibar, the results also have been dramatic. Mosquito nets, moderate insecticide spraying, proper body protection, and distribution of anti-malarial drugs have paid off.

On the power of government to influence or dictate health conditions and enforce behavioral changes, one needs to realize the different sides of the issues involved. Health issues function at three levels, namely, personal, population, and public health (Azevedo and Brackin 2013). Unfortunately, these levels are not clear cut, and the types of services and the needs within each can overlap. On the personal level, individuals are most familiar with personal health services. When a person has a common infection, such as a sore throat, or a minor cut, he or she visits a personal health care provider for treatment. The patient's condition, for the most part, does not affect others. If a disease or condition is producing morbidity in a community, it may be a personal health problem as well as a population health concern. Since providers cannot treat the entire community, such techniques as health education messages may be help prevent or limit the health burden on the affected population. An example of population health control efforts would be messages urging immunization for influenza, along with frequent hand washing and advice to "cover the cough" before and during flu season. Though urged, the action the population takes is voluntary (Azevedo and Brackin 2013).

If routine private health care providers and population health techniques cannot prevent or control a situation, public health may come into play. The distinction of what is considered public health is derived from the statutory authority that created and authorizes public health agencies. One lay definition often cited holds that public health is health that "one cannot do oneself." It is clear, for example, that individuals and individual health care providers do not have the authority to quarantine an infectious patient, inspect a food service facility, or regulate the local water supply. Some efforts of public health agencies overlap the two other forms. On one hand, campaigns to reduce tobacco use or urge potential mothers to seek health care before or early in their pregnancy are actually population-based and not done under the legal authority of a public health agency. On the other hand, regulations on immunizations required for school or day care are authorized under law, and people are compelled to comply. It should be noted, however, that immunization requirements are also aimed at protecting the population at large and the individual (Azevedo and Brackin 2013).

Public health agencies may often be forced to provide personal health services if those needed services are lacking in a community, the enabling statutory authority allows it, and funding is available. Thus, while called a public health clinic, the services provided by a state or county or district health department clinic are in reality personal health services.

The basic distinctions between the three levels or types of health services are important to note when considering approaches to help control unhealthy conditions and their disparities. Therefore, while many conditions, such as infant mortality, are looked on as public health, improvements will mostly come from personal and population health-based efforts. The role of public health may be more in support of the other two.

ASSOCIATED COST

The adverse impact of NCDs on government budgets in Africa has been sky rocketing. Estimates are that loss of income and needed treatment for heart disease and diabetes alone is costing the continent between 1 percent and 5 percent of the annual GDP, estimated at $1.184 trillion (U.S.) in 2012. Despite all of the resources allocated, if Sub-Saharan Africa continues along its present path, the cumulative effect of treatment will not be sustainable in the long run. Estimates are that, presently, 80 percent of the health budget in Africa goes to communicable diseases and the remainder to NCDs.

Diabetes, for example, is a disease Africa can hardly afford. Throughout the continent, patients struggle to buy syringes on their own to self-administer insulin. While in Mali, the cost of a syringe is between twenty cents and sixty cents, in Mozambique it is four cents to twenty cents, and in Zambia one cent to $1.50. A urine glucose test in Mali, where per capita income GDP is $900, costs about eighty-nine cents, and a blood glucose test can be performed for $2.38. Testing, insulin purchase, and transport for a city resident in Mali cost approximately $21.24 a month for diabetes care alone, or $225 a year, of which half, $11 a month, is for just one vial of 100 IU insulin. In Mozambique, the tests are free for labor inpatient members but about twenty-one cents for outpatients. In Zambia, the cost can be as high as $51.06 a month. In Kenya, where per capita GDP is estimated at $1,200 a year, most diabetics, even with government subsidies, are still unable to afford consistent effective health care.

In Sub-Saharan Africa, if leaders and civil society do not make public health a top priorities, the gains made against infectious disease over the last decade will soon be overshadowed. Only the government, assisted by a strong but enlightened civil society, has the power and the human and physical resources to mobilize and improve the health system. Only government can influence behavior in such matters as alcohol consumption, smoking, deficient diet, and physical inactivity through policy, advocacy, creation of conditions that facilitate physical exercise, and the ability to improve health, and curb lobbyists and multinational corporations disguised as promoters of positive globalization. Only a central power, aided by civil society pushing for policies on health, can minimize the impact of second-hand smoking, which is individually uncontrollable, or drunken driving, which has become one of the deadliest weapons against pedestrians or bus riders.

CONCLUSION: PRIORITIES AND STRATEGIES

Many of the issues related to the health of Africans are spelled out in the Millennium Goals that African heads of government pledged to work toward achieving. Much has been done regarding malaria, TB, and HIV, but high risk factors related to maternal and reproductive health, the so-called "silent epidemic in Africa," have been relegated to the backburner. Maternal mortality rates at childbirth are virtually unchanged. This condition can be corrected by realistic and acceptable family planning, the use of effective contraceptives, and the empowerment of women to negotiate their sexual life with husbands and male family members.

What might we include in the strategies for a better and healthier Africa in the years to come? The following is a summary of ideas and strategies recommended by those who have been involved with health and finance in Africa over the years. Needed are:

- awareness campaigns for both infectious and non-communicable diseases;
- more effective disease and risk factors surveillance;
- intensified and more accurate collection of data on reported and non-reported disease incidence;
- emphasis on disease prevention interventions;
- emphasis on primary health care that takes into account maternal and infant mortality;
- containment of vehicular deaths through policies, enforcement, and better infrastructure;
- stronger health through integration of health systems and strategic allocation of funding that focuses on access to health;
- establishment of an integrated approach to health that involves policy, health, urban planning, agriculture, education, and other sectors of life, such as economic development;
- help to build infrastructure in areas that have experienced conflict and war, such as the Democratic Republic of Congo, Sudan, Somalia, Zimbabwe, and Rwanda;
- establishment of accredited schools and programs of public health throughout the continent;
- improved human and physical health infrastructure;

- health financing that balances the budgets needed to reduce the impact of infectious as well as non-communicable diseases;
- improved health policy and leadership;
- elimination of gender inequities and norms;
- provision of means for water sanitation, nutrition, and food security;
- rural/urban infrastructure, where community-based distributions can reach the poorest, the most vulnerable, and the most isolated populations, thus saving scarce resources;
- continued commitment by donors to Africa's fight against infectious and chronic diseases;
- leaders committed to health goals, while involving civil society in governance and priorities, and
- global coordination and burden sharing among the United Nations, international assistance, NGOs, the G8, the World Bank, the International Monetary Fund, and new investors in Africa, such as China and India.

Of all these recommendations, most public health practitioners and academicians agree that prevention and health promotion must be priority number one.

The much discussed paradigm of the double burden of disease in Africa has led some observers to caution those who announce the impending ominous impact of NCDs not to overdo the projections. The claim that many NCDs are "diseases of affluence," as in the West, must be tempered with the disclaimer that they are "rather diseases of poverty, disproportionately affecting the most economically disadvantaged segments of national populations" (Barber 2012, p. 2). The risk factor shift to non-communicable disease must not work to the detriment of the war against such infectious diseases as HIV/AIDS and malaria. Overemphasizing the need to shift to non-communicable diseases seems to imply that the West is right when it says that the continent is rising out of poverty and disease to finally join the consumer capitalist global economy. That belief is reflected in statements such as one quoted by Barber:

> Lifestyle diseases . . . are now beginning to take their tool in Africa. . . . Africa's recent economic growth has created an emerging middle class that has adopted many of the West's most damaging lifestyle choices. . . . A sedentary lifestyle has been encouraged with wider car ownership and leisure hours spent watching computer screens and TV's. . . . Fast-food chain outlets are proliferating and are popular with office workers grabbing a quick lunchtime meal. Many will, on their way home from work, also buy a takeaway for their evening meal in front of the TV, forsaking traditional African diets that tend to be more nutritionally balanced. (Barber 2012, p. 2)

Africa must face the double burden of disease with determination, not accepting the status quo in health and health systems. Needs to eradicate transmissible diseases must be balanced with needs to stem the tide of non-communicable diseases. This will require the mobilization of physical, financial, and human resources directed towards awareness campaigns, changes in behavior, adjustment or eradication of certain cultural practices. Priorities must be aligned with new realities that tend toward producing an unhealthy and therefore unproductive population. There must be reverence for human rights and a keen sense for equality. Africa must resist the blind importation of some of the most nefarious, violent, materialistic, and explicit sex-related cultural elements that bombard our children's television screens in our own homes.

As Chukwuma puts it, "What is at stake is our health as populations, our wealth as nations, and our development as a region" (Chukwuma 2012).

BIBLIOGRAPHY

AllAfrica (2013). "Uganda: HIV Vaccine Trial Ends in Failure," April 26, 2013. Available at http://allafrica.com/stories/201304261192.html. Accessed 18 July 2013.

Allen, F.R. (1943). "Development of the Public Health Movement in the Southeast," *Social Forces*, 22 (1): pp. 67–75.

Arendt, H. (1993). *Between Past and Future*. Baltimore: Penguin Books.

Azevedo, M.J., and Johnson, B. (2011). "The Impact of Globalization Determinants and the Health of the World's Population." In P. Pachura, ed., *New Knowledge in a New Era of Globalization*. Croatia: INTECK, pp. 165–182.

Azevedo, M.J. (2011). "Diabetes in Sub-Saharan Africa," *Journal of Diabetes in Developing Countries*, 13.

Azevedo, M.J., Prater G., and Hayes, S. (2010). *The State of HIV/AIDS/TB Co-Infections in Kenya: The Impact of Environment, Resource Management, and Culture*. Lap Lambert Academic Publishing, Saarbrucken, Germany.

Barber, Nicholas. (2012). "'Africa Rising' and the Shifting Disease Burden." Available at http://www.africasacountry.com/2012/11/28/Africa-rising-and-the-shifting-disease-burden/. Accessed 4 June 2013.

Bennett, J.D.C. (1990). "Medical Advances Consequent to the Great War 1914–1918," *Journal of the Royal Society of Medicine*, 83: pp. 738–742.

Bhuiyan, A.R. et al. (2013). "Infectious and Communicable Diseases in Mississippi." In Azevedo, M.J., ed., *The State of Health and Health Care in Mississippi*. Publication pending, Jackson, MS: University Press of Mississippi.

Brewer, I.W. (2009). *Rural Hygiene: A Handbook of Sanitation Designed for the Use of Students and for the Residents of the Rural Districts in the U.S.* New York: Cornell University Library.

Brownson, R.C., Remington, P.L., and Davis, J.R. (1998). *Chronic Disease Epidemiology and Control*. Washington, DC: American Public Health Association.

Caims, G. (2012). "Magical Thinking? FEM-PrEP Trial May have Failed Because Participants Used Testing as Prevention." Available at www.aidsmap.com/Magical-thinking-FEM-PrEP. Accessed 18 July 2013.

Charatz-Litt, Ca. (1991). "A Chronicle of Racism: The Effects of the White Medical Community on Black Health," *Journal of the National Medical Association*, 84 (8): pp. 717–725.

Centers for Disease Control and Prevention (2008). "Public Health Reports." Atlanta: CDC.

Chukwuma, A. (2012). "Facing the Double Disease Burden in Sub-Saharan Africa: Is this Inevitable?" Consultancy Africa Intelligence (CAI). Available at http://.policy.org.za.

Cooke, J.C. (2009). *A Report of the CSIS Global Health Policy Center*. Washington, DC: Center for Strategic and International Studies (CSIS).

Curtis, V., et al. (2003). "Hygiene in the Home: Relating Bugs and Behaviour," *Social Science and Medicine*, 57 (4, August): pp. 657–672.

Dittmer, J. (2009). *The Good doctors: The Medical Committee for Human Rights and the Struggle for Social Justice in Health Care*. New York: Bloomsburg Press.

Dickson, K. et al. (2011). "Voluntary Medical Male Circumcision: A Framework Analysis of Policy and Program Implementation in Eastern and Sothern Africa" PLOS Med 8 (11): e1001133.doi.1371/journal.pmed.1001133.

Goldman, R. (2013). "Campaign to Promote Circumcision Wastes Resources: Lack of Open Debate Results in Flawed Policy." News Release, Circumcision Resource Center. Available at www.circumcision.org/72112NewsRelease.htm. Accessed 18 July, 2013.

——— (1997). *Circumcision: The Hidden Trauma*. On-Line Vanguard Publications. Amazon Distributor, 2013.

Gostin, L.O.F. (2002). *Law and Ethics: A Reader*. Los Angeles: Center for Law and the Public's Health, University of California Press.

Griffiths, I. (1984). *An Atlas of African Affairs*. London: Cambridge University Press.

Grove, A.T. (1989). *The Changing Geography of Africa*. New York: Oxford University Press.

Guardian (2013) (March 25). "UN Reports Urges Africa's Leaders to Put Environmental Health Policies First," U.K. *Guardian* blog, March 25, 2013. Available at http:/// www.guardian.co.uk/environment/blog/2013/mar/25/un-eport-africa-health-policies. Accessed 13 July 2013.

Hance, W. (1999). *The Geography of Africa*. New York: Columbia University Press.

Innes, E. (2013). Available at http://www.dailymail.co.uk/health/article-2335070/New-non-surgical-male-circumcision-device-reduce-HIV-infection-rate-60.html#ixzz2ZhJj8Omv. Accessed 21 July 2013.

International Scientific Forum for Home Hygiene (IFG) (2009). *Hygiene*. Norwhich, Cheschire, United Kingdom.

IRIN News Agency (2013). "Mozambique's first HIV Vaccine Trial Heralds New Era in Local Research." Available at http:www.irinnews.org/report/97657/Mozambique-s-first-hiv-vaccine-trial-heralds-new-e…. Accessed 18 July 2013.

——— (2010). "Kenya: Stigma Hinders Participation in Clinical HIV Trials." Available at http://www.irinnews.org/report/94513/kenya-stigma-hinders-participation-in-clinical-hiv-tr... Accessed 18 July 2013.

——— (2009). "Global: HIV Vaccine Trial Results Raise More Questions." Available at http://www.irinnews.org/report/86685/global-hiv-vaccine-trial-results-raise-more-questions. Accessed 18 July 2013.

Kirwa, C., and Werthman, M. Jr. (1978). "Neonatal Circumcision and Penile Dorsal Nerve Block—A Painless Procedure," *Journal of Pediatrics*, 92 (6): pp. 998–1000.

Krieg, E., and Faber, D. (2005). "Not so Black or White: Environmental Justice and Cumulative Impact of Assessments." *Environmental Impact Assessment Review*, 24, (7–8, October–November): pp. 667–694.

Labonte, R., et al. (2004). *Fatal Indifference: The G8, Africa and Global Health*. Landsdowne, South Africa: University of Cape Town Press.

Healy, M. (2013). "Researchers Halt HIV Vaccine Trial," *Los Angeles Times*, April 26, 2013.

Maugh, T.H. (2010). "Poverty and HIV are Strongly Linked, CDC Survey Finds." *Los Angeles Times*.

McCally, M., et al. (1998). "Poverty and Ill Health: Physicians Can, and Should, Make a Difference," *Annals of Internal Medicine*, 129 (9): pp. 726–733.

Mirabadi, T. (2011). See text at http://www.howtohint.com/diseases/diseases/article-573-what-are-the-common-diseases-f... Accessed 30 May 2013.

Mulekya, F. (2013). "State of Health in Uganda." Seminar paper presented 19 June 2013, Fort Portal, Uganda.

Nakajima (1996). *Fighting Disease, Fostering Development*. Geneva: WHO.

National Institute of Allergies and Infectious Diseases (NIADI) (2013). "Regulatory Officials Informed of HVTN 503." Bethesda, MD: NIH.

Nelson, R. (2003). "Antiobiotic Development Pipeline Runs Dry," *Lancet*, 362: pp. 1726–1727.

Okasha, A. (2005). "Globalization and Mental Health: A WPA Perspective," *Journal of World Psychiatry Association*, 4 (1): pp. 1–2.

Opoku, S. Y., Benwell, M., and Yamey, J. (2012). "Knowledge, Attitudes, Beliefs, Behavior, and Breast Cancer Screening in Ghana, West Africa." *Pan African Medical Journal*, an on-line publication of AFENET: pp. 1–10.

Pannenborg, O. (1995). "An Economic and Financial Look at Health in Low and Middle Income Countries." In *Health Matters: Public Health in North-South Perspective*. Amsterdam: Royal Tropical Institute.

Peltzer, P. (2012). "Hygiene Behavior and Health Attitudes in African Countries." Turfloop, South Africa: University of Limpopo.

Public Health Rep. (2008). 123 (1): 9–20. Available at PMCID: PMC2099321.

Rosen, G. (1993). *A History of Public Health*, 1993 ed. New York: Johns Hopkins University Press.

Schneider, M. (2011). *Introduction to Public Health*, 3d ed. Boston: Jones and Bartlett Publishers.

Smit, J. et al. (2005). "Socio-Behavior Challenges to Phase III HIV Vaccine Trials in Sub-Saharan Africa," *African Health Sciences*. Kampala, Uganda: Makerere Medical School.

Starr, P. (1982). *The Social Transformation of American Medicine: The Rise of a Sovereign Profession and the Making of a Vast Industry*, 3d ed. Philadelphia: University of Pennsylvania, Basic Books.

Stock, R. (1995). *Africa South of the Sahara: A Geographic Interpretation*. New York: Guilford Press.

Thomson, M. (2013). "Climate and Disease in Africa." Accessed 13 July 2013.

Tulchinsky, T., and Varavikova, E. (2000). *The New Public Health*. New York: Academic Press.

Tumwebaze, S. (2013). "Uganda Joins HIV Vaccine Trial Tests," Kampala, Uganda, *Daily Monitor* May 17, 2013.

Turnock, B. (2009). *Public Health: What it is and How it Works*. Boston: Jones and Bartlett Publishers.

UNAIDS (2013). "*How Africa Turned AIDS Around. UNAIDS Report* and *Joint United Nations Program on HIV/AIDS Report*. New York: United Nations.

UNILEVER (2012). "UNILEVER Announces New Initiative Helping 1 Billion People Improve their Wellbeing," press release. London: UNILEVER House.

United Nations (2013). "Information Sheet 2: "Disease and Environment." New York: UN, pp. 1–5.

——— (2012). "Drinking Water, Sanitation and Hygiene." New York: World Water Assessment Program (WWAP).

United Nations Children's Fund (2012). "Africa: On Global Handwashing Day UNICEF Says—It's Not Complicated, But It's Crucial." New York: United Nations.

U.S. Department of Health and Human Services (2010). "Healthy People 2010 and Healthy People 2020." Available at http://www.health.gov/healthypeople or healthypeople.gov/2020/default.aspx. Accessed 17 July 2012.

Wagstaff, A. (2002). *Reflections on and Alternatives to WHO's Fairness of Financial Contribution Index*. Hoboken, NJ: Wiley & Sons.

World Health Organization (2013). "Water Sanitation and Health." New York: United Nations.

——— (2002). "Poverty and Health Sector Inequities." *WHO Bulletin*, 80 (2).

——— (2000). "Millennium Development Goals." United Nations Millennium Declaration Resolution, adopted September 18, 2000. New York: United Nations.

II

Health and Communication Policy

FOUR

Nutrition Education and Communication

A Critical Examination of Research and Practice in India

SubbaRao M. Gavaravarapu

INTRODUCTION

> "Oh, God, give us food which does not cause any disease and also gives us strength." —Yajurveda, one of the four Vedas, the canonical texts of Hinduism

> "He who takes food in proper measure lives long life and lives without disease, gets strength and alertness of mind. His children are born healthy and without any deformity or disease." —Mahabharata, an ancient Indian epic

Another ancient Indian maxim says, "*Annam Brahma*" (Food is divine). More than 2000 years ago, Hippocrates, an ancient Greek physician wrote, "Let food be your medicine, and let medicine be your food." This is an often quoted dictum by nutrition scientists for emphasizing the need for knowledge and proper understanding of nutrition. Over 200 years ago, Anthelme Brillat-Savarin, a French lawyer and politician who gained fame as an epicure, gastronome, and the pioneer of the genre of the gastronomic essay, said, "The destiny of nations is determined by what and how they eat" (Cannon 2002).

These ancient dictums draw people's attention to the need to educate themselves about the importance of food and right nutrition. In fact, the practice of nutrition education is about as old as any of the so-called helping professions, such as nursing and counseling.

The terms *education* and *communication* are often used synonymously in public health nutrition circles. The practice of nutrition education/communication is usually viewed as a deliberate effort to improve nutritional well-being by providing information or other types of educational/behavioral interventions. The earliest nutrition programs taken up in India were mainly aimed at disseminating nutrition information. Authorities used a top-down approach in their attempts to take the message of nutrition to the people.

Realizing that the effectiveness of programs should not be assumed but measured, nutrition educators began to apply nutrition knowledge tests, which evaluated nutrition knowledge. There were few attempts, however, to measure attitudes and practices. Later, more studies were developed to measure affective, behavioral, and cognitive outcomes. The concept of communicating nutrition information has been introduced in the field of nutrition education, both in research and practice. The shift in development communication thinking—from modernization to dependency to multiplicity and participation—can be traced in nutrition communication research and practice.

Given this global context, we will review the studies that used various approaches like social marketing, advocacy, participatory communication, and information and communication technology (ICT) for nutrition education/communication in India.

While there are many definitions of nutrition education, but most acknowledge the characteristic that it is a form of planned change that involves an effort to improve nutritional well-being by providing information or other educational/behavioral interventions (Sims 1987). The following are some of the important definitions found in scholarship on nutrition education:

> Nutrition Education is a means of translating nutritional requirements of food, and adjusting the food choices to satisfy nutritional, cultural, psychological and economic needs. (Albasena 1971)

> The process by which beliefs, attitudes, environmental influences and understandings about food are converted into practices, which are nutritionally sound and consistent with individual's needs, purchasing power, available food sources and socio-cultural background. (Devadas 1977)

> Nutrition education is that group of communication activities aimed at achieving a voluntary change in nutrition related behaviour to improve the nutritional status of the population. (Andrien 1994)

> A set of learning experiences designed to facilitate voluntary adoption of eating and other nutrition-related behaviours, conducive to health and well-being. (Contento et al. 1995)

NUTRITION INFORMATION DISSEMINATION—A HISTORICAL PERSPECTIVE

After the evolution of nutrition sciences as a discipline of study, activities to inform the public about advisable food choices, based on scientific evidence, started at the turn of the twentieth century (Sims 1987). In the United States, Dr. Wilbur Olin Atwater, the first director of the United States Department of Agriculture's (USDA) Office of Experiment Station, is credited with charting a new course for nutrition education at USDA. He used the scientific process to develop dietary guidance to improve the health and well-being of the population. In a "Farmers' Bulletin" published in 1902, Atwater emphasized the importance of variety, proportionality, and moderation in healthful eating (Welsh 1994).

Although nutritionists have been engaged in nutrition education for many years, few have questioned its efficacy. It was assumed that nutrition education would result in such positive outcomes as changes in diet. Even the very few evaluations conducted during the early part of the twentieth century, were subjective and focused more on finding out how well the audience liked a specific program (Gillespie 1981).

NUTRITION EDUCATION—AWARENESS CREATION, OR BEHAVIOR CHANGE?

A review of nutrition program evaluations between the 1930s and 1960s, conducted by McKenzie and Mumford (1965), concluded that only a few of the studies were objectively conducted. Whitehead's (1973) review of studies spanning seventy years found that nutrition education has been directed more towards disseminating nutrition information than towards improving dietary habits. That approach was effective in increasing knowledge, but it was not very effective in changing dietary practices. The assumption was that, if people were given information, they would change their attitudes and behavior reflect their newly acquired knowledge.

Realizing that effectiveness of programs should not be assumed but measured, nutrition educators began to apply nutrition knowledge tests to measure cognitive changes. A review of studies conducted in the 1960s and early 1970s showed that many of these tests only evaluated nutrition knowledge. Few attempted to measure attitudes and practices (Gillespie 1981). Later, more studies were developed to measure behavioral as well as cognitive outcomes. This gave greater insights into the success and failure of the programs.

A meta-analysis conducted by Johnson and Johnson (1985) reviewed all the available research in nutrition education until the mid-1980s to assess effectiveness of nutrition education and to delineate new directions for future research. They reported their observations on the impact of nutrition education in terms of knowledge, attitudes and behavior, since these were the most commonly measured variables. Their meta-analysis of 303 studies found that nutrition education resulted in an overall improvement of 33 percent in knowledge, 14 percent in attitude and 19 percent in dietary practices. They also indicated that a wide variety of instructional procedures were used in the studies and many of the studies involved participants not in designing communication methods but in planning menus and preparing and tasting foods. Finally the meta-analysis concluded that as many as 80 percent of the studies used more than one educational method thus, making it difficult to determine their relative effectiveness.

Exposure to new information or services, which is thought to induce knowledge acquisition, may not result in a change in attitudes or dietary behavior. Literacy level, socio-economic factors, and food belief systems may influence an individual's behavior (Nayak 1999).

The approach used most often in health and nutrition education programs is top-down, with planners designing the media material to provide information to the community from a central point, without taking into consideration regional and socio-cultural differences within the population (Nayak 1999). Smitasiri (1994) suggested that traditional nutrition education efforts were based on the assumption that people lack nutritional knowledge, leading to nutritional problems. When people correctly learn about nutrition, they will act according to their knowledge.

The lack of a theoretical framework has been considered one of the weaknesses in top-down communication programs. Messages were usually medically oriented and mainly addressed nutritional diseases and how to prevent them. The information provided was what the policy makers, program planners, and other implementers perceived as important for the community to know. In most of the less developed countries, inter-personal communication was expected to be the main channel for traditional nutrition education. The volunteers in the existing health set-up, trained in basic nutrition without proper media materials, are key communicators. Such an approach could well be the reason for the failure of intervention programs to make a measurable impact (Nayak 1999).

NUTRITION EDUCATION, COMMUNICATION, AND PROMOTION—THE CHANGING PHASE

A distinction is often made between nutrition education, nutrition communication, nutrition promotion, and information, education, and communication (IEC) (Graeff, Elder, and Booth 1994). In the last two or three decades, a dramatic change has occurred in the definition, as well as in methods of nutrition education. The traditional definition of nutrition education is that it is a process of giving the wisdom of how to acquire, prepare, and consume foods that are good to eat (Gussow and Contento 1984). The focus of education activities is on changing individual behavior. Still, there has been a growing recognition that the health of individuals and their health-related behavior are products of individual interaction with his or her environment. This includes the family, community, culture, social structure, and physical environment (Smith 1997).

Currently, the concept of communicating nutrition has been introduced in the field of nutrition education. Education activities can include information processes, which are generally designed to inform unilaterally, whereas communication is a two-way process. The term *communicate,* is derived from Latin and means "to have a common understanding." A return to the idea of common understanding allows for broader consideration of people as individuals in communities, not as students in a classroom (Smitasiri 1994).

One of the prerequisites of good communication is that it should be continuous and reiterative. Communication research findings suggest that behavior change is a difficult and slow process that requires many messages over a long period of time. Nutrition communication should be phased over a period of time, as people move through steps of behavioral change: unaware; aware; concerned; knowledgeable; skilled; motivated-to-change; trial; and sustained behavior change (Yarbrough 1981).

The creation of an enabling environment is among major factors necessary to bring about positive behavior change. Recognizing this, the Ottawa Charter for Health Promotion, developed by thirty-eight countries, identifies five interdependent domains for action in promoting the health (including diet related health) of individuals, groups, and populations (WHO 1986). They are, first, building public policy on health, second, creating a supportive environment, third, strengthening community action, fourth, developing personal skills through education, and fifth, reorienting health services to promote health as well as treat illness. This gives structural and environmental support to educational strategies that bring about behavior change.

Definitions of health/nutrition promotion that have these domains in mind still have education as a central activity. One definition describes health (nutrition) promotion as a combination of health education and related organizational, economic and environmental supports for enabling behavior change of individuals to promote (nutritional) health (Green and Anderson 1986).

Approaches to Nutrition Education

Countries such as India have a wide array of nutritional problems. Some countries have a mixture of difficulties related to their individual stage of development. Directing nutrition communication interventions precisely at such specific target groups is thus a real challenge. Much of the ongoing work in nutrition education and communication is now viewed from a broader framework as a process, a mechanism for interaction among participants, and as a resource. As a resource, the intention is to apply a coordinated, multisectoral, and interdisciplinary effort toward improving and sustaining the nutritional status of the most vulnerable groups. Several approaches to nutrition education have been developed and applied effectively. These include social marketing, social mobilization, and development-support communication. Stuart and Achterberg (1995) have identified common threads among these approaches. First, the ultimate goal of any approach to nutrition education is to improve the quality of life of people through a participatory process of communication. Second, there is a demand to establish a dynamic relationship among the participants of the program—the subjects of the nutrition education intervention, the policy makers, the planners, and the implementers, as well as the evaluators. Third, IEC strategies are built into the process. The core elements of the process are:

- formative research, assessment, and analysis;
- capacity building; development of a multi-channel communication strategy;
- community organizing;
- networking, alliance building, and co-ordination with linkage and support systems;
- design, pre-testing, and development of messages and materials; and
- monitoring and evaluation.

While nutrition communication has been relying largely on interpersonal communication, finding a multipronged approach to educate the opinion makers, policy framers, and implementers is a top priority. Positive change in behavior needs an enabling environment.

Participation and Nutrition Communication

Many communication scholars believe that involvement of people in the communication process may enhance the likelihood of program success by stimulating two-way communication. Bordenave (1994, p. 43) defines participatory communication "as that type of communication in which all the interlocutors are free and have equal access to the means to express their viewpoints, feelings and experiences. Collective action aimed at promoting their interests, solving their problems, and transforming their society, is the means end."

The rationale behind participatory communication is that it eliminates one-way prescriptive and non-participatory approach to development. It involves development recipients in two-way interactions in the design, development, implementation, and evaluation of projects. Similarly, the involvement of people in a development communication process is very important, since they are the ultimate beneficiaries of the development communication policies and planning.

Participatory actions rest on two-way communication and development. Two-way communication helps eliminate the lacunae of a top-down approach that usually neither involves people in different phases of a development project, nor considers local conditions and constraints. Experience has shown that, when a community is fully involved in the design, implementation, monitoring, and evaluation of nutrition and other development projects, the work is likely to be more effective and sustainable. Such participatory efforts more often meet the real needs of the people in the community and achieve results that can be continued with minimal external inputs (FAO 1994).

Nutrition Communication Strategies

In view of the growing importance of the involvement of people in the development projects, it appears that some nutrition-related projects in various parts of the world have already successfully applied a participatory communication approach (Khadka 2003). In their commentary, Valyasevi and Attig (1994) have listed the four most common strategies for nutrition communication. These are based on the experiences and reports given by representatives of ten South and East Asian countries at the FAO-sponsored Inter-Country Workshop on Nutrition Education for South and East Asian Countries, held at Salaya, Thailand, in February 1993. They are information dissemination, educational communication, participatory action, and participatory communication.

The information dissemination model usually used in least developed and developing nations that have limited communication capabilities. This approach parallels the "knowledge dissemination" model. According to this model, if people receive the knowledge they need to change, then change will automatically follow. However, "knowledge" here is includes information in general, since not all of what is transmitted can be considered true knowledge, at least in terms of how the receiver interprets it.

Educational communication is a mass media approach used to persuade people to adopt a new product, service, and/or behavior. It is close to the information dissemination approach. It is different in that it often goes beyond information dumping to apply a social advertising strategy to encourage people to try something new. However, people are not always told how to use the product properly, and countless experiences have shown that use of mass media alone is not effective in leading to behavior change (Achterberg 1993). At the other extreme, education can occur primarily through face-to-face instruction in non-formal health care clinics. This approach rests largely on a top-down model of communication, in which information is passed down the hierarchy from official or doctor to patient.

Participatory action as a model is premised on the reality that nutrition-oriented development projects cannot be sustained at the grassroots level if they are planned from the top, focused on individual components, and isolated from the total development process. This strategy relies heavily on a participatory action research (PAR) framework and a bottom-up development approach. The participatory strategy is effective on a small scale and has potential on a large scale as long as the momentum continues, and people remain involved.

Participatory communication has two very important characteristics. First, it focuses on people's felt needs, determined through formative research. Data and information are collected to identify important factors that may affect a program's acceptance. These considerations are then incorporated into a communication program's design. The intent is not to confront people with their inappropriate beliefs or resource constraints, but to use these beliefs to build nutrition communication programs.

The second important aspect of participatory communication is that it focuses on changing the environment in which people see themselves. Social mobilization is based upon creating a local need and demand for change. It initially focuses on how people view their environment, rather than how they view themselves. This need and demand again rest on formative research into the needs of the people. In this context, the term *people* means both vulnerable target groups and target audiences. The general public is not a uniform mass and should not be treated as one. Rather, it should be separated into specific groups according to their characteristics, needs, wants, and predispositions (Achterberg 1993).

NUTRITION EDUCATION AND COMMUNICATION RESEARCH IN INDIA

In proposing his nutrition research plan in India in the 1900s, Sir Robert McCarrison, the first director of Nutrition Research Labs (NIN), included community nutrition education as one of the activities. To this end, he prepared popular-level books and pamphlets. Providing textual materials was continued by his successor, Dr. Wallace R. Aykroyd. Although there were many such scattered efforts, there was hardly any concerted strategy for education.

There is evidence that individual nutrition scientists considered developing "appropriate" methods of nutrition education consistent with the socio-economic and cultural background of the population (Narsinga Rao 2005). In the early 1960s, many studies carried out by the scientists of NIN emphasized nutrition education for school children. Studies examined various aspects of the possibilities. They looked at the idea of a nutrition component in school syllabi and teaching nutrition in schools (Chapakam and Balasubramanian 1967 a,b,c).

In 1970s, studies looked for effective media that could carry the message of nutrition to various groups of people (Devadas 1977). Nutrition counseling was studied for use as a tool to disseminate nutrition information (Dastur et al. 1976). Berg (1970) wrote that the Indian preference was to approach nutrition education, not so much as a nutrition problem, but more as a communication problem. Earnest efforts were made through the mass media and by commercial advertising agencies to go beyond the "four food groups" clichés of standard nutrition posters.

Hardly any studies evaluated this communication drive. Some 1980s studies looked into the use and relative effectiveness of mass media for disseminating nutrition messages (Kaliperumal 1986; Mathur and Joseph 1986). Studies conducted by Parvati Rau (1991, 1994) proved that folk art forms could also be used as effective media for nutrition education. During the 1980s, the Indian Council of Medical Research (ICMR) funded a string of projects on nutrition education (Narsinga Rao 2005). Most of them aimed at providing nutrition education interventions and assessing incremental changes in knowledge.

The studies concluded that, due to economic factors, people were unable to put knowledge to use. In this connection, there are lessons to be learned from the Tamil Nadu Integrated Nutrition Program (TINP), in operation since the 1980s. TINP made integrated health and nutrition interventions that included a major communication component. The communication strategy segmented the audience into primary and secondary targets.

Strategies were carefully planned for both. Two-pronged communication was used for the primary target group and one-way communication for the secondary audience. The primary target group was mothers, mothers-in-law, and fathers. Counseling was used, supported by flip charts and flash cards. The secondary target group was the rest of the population. Films incorporating popular film tunes, filmstrips, and slides were used for this wider audience were. Pamphlets were available for the literate and the popular folk medium, villupattu, was used.

Although no separate evaluation of the communication strategy was conducted, it was well accepted that a major contribution of the communication strategy was to increase the community's use of services. It was emphasized that communication activities should be supported by other services and strategies that make it possible to act on the messages (Vijayaraghavan 1997).

Studies by NIN have also used social marketing techniques for imparting nutrition education (Nayak 1999). In studies conducted over the past decade, internationally accepted school-based education modules, computer-mediated education tools, and small media, such as skits, plays, and folk media, have also been used for nutrition education (SubbaRao et al. 2006; Vijayapushpam et al. 2003; Raghunatha Rao et al. 2007; Gavaravarapu and Thangiah 2009).

NUTRITION EDUCATION/COMMUNICATION—A MULTI-PRONGED APPROACH

Today, nutrition education and communication are regarded more broadly as a mechanism for interaction among participants and as a resource, applying a coordinated, multisectoral, and interdisciplinary effort (Stuart and Achterberg 1995). Nutrition communication is now an umbrella for a wide range of education and other approaches that aim to influence nutritional status (Smitasiri et al. 1993). Social marketing, advocacy, participatory communication, "edutainment" using information and communication technology, and using food labels for nutrition communication have been tried experimentally.

One reason why *social marketing* has become popular in recent years is that nutrition communication's goal is to facilitate change in nutrition-related practices and status. This usually requires increasing the demand for specific foods and practices (Smitasiri et al. 1993).

Social marketing uses business marketing principles to advance a social cause or idea (Kotler and Zaltman 1971). As a social change management technology, it involves the design, implementation, and control of programs. These programs are aimed at increasing the acceptability of a social idea or practice in one or more target groups (Kotler and Roberto, 1989). The strategy adopts the four "Ps" of marketing—product, price, place, and promotion. In the 1990s, this strategy was successfully used in Thailand to promote Vitamin A rich foods (Smitasiri et al. 1993). In India, this strategy also was successfully used to promote Vitamin A rich foods among rural households in the south Indian state of Andhra Pradesh (Nayak 1999). Elsewhere, many examples can be found of the social marketing of breast-feeding, weaning foods, oral rehydration salts, and immunization (McKee 1992). Social marketing increased awareness and better practices of including nutritious foods in daily diets (Vijayaraghavan 2000).

Advocacy is a planned communication effort to persuade decision makers at policy, planning, and management levels to adopt necessary policies and allocate resources for a cause (Stuart and Achterberg 1997). In the Indian context, such international organizations as WHO and the United Nations Children's Fund (UNICEF) have been using this strategy to encourage various stakeholders from different sectors of government to realize their role in implementing food and nutrition plans and policies. Workshops for representatives from seven Southeast Asian countries advocated for multisectoral collaboration to promote nutrition in

India and other Southeast Asian Countries (WHO 2005; SubbaRao et al. 2009).

Other efforts involve mobilizing support for policy makers by depicting the effects of malnutrition as functional and economic consequences. International organizations like CARE-India, with the support of WHO-prepared advocacy material based on the PROFILES program, developed by the Academy for Education Development in the U.S. These material show the cost-benefit ratio of investments needed to save a country from impending economic losses due to less productive malnourished manpower (SubbaRao et al. 2005; Shah et al. 2012).

Bordenave (1994) defines *participatory communication* as that type of communication in which all the interlocutors are free and have ways to express their viewpoints, feelings, and experiences. It is believed that participatory communication may enhance the likelihood of program success by stimulating two-way communication in the program. It involves people in dialogue, collaboration, and decision making, while considering them to be the ultimate and most important beneficiaries of development. As a result, such a communications process can address a whole range of social, cultural, political, economic, and environmental issues affecting people's nutrition and health (Khadka 2003).

Experience has shown that when a community is involved in designing, implementing, monitoring, and evaluating, nutrition and other development projects are more likely to be effective and sustainable. Such participatory efforts more often meet the real needs of the people in the community and achieve results that can be continued with minimal external inputs (FAO 1994).

An innovative approach to participatory community learning was "positive deviance." This phenomenon exists in many resource-poor communities. A few individuals and families employ uncommon, beneficial practices that allow them and their children to have better health as compared to their similarly impoverished neighbors (Marsh and Schroeder 2002). Learning through experience sharing with such individuals and families, as well as incorporating these practices in planning and implementng some of the nutrition supplementation programs in India was extremely beneficial, especially in the northern states of India (Sethi et al. 2003; Bamji 2003; Levinson et al. 2007).

Edutainment using information and communication technology is an increasingly important approach. While the multimedia CD-ROM market is exploding with programs for children, there are only a few nutrition education programs. Although the ability of multimedia programs to capture children's attention, increase their knowledge, and change behavior is widely documented in the developed world, very few studies have compared the efficacy of teaching tools in experimental designs. A study carried out by Turnin et al. (2001) concluded that using computer-based nutritional teaching methods at school provides an additional support to conventional teaching. In the Indian context, Vijayapushpam et. al. (2003) documented that CD-ROM-based intervention brought about significant improvement in the knowledge of school children. Contrary to this observation, a study by Ragunatha Rao et al. (2007) countered that the CD-ROM intervention did not show more value than classroom-based intervention. It has also been observed that a majority of a studied group of adolescent girls paid attention to the classroom lecture of a science teacher who used folders, slides, and charts, and they interacted more with the teacher. When they used audio-visual CDs, the attention of the adolescent girls was very low. The authors said that this could be because the girls mostly viewed computers as entertainment devices, rather than educational devices.

Food labels for nutrition communication has become standard in the West as important modes of communication. This is one potentially powerful tool of communication not often considered when traditional channels are discussed (Goldberg 1992). In addition to the ingredients list, the nutrition-labeling panel gives important information about nutrient content, enabling the consumers to make healthy choices.

This is important in the Indian context where over 59 percent of households buy packed foods at some point (Polasa et al. 2006). Studies in other parts of the world have reported that about 40 percent of the studied consumers did not check the food labels (Surujlal and Badrie 2004; Yang et al. 2000). However, women, especially those with higher educational levels, have been observed to be more likely to check food labels than men (Yang et al. 2000). In studies conducted in India (SubbaRao et al. 2007, 2009; Laxmaiah et al. 2011; Sudershan et al. 2013), literate persons generally were more likely to check label information. The study concluded that efforts can be intensified to familiarize quality symbols on food labels, which can even be identified by illiterates in India.

NUTRITION COMMUNICATION—CRITICAL EXAMINATION OF INSTITUTIONAL APPROACHES

Taking a macro perspective, Gavaravarapu and Pavarala (2014) have critically examined how various organizations that are engaged in nutrition communication in India perceive, develop, and implement communication processes. Through case studies of organizations from government, voluntary, and research sectors, they have concluded that nutrition communication programs are usually top-down, expert-driven and often lacking in planning, evaluation, or adequate financial allocation. They suggest that perceptions of the key communicators, their motivation levels and personal biases also affect the design and implementation of nutrition communication programs. Examining the context in which the organizations function, the authors conclude that the framework for communicative processes for government and research organizations is created by the centers of authority, such as the state, UN agencies, or funding agencies. These centers often define nutrition priorities and frame solutions. The institutions, operating in tandem with the priorities set by the state or other centers of authority, invariably have to work in a predetermined framework. Juxtaposing these top-down programs with participatory approaches adopted by some voluntary organizations, they find that the participatory communicative processes are designed based on articulations that emerge from within the context of the audience. The authors suggest that, in efforts related to promoting nutrition, communication's role should be seen as going beyond the production of materials for information dissemination or as one option. Communication should become a fundamental component of all health and nutrition programs, with appropriate provision for budget and a strong evaluation component, incorporated at the planning stage.

THE WAY FORWARD

As the National Nutrition Policy of the government of India recognizes that "Nutrition affects development as much as development affects nutrition . . ." (FNB 1993, p. 2), nutritional concerns are being integrated into various developmental policies and programs being taken up at various levels by the government. Non-governmental organisations (NGOs) and international organizations such as WHO, UNICEF, and FAO are also exerting effort to take the message of nutrition to the community. In some cases, government, voluntary, and international organizations are working together. All are emphasizing the need to involve the beneficiaries in the process of developing and implementing programs. But in many of these endeavors, there has hardly been any separate evaluation of the nutrition education/communication components. There is even a dearth of published literature regarding the scattered studies and smaller experiments conducted by NGOs and university departments and students. Systematic documentation of all nutrition education and communication programs is certainly needed.

This review indicates that nutrition education is a necessary but not a sufficient condition for bringing about the desired behavior change. Hence, emphasis should be laid on creating an enabling environment for adapting and maintaining positive change.

The following conclusions, arrived at by an earlier review done by Stuart and Achterberg (1997), also apply:

- Nutrition education and communication should be thought of as an integral part of a country's development plan.

- Changing food and nutrition behavior to improve national nutrition is a long process, comprising many steps, in many sectors, at many levels.
- Nutrition education and communication programs need to be comprehensive and coordinated.
- Nutrition education and communication problems need to be participatory in nature. In different nutrition communication programs, the extent of participation will vary, and the model adopted is likely to differ accordingly. In a country such as India, which is in transition, more studies are needed to evaluate the efficacy of participatory communication strategies in raising the nutritional status of the people. More studies are also needed to evaluate the effectiveness of ICT and food labels as media of nutrition communication.

The Indian experience clearly indicates that multiple, integrated strategies can work. A combination of different actions is widely seen as responsible for the success of one communication strategy. Communication strategies have successfully used interpersonal and mass communication interventions in many a project. In most of those projects several stakeholders and organizations worked in multiple ways towards a common objective. However, a strategy that works in one context may not be successful in others. Communication strategies that aim to mobilize communities for the cause of nutrition must adopt different characteristics in different circumstances, based on the context and felt needs.

Moving away from top-down models of communication that concentrated on the effects and effectiveness of an intervention, the focus now seems to be on various measures for success. Beneficiaries, the consideration of various stakeholders, participation, outcomes, data gathering, analysis, and a multi-channel versatility all need to be looked at. However, the strategies or approaches decide the content, while the content is largely decided by the context.

Hence, there is a need to critically examine different models, approaches, and content for communicating nutrition in different contexts, both at micro and macro levels. While attempting to do so, it is also pertinent to critically examine the context in which key actors in nutrition communication work and their considerations for choice of a model or approach for nutrition communication.

BIBLIOGRAPHY

Achterberg, C. (1993). "Update on Nutrition Communication," Report of the Inter-Country Workshop on Nutrition Education for South and East Asian Countries, Salaya, Thailand, 22–26 February, 1993. Rome: Food and Agriculture Organization.

Albasena, N.G. (1971). "A Giant Step in Nutrition Education," *School Lunch Journal*, 25: p. 106.

Andrien, M. (1994). *Social Communication in Nutrition. A Methodology for Intervention.* Rome: Food and Agriculture Organization.

Bamji, M.S. (2003). "Early Nutrition and Health—Indian Perspective," *Current Science,* 85 (8): pp. 1137–1142.

Berg, A.D. (1970). "Nutrition as a National Priority—Lessons from the India Experiment," *The American Journal of Clinical Nutrition,* 23 (1): pp. 1396–1408.

Bordenave, J.D. (1994). "Participative Communication as a Part of Building the Participative Society." In S.A. White, S.K. Nair, and A. Ascroft, eds. *Participatory Communication Working for Change and Development.* London: Sage.

Cannon, G. (2002). "Nutrition: The New World Order," *Asia Pacific Journal of Clinical Nutrition,* 11 (Suppl): pp. S498–509.

Chapakam, S., and Balasubramanian, S.C. (1967a). "Nutrition in the Syllabi and Textbooks of Elementary Schools," *Journal of Nutrition and Dietetics,* 4: pp. 36–40.

———. (1967b). "An Assessment of Teaching Nutrition in Elementary Schools in Hyderabad," *Journal of Nutrition and Dietetics,* 4: pp. 41–50.

———. (1967c). "Impact of Nutrition Education on Prospective Teachers," *Journal of Nutrition and Dietetics,* 4: pp. 323–330.

Contento, I., et al. (1995). "The Effectiveness of Nutrition Education and Implications for Nutrition Education Policy, Programs and Research: A Review of Research," *Journal of Nutrition Education,* 27: pp. 284–418.

Dastur, K.S., Kundarpur, S., and Easwaran, S. (1977). "Nutrition Education in Community," *Proceedings of the Annual Meetings of the Nutrition Society of India,* 21: 10–19.

Devadas, P.R. (1977). "Need for Nutrition Education," *Proceedings of the Annual Meetings of the Nutrition Society of India,* 1977, 21: pp. 1–9.

Food and Agriculture Organization (1994). "The International Conference on Nutrition." In J.L. Albert, ed. *Food, Nutrition and Agriculture.* Rome: Food and Agriculture Organization of the United Nations.

———. (1994). "The International Conference on Nutrition." In J.L. Albert, ed., *Food, Nutrition and Agriculture.* Rome: Food and Agriculture Organization of the United Nations.

Food and Nutrition Board (1993). "National Nutrition Policy." New Delhi: Food and Nutrition Board (FNB), Department of Women and Child Development, Ministry of Human Resource Development, Government of India.

———. (1995). "National Plan of Action on Nutrition." New Delhi: Food and Nutrition Board (FNB), Department of Women and Child Development Ministry of Human Resources, Government of India.

Gavaravvarapu, S.M., and Pavarala, V. (2014). "Communicating Nutrition in Community Settings—Case Studies in Critical Examination of Institutional Approaches in India," *Journal of Creative Communications* 9(1): 39-64.

Gavaravarapu, S.M., and Thangiah, V. (2009). "Nutrition Education for Student Volunteers Using a Videotaped Folk Dance Format," *Journal of Nutrition Education and Behavior,* 41 (6), pp. 436–437.

Gillespie, A.H. (1981). "Applying communication theory in nutrition education," *Journal of Nutrition Education,* 13 (1) (Suppl.): pp. S29–S33.

Goldberg, J.P. (1992). "Nutrition and Health Communication: The message and the media over half a century," *Nutrition Reviews,* 50 (3): pp. 71–77.

Graeff, J.A., Elder, J.P., and Booth, M.B. (1994). *Communication for Health and Behaviour Change.* Washington: Academy for Educational Development.

Green, W.W., and Anderson, S.C. (1986). *Community Health.* St. Louis: Times Mirror/ Mosby College Publishing.

Gussow, J.D., and Contento, I. (1984). "Nutrition education in the changing world: A conceptualization and selective review," "Nutritional Considerations in a Changing World," *World Review of Nutrition and Dietetics,* 44: pp. 1–47.

Indian Council of Medical Research (1989). "Evaluation of National Nutritional Anaemia Prophylaxis Program," ICMR Task Force study. New Delhi: Indian Council of Medical Research.

Johnson, D. W., and Johnson, R. T. (1985). "Nutrition Education: A Model for Effectiveness, a Synthesis of Research," *Journal of Nutrition Education,* 17 (suppl.): pp. S1–S44.

Kaliperumal, K. (1986). "Communication—Methods and Media for Rural Areas in Education for Better Health of Mother and Child in Primary Health Care." In *Proceedings of the First South East Asia Conference, IUHE, November 1986, Chennai,* pp. 312–320.

Khadka, N.B. (2003). "Participatory Nutrition Communication: Rhetoric or Reality? A Case Study of Nepal," Paper presented at Designing Communication for Diversity Conference, Brisbane, July 2003, Brisbane: Australia, New Zealand Communication Association. Available at: http://www.bgsb.qut.edu.au/community/ANZCA03/Proceedings/papers/khadka_full.pdf. Accessed 14 February 2007.

Kotler, P., and Roberto, E. (1989). *Social Marketing: Strategies for Changing Public Behavior.* New York, Free Press.

Kotler, P., and Zaltman, G. (1971). "Social Marketing: An Approach to Planned Social Change," *Journal of Marketing,* 35: pp. 3–12.

Levinson, F.J., et al. (2007). "Utilization of Positive Deviance Analysis in Evaluating Community-based Nutrition Programs: An Application to the Dular Program in Bihar, India," *Food and Nutrition Bulletin,* 28 (3), pp. 259–265.

Marsh, D.R., and Schroeder, D.G. (2002). "The Positive Deviance Approach to Improve Health Outcomes: Experience and Evidence from the Field," *Food and Nutrition Bulletin,* 23 (4), pp. 3–6.

Mathur, M.S., and Joseph, A. (1986). "Effectiveness of Different Educational Aids in Changing Knowledge." In *Proceedings of the First South East Asia Region Conference, IUHE, Nov. 1986, Madras,* pp. 384–395.

McKee, N. (1992). *Social Mobilization and Social Marketing in Developing Countries.* Penang, Malaysia: Southbound.

McKenzie, J.C., and Mumford, P. (1965). "The Evaluation of Nutrition Education Programs: A Review of the Present situation," *World Review of Nutrition and Dietetics,* 5: pp. 21–31.

Narsinga Rao, B.S. (2005). *Development of Nutrition Science in India.* New Delhi: Allied Publishers.

National Institute of Public Cooperation and Child Development (1992). *National Evaluation of Integrated Child Development Services.* New Delhi: NIPCCD.

Nayak, U.M. (1999). "Social Marketing Strategy for Nutrition Education to Combat Vitamin A Deficiency in the Rural Community," PhD thesis submitted to Sri Padmavathi Mahila Visvavidyalayam, Tirupathi, India.

Polasa, K., et al. (2006). *KABP Study on Food and Drug Safety in India—A Report.* Hyderabad: Food and Drug Toxicology Research Centre, National Institute of Nutrition (NIN).

Raghunatha Rao, D., et al. (2007). "Dietary Habits and Effect of Two Different Educational Tools on Nutrition Knowledge of School Going Adolescent Girls in Hyderabad, India," *European Journal of Clinical Nutrition,* 61: pp. 1081–1085.

Rau, P. (1968). "Socio-cultural Factors and Malnutrition in Telangana Region of Andhra Pradesh," *Proceedings of the Nutrition Society of India,* 6: pp. 37–43.

———. (1991). "Some Folk Forms in Andhra Pradesh and Their Use in Nutrition Education—A review," *Nutrition,* 25 (4): pp. 3–14.

———. (1994). "Role of Folk Media in Nutrition Education," *Cajanus,* 17: pp. 368–374.

Sarma K.V.R. et al. (1992). *Integrated Child Development Services: Status Appraisal in Four States,* Hyderabad: National Institute of Nutrition.

Sethi, M.V.; Kashyap, S.; and Seth, V. (2003). "Effect of Nutrition Education of Mothers on Infant Feeding Practices," *The Indian Journal of Pediatrics,* 70 (6), pp. 463–466.

Sims, L.L. (1987). "Nutrition Education Research: Reaching Toward the Leading Edge," *Journal of American Dietetic Association,* 87 (9) (Suppl.): pp. S10–18.

Smitasiri, S. (1994). *Nutrition—Action—Analyses Going Beyond Good People and Adequate Resource,* Bangkok, Thailand: Institute of Nutrition, Mahidol University, pp. 17–31.

Smitasiri, S., et al. (1993). *Social Marketing Vitamin A Rich Foods in Thailand—A Model Nutrition Communication for Behaviour Change Process.* Bangkok, Thailand: The Institute of Nutrition, Mahidol University.

Smith, B. (1997). "Past Experiences and Needs for Nutrition Education: Summary and Conclusions of Nine Case Studies." In *Nutrition Education for the Public: Discussion Papers of the FAO Expert Consultation (Rome, Italy, 18–22 September 1995),* FAO Food and Nutrition Paper 62. Rome: Food and Agriculture Organization. Available at: http://www.fao.org/docrep/ W3733E/w3733e02.htm. Accessed 5 March 2007.

Stuart, H.T., and Achterberg, C. (1997). "Education and Communication Strategies for Different Groups and Settings." In *Nutrition Education for the Public. Discussion Papers of the FAO Expert Consultation (Rome, Italy, 18–22 September 1995),* FAO Food and Nutrition Paper 62. Rome: Food and Agriculture Organization of the United Nations. Available at: http://www.fao.org/docrep/w3733e/w3733e04.htm#introduction. Accessed 13 May 2013.

SubbaRao, G.M., et al. (2007). "Food Safety Knowledge, Attitudes and Practices of Mothers—Findings from Focus Group Studies in South India," *Appetite,* 49: pp. 441–449.

———, et al. (2006). "Evaluation of the Food and Agriculture Organization's Global School-based Nutrition Education Initiative: Feeding Minds, Fighting Hunger (FMFH), in Schools of Hyderabad, India," *Public Health Nutrition,* 9 (8): pp. 991–995.

———. (2005). "Micronutrient Deficiencies—A Drain on Indian Economy: Use of PROFILES and Scope for Advocacy." In *Proceedings of the One-day State-Level Workshop on Micronutrient Deficiencies—A Drain on Indian Economy, Hyderabad, September 2005.* Hyderabad: Food and Nutrition Board.

———, et al. (2009). "Focus Group Studies on Food Safety Knowledge, Perceptions, and Practices of School-going Adolescent Girls in South India," *Journal of Nutrition Education and Behavior,* 41 (5), pp. 340–346.

———, et al. (2009). "Issues Concerning Implementation of Inter-sectoral Food and Nutrition Plans and Policies in Southeast Asian Countries," *Annals of Nutrition and Metabolism.* 2009: 5 (Suppl. 1): p. 263.

Sudershan, R.V., et al. (2013). "Use of Food Label Information by Urban Consumers in India—A Study Among Supermarket Shoppers." *Public Health Nutrition* (in press).

Surujlal, M., and Badrie, M. (2004). "Household Consumer Food Safety in Trinidad, West Indies," *Internet Journal of Food Safety,* 3: pp. 8–14.

Turnin, M.C., et al. (2001). "Evaluation of Microcomputer Nutritional Teaching Games in 1,876 Children at School," *Diabetes and Metabolism,* 27: pp. 459–464.

Valyasevi, A., and Attig, G. (1994). "Nutrition Communication in South and East Asia—Experiences and Lessons Learned." In *Report of the Inter-country Workshop on Nutrition Education for South and East Asian Countries, Salya, Thailand, 22–26 February 1993.* Rome: Food and Agriculture Organization.

Vijayapushpam, T., et al. (2003). "A Qualitative Assessment of Nutrition Knowledge Levels and Dietary Intake of Schoolchildren in Hyderabad," *Public Health Nutrition,* 6 (7): pp. 683–688.

Vijayaraghavan, K. (1997). "The Tamil Nadu Nutrition Project: A Case Study of the Communication Component. In: Smith, B., ed. *Nutrition Education for the Public. Discussion papers of the FAO Expert Consultation (Rome, Italy 18–22 September 1995),* FAO Food and Nutrition Paper 62. Rome: Food and Agriculture Organization of the United Nations. Available at: http://www.fao.org/docrep/W3733E/w3733e02.htm. Accessed 5 March 2007.

Welsh, S. (1994). "Atwater to the Present: Evolution of Nutrition Education," *Journal of Nutrition,* 124 (Suppl): pp. 1799S–1807S.

White, S.A. (1994), "The Concept of Participation: Transforming Rhetoric to Reality." In A.S. White, K.S. Nair, and A. Ascroft, eds., *Participatory Communication Working for Change and Development.* London: Sage.

Whitehead, F.E. (1973). "Nutrition Education Research," *World Review of Nutrition and Dietetics,* 17: pp. L91–149.

World Health Organization (1986). "Ottawa Charter for Health Promotion," First International Conference on Health Promotion, 21 November, 1986.: Available at http://www.who.int/healthpromotion/conferences/previous/ottawa/en/. Accessed 13 May 2008.

———. (2005). "Updating and Implementing Intersectoral Food and Nutrition Plans and Policies—Report of an Inter-country Workshop, Hyderabad, India, 4–8 April 2005," New Delhi: WHO Regional Office for South-East Asia.

Yang, S.; Angulo, F.J.; and Altekruse, S.F. (2000). "Evaluation of Safe Food Handling Instructions on Raw Meat and Poultry Products," *Journal of Food Protection,* 63 (10): pp. 1321–1325.

Yarbrough, P. (1981). "Communication Theory and Nutrition Education Research," *Journal of Nutrition Education,* 13 (1): pp. S16–S27.

FIVE

Communicating HIV and AIDS Prevention in India

Identifying Appropriate Health Management Policies for Sustainable Development

Ravindra Kumar Vemula

INTRODUCTION

HIV/AIDS has over-burdened the health systems in India since 1986. Most of the funding agencies are spending a lot of money to counter the pandemic but are failing to focus on other life-threatening diseases and structural factors. International fund projects, extensive media coverage, and the introduction of many new terms are a few spillovers of the situation.

This chapter argues that few of the health communication campaigns in India are successful, but the success of the HIV/AIDS campaigns largely depends on the communication needs of the marginalized people. Campaigns are now impeded by a lack of understanding of the target population among policy makers. Inequalities in income, education, and access to health services are not adequately factored into the design and delivery of health programs, while regional and gender disparities further undermine the effort.

After independence in 1947, India embarked on ambitious five-year plans for development, with both long term and short term planning. The first five-year plan (1952–1957) brought the realization that the population growth had to be checked in order to make development programs work. India became the first country in the world with an official family planning program (Bose 1998). The entire thrust of health communication strategies emanated from the deliberations in the Health and Family Welfare Ministry. The effort was designed around three premises: 1) The government needed to identify qualitative and geographical characteristics common to population areas and to tailor information, education, and communication to encourage behavioral change in each. 2) Information dissemination was necessity driven. 3) Use of media would fit the media consumption pattern of each people group.

Planning of population control schemes was at the district level and implementation was at the village or local level. Central government only helped to facilitate. This obviously needed a more region specific Information Education Communication (IEC) policy (Goswami 2002).

India has successfully carried out campaigns on family planning, leprosy, tuberculosis, malaria, leprosy, mother and child health, and polio as part of its five year plans. Population control programs, promoted with extensive campaigns, are credited with stabilizing India's population. Single- or two-child families have become common. The scheme started with the concept of a small family and the slogan *Hum do Hamare do* ("We two and our two."). A red inverted triangle symbol was created during the fourth five-year plan (1969–1974) as a branding effort to familiarize and popularize the idea of family planning. Social messages were used to sensitize the people to the need for family planning.

The use of communication by the leprosy program in India offers valuable lessons for other programs, both in its successes and its challenges.

Multidrug therapy for leprosy was introduced in 1982 with rifampicin, clofazimine, and dapsone. This regimen was adopted throughout the country with remarkable success. A very rapid and steep drop in prevalence of the disease was seen (Desikan 2012, p. 4)

News of the effectiveness of multidrug therapy raised awareness about the signs and symptoms of leprosy and the importance of seeking early treatment. Social stigma associated with the disease was reduced. Early efforts at communication were hampered by the lengthy treatment, uncertain outcomes, and limited media options, but the Modified Leprosy Elimination Campaigns (MLECs) scaled up interpersonal communication and used mass media. Communications efforts have helped enormously to promote of the news that leprosy can be cured, increase awareness of the free availability of treatment, and diminish the stigma associated with the disease.

Tuberculosis (TB) was another major public health problem that could be abated in India. India accounts for one-fifth of the global TB incident cases. Since 1993, the government of India has been implementing the WHO-recommended Directly Observed Treatment Course Strategy (DOTS) via the Revised National Tuberculosis Control Program

(RNTCP). Communication campaigns have worked in tandem with the government in informing people about it and bringing down the prevalence levels of TB all around the country. The increasing rate of Human Immuno Deficiency Virus (HIV) infection in many countries has had an impact on TB epidemiology as well. While TB prevalence has remained stable through the past ten years (2002–2012), TB incidence continues to rise, especially in countries most severely affected by the HIV epidemic. It also affects those facing political turmoil, migration, poverty and unemployment and residents of areas where intravenous drug abuse is rampant (Swaminathan and Narendran 2008, p. 527).

India's National Malaria Control Program was implemented from 1953 to 1958. It eventually became a disease eradication program. Aggressive campaigns using DDT were launched in India, leading to the rapid eradication of malaria. The DDT campaign was backed up media messages through radio, wall frescos, and through village-level health workers. Although the campaign was unsuccessful in eradicating malaria completely, malaria prevalence was drastically reduced (Cutler et al. 2010).

In 1995, following the 1988 Polio Eradication Initiative of the WHO, India launched Pulse Polio Immunization Program. Pulse Polio is an immunization campaign established by the government in 1995–1996 to eradicate polio in India by vaccinating all children under the age of five years. The Pulse Polio campaign is counted among the most successful health communication campaigns in India. The entire program used all of the available media resources.

With the advent of HIV/AIDS, health concerns in India received international attention. HIV affects everyone in world, without regard for where they come from. HIV/AIDS also initially carried the "foreign" tag, so international concern was very high because sexual intercourse was its transmission mode. This differs from other diseases discussed. Malaria, leprosy, TB, and polio are region-specific and are most commonly found in the tropical climate of South Asia. Thus, an international concern is not pertinent. Policy regarding HIV/AIDS was originally steered by the WHO. It became the only disease with a dedicated UN agency, the joint program of HIV/AIDS (UNAIDS).

HIV/AIDS also has seen an unprecedented inflow of foreign funds. Mainstream media images from the Western world stressed it further. HIV/AIDS became the first "televised disease." At least in India, HIV/AIDS has been viewed as the first epidemic of the information age and it was widely covered in the media. Discussions about sex and sexuality became a focal point during the media debates. In a way it allowed public health professionals to define images of HIV/AIDS using sophisticated information technologies in ways that targeted certain people (Connelly and Macleod 2003).

HIV/AIDS IN INDIA: DECONSTRUCTING FOUCAULT

Health education also represents a singular contribution to the exercise of bio-power (Foucault 1976). Its involvement with prevention and health promotion, as well as its education nature, enhance the set of power techniques that come into play in the management of individual and social bodies.

Health Education dates from the turn of the twentieth century, when the medical paradigm underwent a shift. In the nineteenth century, the predominant model was hospital medicine, concentrating on symptoms and signs that together configured pathology. This model maintained its influence into the twentieth century, but gradually a new paradigm, surveillance medicine, has been recreating the concepts of health, illness, and normality (Armstrong 1995). Surveillance medicine moves the attention of medicine from pathological bodies to every member of the population. The categories of health and illness give way to the notion of risk. Illness is not a problem per se, but a significant portion of health is redefined as an "at-risk state," much witnessed in the context of HIV/AIDS (Armstrong 1995; Petersen 1996).

The borders between health and illness have also been reshaped. Healthy people can become even healthier, and a person can be healthy and ill at the same time. Because ill and healthy people are at risk, the old tradition of teaching hygiene has proven to be insufficient and has been transformed into the promotion of health (Armstrong 1995). Health education has become part of a whole strategy to promote health for all human beings, a strategy supported by the WHO.

In Foucault's view, biological life is a political event: Population reproduction and disease control are central to economic processes and are therefore subject to political control. Bio-power refers to the mechanisms employed to manage the population and discipline individuals. In this century, health has become increasingly political as a point of contact between government and population. Health education practices that concentrate on individual responsibility for health and disease prevention will be called *traditional health education*. Those practices that focus on empowering people to control their own health will be called *radical health education* (Gastaldo 1997).

The concept of radical health education figures in movements for health promotion, new public health, and health public policy. It focuses on empowering people to control their own health. It is also committed to combating social inequality in a broad way and promoting community participation in health issues. Within this framework, health education can be seen as a political practice that enables individuals and groups in society to organize themselves to develop actions based on their own priorities (Gastaldo 1997). Radical and traditional forms of health education share an underlying notion that there is empowerment through education and subjugation through ignorance. Both are based on the understanding that human beings are liberated beings unless something oppresses them. Empowering them through education is a way to remove the chains of oppression—be it ignorance, lack of political understanding, or submissive behavior.

What health education does construct is identity. Health education is an educational experience that gives professionals and patients/clients elements for building up representations of what is expected from healthy and sick people. These social roles are reinforced by a complex system of rewards and punishments. Health education governs from the outside and encourages self-discipline. From inside, health education is a constructive exercise of power that improves the medical gaze. The promotion of health moves into spheres that are new to bio-medicine. Several scholars have advocated a health communication research program grounded in cultural theory, which would complement existing approaches (Tulloch 1992). The development of praxis and the articulation of knowledge derived from these dominant theories/models take for granted the voices of marginalized people. Persuasive campaigns are based on dominant values, morals, and ideologies. Further, these transmission-based models that seek to modify individual behavior via persuasion impose messages from outside that focus on changing cultural beliefs and practices (Dutta 2006).

The culture-centered approach provides a point of departure from the dominant approach by articulating the very absences in the dominant approach and by emphasizing context in the construction of health meanings. With their focus on individual-level behavior change, the dominant approaches fail to account for the context that encompasses human existence and, therefore, silence the voices of marginalized people by not including them in problem definition. The health problem is preconceived by funding agencies and campaign scholars instead of being developed in dialogue with members of community.

The singular commitment to a particular behavior constrains the ability of the scholar to see the whole picture of health, to really understand the narrative, and to understand the true risk faced by the people of the culture. Instead of focusing on communicative meanings, the models impose a dominant worldview on the receiving population. The voices of cultural participants are no longer listened to. The participation of the receiving population in formative and evolution research serves the dominant framing of health problems. Research and models based on it do not articulate a community based problem. Throughout history, nations and other organized communities have used a variety of communicative tools, including oral and written persuasion, in an attempt to guide or control social change (Wilkins 2003).

The power structures within development processes also need to be critically analyzed in the context of location (Wilkins 2000). Power structures may be conceptualized in a variety of ways, for example, through political-economic contexts. In this approach, development discourse becomes a struggle over the representation of problems, communities, and solutions. Powerful development institutions conceptualize social problems in ways that benefit their own institutional and political-economic interests.

Daniel Lerner's (1958) quintessential treatise on the "passing of traditional society" in the Middle East established a framework for understanding the relationship between media and modernization. Lerner proposed that media exposure makes people more empathetic to ideas that are beyond their local conditions. This enables them to participate in more democratic forms of political governance and more entrepreneurial economic activities. The literature of this historical period promoted a version of modernity that highlighted free-market capitalism, democratic governance, strong national identity (transcending cultural and ethnic differences), and faith in science and technology (e.g., Rogers 1976; Schramm 1963). The characteristics of the U.S. experience at the time were proposed as a universal model for all other societies.

By the 1970s, Asian and Latin American scholars began to critique the ethnocentric nature of this domination. Critical scholars also recognized the limitations of seeing development as an isolated pursuit, drawing attention to the constraints in the global sphere that shaped development processes. As victims of cultural imperialism and dependency on wealthier nations, poor nations found it difficult to set autonomous development policies on health that were in accord with their own cultural histories and societal interests. The critical analysis by such scholars as Everett Rogers (1976) helped open discussion to consider alternative approaches to development. In response to a critique that the dominant model generally assumed to top-down flow of information, participatory approaches emphasized working at the level of local communities. Information generated at the local level would go to government agencies. Participatory approaches argue for local agency in defining both social problems to be addressed and appropriate solutions (Melkote and Steeves 2001).

Vishwanath and Finnegan (2002) point out those low socio-economic status groups, which face the greatest threats of ill health, fail to benefit equally with higher socio-economic groups. The at-risk populations are most often left behind while campaigns continue to benefit the health rich: A substantive body of evidence on knowledge gap theory points out that health communication campaigns contribute to the existing gaps between the rich and the poor (Finnegan and Vishwanath 1997; Freimuth 1990; Vishwanath and Finnegan 1995). Addressing the increasing societal chasm between the have and have-nots, health communication scholars have called for a reconfiguration in campaigns that focuses on serving marginalized people (Marshal and McKeon 1996). Such a reconfiguration has called communicators to reflect on how effective campaigns can be in controlling behavioral change. New individual campaigns efforts have already been initiated in India in various fields of health communication and public health to address leprosy, polio, and HIV/AIDS.

Although the alternatives to extant health communication approaches have developed into individual campaigns, they have hitherto been systematically integrated within a single framework and positioned against the backdrop of the dominant approach of the campaigns. Entertainment-education campaigns are particularly suitable for this critique because they are implemented by Western interventionists in the Third World. Such campaigns reflect the power difference between the West and the Third World in available access to the means of communication. The voices of the West are heard loudly in addressing Third World problems.

For several decades information-education-communication (IEC) has been associated with population and family planning programs around the world. UNFPA was among the first to use the term in its communication activities in 1969. The terms *birth control* and *family planning* frequently were used to advance concerns over the increasing population. The traditional approach to IEC campaigns and community mobilization used information to try to influence people's contraceptive behavior to comply with policies generated by governments and population authorities (Colle 2009). Campaigns linked population issues to HIV/AIDS, assistance to infertile couples, and to development in general. Along with these issues, different approaches were introduced for reaching population including social mobilization, social marketing, advocacy, and interventions emphasizing participation and empowerment. Within many agencies, the emphasis began shifting from agency-dictated goals to goals jointly determined by the agency or government and the broader health-related needs of the people.

HIV/AIDS IN INDIA: PROGRAMMATIC AND POLICY ISSUES

India's National AIDS Prevention and Control Policy (2003, p. 5) acknowledges that

> HIV/AIDS is not merely a public health challenge, it is also a political, and social challenge. Change in behaviour will not occur without a significant change in social and political environment. Unequal gender and power relation, taboos in frank and open communication about sexual health and stigma and discrimination are particularly significant obstacles.

Family population control and the HIV/AIDS campaigns in India are far from being people's movements. Both are bureaucratic programs, designed, financed, controlled, and monitored from New Delhi. The National Health Policy of 2002 and the AIDS policy of 2003 invariably discuss how the prevention mechanism promoted will be carried forward among the poor and marginalized communities who are at the highest risk. The at-risk populations received "targeted interventions," while the rest of the population was called the "general population."

The use of such disassociating language to set marginal people apart can be formal or technical or literally foreign. This language is magnified in health ministries and organizations involved in sexual health promotion and disease prevention. In these organizations, staff and other participants quickly learn to use the international vocabulary of sexual health, which includes phrases such as "high risk" and a proliferation of acronyms such as STI (Sexually Transmitted Infection), MSM (Men who have Sex with Men) and CSW (Commercial Sex Worker). International terms may seem to be neutral, but using them affects development and understanding of. Inevitably the use of these terms also imposes their category referents (Lambert 2001, Foreman 2004).

Rather than utilizing and building on local discourses of sexual health, a new language is developed in which local input becomes meaningless. Communication using language derived from existing local parlance about sexual health (as locally understood) may be less exclusionary and more effective in developing new knowledge than that which uses language rooted in international health vocabulary. The language of sexual health used by international and local health agencies takes a highly particular, essentially biomedical form that may have no precise local referents. Local discourse draws on indigenous definitions of health. Local terminology helps researchers understand how sex and sexuality are locally conceived, and how the people's concerns about sexual regulation and propriety. With this understanding, HIV preventive strategies may be more fruitful (Lambert and Wood 2005).

When this narrowly cultural approach is translated into HIV prevention interventions, it is often manifested in attempts to fit the look and sound familiar to the target population. It addresses locally relevant themes within the intervention's content (Wilson and Miller 2003).

However, these strategies are not informed by, and do not address, the cultural and structural contexts in which people live their sexual lives. Political economy and structural conditions, as well as socio-cultural milieu, influence the dynamics of socio-medical crises such as HIV/AIDS (Parker 2000; Kalipeni et al. 2004). Educational interventions based primarily on individual and social normative approaches, for example, changing awareness and consciousness, improving communication skills and shifting group norms, may not succeed on a major scale. Even if appropriately tailored to local cultural assumptions, they may neglect the underlying dimensions of sexual ill-health.

The resolution on HIV/AIDS adopted by the United General Assembly in 2001 brings this fact out. It "recognises that poverty, underdevelopment and illiteracy are among the principal contributing factors to the spread of HIV/AIDS and notes with grave concern that HIV/AIDS is compounding poverty and is now reversing or impeding the development in many countries."

There are theoretical debates in the social sciences about the individual's capacity to act against the structural determinants and the influence of these determinants on the individual's capacity for action. Nevertheless, the economic and structural drivers must be carefully studied as a part of the daily context in which people live, become infected, and respond to HIV. Most communication campaigns have not attempted to look at HIV/AIDS as an entirely medical problem, since it also is a social problem that affects the society at large.

In the area of population control, it was argued that nations that control their population problem will be better able to manage their resources and citizens.

This nation would more likely fit a global climate. Population control serves transnational hegemony by fostering conditions for sustainable development. This, in turn, promotes economic growth and new opportunities for businesses. The concepts of population control programs embody other ideological biases. The attention has shifted to serving the status quo by focusing on individual-level behavior change among the subaltern classes. In these classes are undesirable groups whose vastly growing masses need to be managed and controlled (Dutta 2006). By focusing on population control as the solution to problems of global peace and stability, the funding agencies and interventionists advance national and international elite privilege. Attention is shifted from the possibilities of really changing the condition of subalterns. Groups are further marginalized while the positions of the elite are supported (Dutta-Bergman 2004). The targeted approach towards population control ensures the political agenda of maintaining the wealth and access to resources in the hands of a small minority while marginalizing the subaltern classes (Klugman 1991).

CONCLUSION

Myths, misinformation, and misconceptions still abound about HIV/AIDS in India. It is still associated with death and dirty, bad, morally wrong actions. The general impression is that "everyone is doing it" and that it is OK to have sex in pre- and post-marital situations. That impression has gotten added impetus, largely due to liberal media and easy access to money and the revolution in information technology. In such a scenario, communication cuts across and plays a strategic role in all components of HIV/AIDS prevention. There must be comprehensive sex education (awareness) at the school level. A problem is that Indian languages do not have a clinical vocabulary for discussing sex, sexuality, and sexually transmitted diseases. Another problem with dividing populations by risk category is that society is not static—a low-risk rural farmer can become a high-risk urban slum dweller or a truck driver overnight.

As this chapter has attempted to show, the issue is not only about HIV/AIDS but also about the politics of the human sexual relationships that serve as the prime carrier of HIV. These have been largely ignored. The primary objective of the HIV/AIDS campaigns is to limit the status of the disease as an epidemic. What is needed is a value orientation rather than information orientation, because knowledge is a necessary, but not a sufficient, condition for preventing HIV/AIDS. This implies that campaigns should be designed, not just to increase knowledge about HIV/AIDS, but also to stress attitude and behavior change. There must also be emphasis on improving gender sensitivity on the part of both men and women and on improving the negotiating skills of women with regard to casual sexual encounters. Several Communication Needs Assessment (CNA) studies have noted the influence of gatekeepers. To date, most of the HIV/AIDS campaigns have focused on film and sports personalities, but there is a need to appeal to different sets of audiences. Non-mass media approaches need to be brought into play.

Management for HIV/AIDS requires an insightful behavioral analysis. Since talking about sex is personal, social sensitivity is the prime concern, at least in India. Individual and socio-cultural aspects play a very important role in designing the messages. Changing behavior, in contrast to changing knowledge, requires formative research that focuses on in-depth behavioral analysis. Researchers must uncover why current behaviors persist and why new behaviors are resisted. Tackling HIV/AIDS also requires an active and coordinated inter-discipline involvement, particularly among education and industry entities that can magnify the impact of health sector programming. A thorough documentation of the behavioral interventions will definitely aid in planning communication campaigns.

Singhan and Rogers (2003, pp. 73–74) observe:

> HIV is not a common everyday infectious disease. It cannot be transmitted in contaminated water and food, like cholera or typhoid. The virus cannot be transmitted by an insect, as are plague and malaria. HIV is not transmitted through air, like influenza and tuberculosis, nor through physical touch, like fungal infections. HIV transmission usually requires the active participation of an individual in activities in which bodily fluids (semen or blood) are exchanged. Theoretically, HIV's spread can thus be controlled.

HIV prevalence in India is measured through the data coming out of the surveillance of antenatal and sexually transmitted disease clinics. These data cannot provide real insight into where transmission is occurring or guide program strategy. The factors that influence the Indian epidemic are the size, behaviors, and disease burdens of high-risk groups, as well as their interaction with sub-populations. The interplay of these forces has resulted in substantial epidemics in several pockets of many Indian states that could potentially ignite sub-epidemics in other, currently low-prevalence parts of the country (Chandrasekaran et al. 2006).

Until HIV is contained, the disease will continue to have consequences for India's development. India's national response to HIV began in 1992 and has shown early success in some states. The priority is to build on those successes. That means increasing prevention coverage of high-risk groups to saturation level, enhancing access and uptake of care and treatment services, ensuring systems and capacity for evidence-based programs, and building in-country technical and managerial capacity. Peter Piot, the director of UNAIDS aptly sums up the HIV/AIDS scenario in India when he states that India faces enormous challenges in overcoming HIV/AIDS. However, he sees ample quantities of all the resources needed to achieve universal access to HIV prevention and treatment. This will require a significant intensification of efforts in India, just as it will in the rest of the world (UNAIDS 2006; cited in Kodandapani and Alpert, 2007).

BIBLIOGRAPHY

Armstrong, D. (1995). "The rise of surveillance medicine," *Sociology of Health and Illness*, 17 (3): pp. 393–404.

Bose, Ashish. (1998). *From Population to People*, 2 vols. Delhi: BR Publishing Corporation, p. 574.

Chandrasekaran, P., et al. (2006). "Containing HIV/AIDS in India: the Unfinished Agenda," *The Lancet Infectious Diseases*, 6, pp. 508–521.

Colle, R. (2002). "Threads of Development Communication" In J. Servaes, ed., *Communication and Development for Social Change*. Paris: UNESCO, pp. 96–157.

Connelly, M., and Macleod, C. (2003). "Waging War: Discourses of HIV/AIDS in South African Media," *African Journal of AIDS Research*, 2 (1): pp. 1–11.

Cutler, D.M., et al. (2007). *Mosquitoes: The Long-Term Effects of Malaria Eradication in India*. Cambridge, MA: John F. Kennedy School of Government, Harvard University.

Desikan, K.V. (2012). "Elimination of Leprosy and the Possibility of Eradication: The Indian Scenario," *The Indian Journal of Medical Research*, 135 (1): p. 3.

Dutta, M. J. (2006). "Theoretical Approaches to Entertainment Education Campaigns: A Subaltern Critique," *Health Communication*, 20 (3): pp. 221–231.

Dutta-Bergman, M. J. (2004). "The Unheard Voices of Santalis: Communicating About Health from the Margins of India. *Communication Theory*, 14 (3): pp. 237–263.

Finnegan, J. R., and Viswanath, K. (1997). "Communication Theory and Health Behavior Change: The Media Studies Framework." In K. Glanz; F. M. Lewis; and B. K. Rimer, eds., *Health Behavior and Health Education: Theory, Research and Practice*. San Francisco: Jossey-Bass, pp. 313–341.

Freimuth, V.S. (1990). "The Chronically Uninformed: Closing the Knowledge Gap in Health." In T.E.B. Ray and L. Donohew, eds., *Communication and Health: Systems and Applications*. Hillsdale, NJ: Lawrence Erlbaum Associates, pp. 171–186.

Foreman, M. (2004). "Males, Men and MSM," *Pukaar*, 45: pp. 3–4.

———. (1976). "Governmentality," *Ideology and Consciousness*, 6: pp. 5–21.

Gastaldo, D. (1997). "Is Health Education Good for You? Re-thinking Health Education Through the Concept of Bio-power." In A. Petersen and R. Bunton, eds., *Foucault, Health and Medicine*. London: Routledge.

Goswami, Shaswati. (2007). *Media and Communication in Post-independence India*. Salford, UK: The Media, Communication and Cultural Studies Association.

Kalipeni, E., et al., eds. (2004). *HIV and AIDS in Africa: Beyond Epidemiology*. Oxford: Blackwell.

Klugman, B. (1990). "The Politics of Contraception in South Africa," *Women's Studies International Forum*, 13 (3): pp. 261–271).

Kodandapani, K., and Alpert, P.T. (2007). "AIDS in India: When Denial Kills," Home, Health Care Management *and* Practice, 20 (1): pp. 21–26.

Lambert, H. (2001). "Not Talking About Sex in India: Indirection and the Communication of Bodily Intention." In J. Hendry and B. Watson, eds., *An Anthropology of Indirect Communication*. London: Routledge.

Lambert, H., and Wood, K. (2005). "A Comparative Analysis of Communication About Sex, Health and Sexual Health in India and South Africa: Implications for HIV Prevention," *Culture, Health and Sexuality*, 7 (6): pp. 527–541.

Lerner, D. (1958). *The Passing of the Traditional Society*, Glencoe, IL: Free Press.

Melkote, S.R., and Steeves, H.L. (2001). *Communication for Development in the Third World*, 2d Ed. New Delhi: Sage.

National Aids Control Organisation (India) (2003). "National Blood Policy," Government of India Ministry of Health and Family Welfare, New Delhi: NACO. Available at http://upsacs.nic.in/bs%20doc/bs%20National%20Blood%20Policy.pdf, New Delhi: NACO.

Parker, R. (2000). "Administering the Epidemic: HIV/AIDS Policy, Models of Development, and International Health." In *Global Health Policy, Local Realities: The Fallacy of the Level Playing Field*. Boulder, CO: Lynn Reinner Publishers, pp. 39–55.

Peterson, A. (1996). "Risk and the Regulated Self: the Discourse of Health Promotion as Politics of Uncertainty," *Australia and New Zealand Journal of Sociology*, 32 (1): pp. 44–57.

Rogers, E.M. (1976). *Communication and Development: Critical Perspectives*. Hills, CA: Sage.

Swaminathan, S., and Narendran, G. (2008). "HIV and Tuberculosis in India," *J Biosci*, 33 (4): pp. 527–537.

Tulloch, J. (1992). "Using TV in HIV/AIDS Education: Production and Audience Cultures," *Media Information Australia*, 65: p. 10.

Viswanath, K., and Finnegan, J. R. (1995). "The Knowledge Gap Hypothesis: Twenty-five Years Later." In B. Burleson, ed., *Communication Yearbook* 19. Thousand Oaks, CA: Sage, pp. 187–228.

———. (2002). "Reflections on Community Health Campaigns: Secular Trends and the Capacity to Effect Change." In R. Hornik, ed., *Public Health Communication*. Mahwah, NJ: Lawrence Erlbaum Associates, pp. 289–313.

Wilkins, K. (2000). *Redeveloping Communication for Social Change: Theory, Practice and Power*. Boulder, CO: Rowman & Littlefield.

Wilson, B.D., and Miller, R.L. (2003). "Examining Strategies for Culturally Grounded HIV Prevention: A Review," *AIDS Education and Prevention*, 15 (2): pp. 184–202.

SIX

Communication for Organizational Adjustment

How to Position Development Institutions for Enhanced Health Communication

Emmanuel K. Ngwainmbi

Communication is now regarded by many as an instrument that brings the world and its cultures into one space. With the new world order stance, new questions must be asked, including this: How well does the management of information and communication methods and channels in health practices fit into the space?

This chapter looks at the way health information is communicated in developing countries to affected populations and within international organizations serving in those countries. It describes the strengths and weaknesses in the management of information, communication methods, and channels in health practices and offers contexts for healthcare practitioners and their media staff. Contexts are required to convey constructive messages that sensitize the populations affected by crucial health challenges, and for proper coordination with their partners.

OPERATIONAL DEFINITION OF CORPORATE COMMUNICATION

The future of any corporation, company, or organization depends on how it is viewed by key stakeholders, such as investors, consumers, employees, and members of the community in which the company operates. Corporate communication is used interchangeably and lavishly in this chapter to mean organizational communication, global communication or communication in international development organizations. It is the way an organization uses communication tools and channels to convey identity, build its brands and develop its reputation or image. Global communication involves sharing information with the organization's stakeholders aimed at promoting transparency, coherence, credibility, and its brand. A corporate culture, coherent corporate identity, and corporate philosophy are inherent in messages communicated. Global communication may also involve a professional relationship with the press and the application of communication channels, tools, and technologies to obtain the results desired.

Global communication presents quick, responsible ways of sharing and facilitating decision making in a crisis. A well-functioning corporation provides a framework for effective coordination of internal and external communication. This framework is needed for establishing and maintaining favorable reputation and positive feedback from stakeholders upon whom the organization depends.

Corporate communication is characterized by immediacy and instant gratification. Information products and channels continue to be updated and improved upon, allowing consumers to reach and exchange data with multiple groups in an instant. This is a "new world information and communications order," a program sponsored by UNESCO to sanction the control of news organizations by governments all over the world. This new order is considered by a fleet of development communication experts to have suppressed, but not eliminated, centuries-old cultural, communication styles among religious, social, and ethnic groups in developing countries (Milne 2012; McDaniel, Samovar, and Porter 2012; Ngwainmbi 1999, 2004, 2005a, 2005b; Mowlana 1997, 1996).

However, this is not the case with the media, which, in recent memory, have played a major role in informing various aspects of individual lives, including access to health information. The volume of social media use for socialization through such outlets as Twitter, MySpace, LinkedIn, or Facebook continues to grow throughout the world, while in health messaging it remains an enigmatic practice. Social networking Websites allow individuals to instantly communicate with large networks of friends, acquaintances, colleagues, and groups of people—including those who are vulnerable to health issues. Newbold and Campos (2011) have found that social media allow personalized, tailored messages to reach target audiences. There is the opportunity for the participation of health consumers. These media also create the context for appealing messages that can be presented in multiple formats to a variety of users. Interaction is practical among the healthcare expert and communication office, the affected population, and the ministry of health.

Newbold and Campos (2011) and other health scholars still consider the use of interactive media to be an exciting new concept in public health, where information has traditionally been disseminated in a one-way manner from gatekeeper to consumer (pp 24–25). However, the threat of new information technologies to the survival of indigenous customs must not be ignored, even if such communication tools, properly used, support healthy living standards. Questions are being raised as to whether social media can be used to effectively improve public health (Uittenhout 2012).

Whatever the verdict, social media are becoming the most widely used medium for reaching various audiences. Health and communication experts ought to pay attention and begin to consider how best to exploit this technology to share information, package feedback, and redistribute strategic information to target groups. It is not too late for the national governments in developing regions to use social media channels as a mechanism for trained midwives, birth attendants, nurses, and doctors to share knowledge and ideas on causes and trends in infectious diseases with healthcare administrators and traditional doctors in their respective provinces. This sort of mediation could, in fact, help healthcare providers to better monitor diseases and engage in a constructive dialogue on response and prevention techniques with the international health and medical community.

Despite their ability to document acute poverty levels in agrarian, arid, and urban communities, development agencies and financial donors seem to avoid investing in information technology when implementing activities to change behaviors. Consultants and other private contractors have observed that most development organizations use information and communication channels to market their respective brands, achievements, and images. They do not use such channels to educate the community. With the exception of Kenya, where social media are reportedly being used to share information on some thirty-six M4 Healthcare projects, there are few reports of field workers in developing countries using twitter or cell phones to share messages about disease prevention.

REFLECTIONS ON GLOBAL COMMUNICATION

Organizations operating on a global scale consider marketing and government relations to be the lifeblood of their existence. Whether they operate on a profit or non-profit basis, international organizations have found the need to promote their image by budgeting financial and human capital and enhancing diplomatic ties with their host country. It is not uncommon to find press or communication officers (COs) representing an international organization in a meeting hosted by local national government. There is at least one specialized UN agency operating in each of 193 member countries of the United Nations. Each agency has a mechanism for sharing news and/or information about its work. In some of the agencies, such as UNESCO or UNICEF, there may be as many as fifteen media and communication officers, each specialized in some area of message packaging, communication management, media, or information dissemination. Some of their communication and information dissemination strategies and platforms have targeted specific audiences. An example is the United Nations Population Fund (UNFPA) sensitization campaigns to reduce fistula and gender mutilation of millions of girls and young women, especially in thirty countries in Africa and the Middle East. Still questions are being raised about the effectiveness of the techniques being used in the campaigns to reach the vulnerable groups.

Marketing

Marketing is an important tool for every organization—business or healthcare, nonprofit or retail. In corporate communications, marketing addresses consumers and clients as external audiences. Marketing plays an integral role in "putting the face" on a company's image, offerings, and products. It defines how the company portrays itself on its Website and in product packaging, logo, messages, and advertising. A corporate communications office will devote a great deal of time, and most likely different staff, to handle marketing, since it can directly affect financial success. Most organizations invest at least one-quarter of their budget for the branding of their products and their image.

Government Relations

Government relations in corporate communications strategy involves external audiences—lawmakers, lobbyists, and watchdog groups, and, of course, the government itself. Communications departments that deal with government relations usually delegate this role to a specialized individual or team. A government relations professional will need extensive knowledge of government processes, have relationships with key lawmakers, and understand how to work with lobbyists. A company might even employ a lobbyist to represent its interests and to influence decision makers. The organization's communications include materials outlining a company's industry and needs, and the effect certain laws might have (Huber 2013). Particularly in the United States companies and organizations hire lobbyists to represent their interests and attempt to influence policy makers. While this act may be considered unethical, the lobbyists have helped the organizations to accomplish their goal.

DEVELOPMENT INSTITUTIONS AND COMMUNICATION MANDATE IN A GLOBAL ENVIRONMENT

Any organization should be conscious of its reputation and the impact of its programs on those it seeks to save. That is the case, even if the organization is operating with no interest in commercial benefits, but rather with a mandate to provide development services. Without a good reputation, the organization's relationship with the service recipients cannot be sustained. Hence, the reputation of an organization is inextricably linked to the quality of its services and the consistency with which the target group delivers such services.

UNFPA Executive Communication

International organizations positioned in countries are better known when they develop infrastructures, end dependence on foreign assistance, and lift people out of poverty and improve their overall well-being. These traits and attributes build the organization's positive qualities to the public and solidify its competitive advantage.

The executive approach to improving internal and external communication makes sense, as it shows that corporations are recognizing the usefulness of communication actions at the highest level. In an effort to strengthen organizational priorities for the year, the executive director of the UNFPA, in a memorandum to staff dated February 13, 2013 to all staff, stressed the need to continue the roll-out of the UNFPA communications strategy, to improve (its) organizational culture and systems and to "deliver coherent, professional, timely internal and external communication." The memorandum identifies activities at the global level to include "training roll-out, enhancement of the internal and external web sites, and increased deployment of communications advisors at country and regional levels." As part of improving communication, the executive director states that a new virtual tool would be launched in 2013. It would have advanced features to support fund-wide communications initiatives and advance messaging and collaboration among staff.

The regional office of the UNFPA in Johannesburg, South Africa, has implemented the communication strategy, however, with recent budget cuts, is not clear whether the virtual tool proposed in the February 2013 memorandum has been launched. The executive approach to improving internal and external communication makes sense, as it shows that corporations are recognizing the usefulness of communication actions at the highest level. The regional office of the UNFPA in Johannesburg, South Africa, has implemented the communication strategy. At this writing, it is not clear what mechanisms will be exploited to ensure or that the virtual tool proposed in the February 2013 memorandum was ever launched (United Nations Population Fund (UNFPA 2013a).

Experts, UNFPA media officers, and senior health experts met with journalists covering health in Africa in Kampala, Uganda, on March 16–23, 2013, to brainstorm. Their objective was to think of ways the UNFPA could be recognized as a "thought leader and catalyst for action on reproductive health, MDG 5 and youth issues" (UNFPA 2013b). The meeting addressed the need for its communication staff to use strategies developed from the local culture and systems to enable professional, timely, and effective internal and external communication.

That the conference took place speaks to the importance the UNFPA attaches to health communication and proper population growth. The population development agency assembled resource people from various backgrounds for a week to share knowledge and chart a course for coordinated delivery of health messages.

Global Corporate Communication and Social Mobilization Contexts

Today's processes of social organization and mobilization, including those derived from gender, culture, class, ethnicity, nationality, and generational cleavages, dominate the media agenda. These processes shape access to and control social media, resulting in a complex set of misunderstandings.

In global corporate communications, the overall economic capital of a country is based on the psychophysical and emotional health of its people. It is not just a simple compilation of costs and investments.

There are a number of compelling psychological reasons for conducting face-to-face business meetings. Face-to-face meetings allow members to engage in and observe verbal and nonverbal behavioral styles not captured in most computer-mediated communication devices (Arvey 2013).

Videoconferencing does not capture all of the dynamics of group members (e.g., the expressions of others while one member is talking).

Another feature is simply that face-to-face business meetings provide human contact among members. Similarly, business meetings allow participants opportunities to develop important relationships with one another.

Professor Richard D. Arvey of the University of Singapore's School of Business states that face-to-face meetings provide a forum for members to obtain and give social support in the form of emotional support that might be less convincing in computer media communications. Organizational life is often lonely, and face-to-face meetings can help to alleviate feelings of isolation and stress. They allow the direct expression of humor in a way that is not always conveyed in computer-mediated communications. Strauss and McGrath (1994) agree when they argue that computer-mediated communication compromises the persuasions that visual, emotional activities.

THE ROLE OF TIME IN NEGOTIATING KNOWLEDGE SHARING

Social media have revolutionized global communication. In fact, social media have become a popular contact agent in nearly all communities. These portals provide a context where people can communicate, exchange messages, share knowledge, and interact with each other, regardless of the distance that separates them. Social media can enhance intercultural adaptation by promoting knowledge sharing and understanding through interaction to increase convenience, so that the demands of a new cultural expectation can be met. In the same way that cultures around the world value their individual traditions, customs, beliefs, and norms, social media connect people everywhere regardless of time differences and geographical boundaries. Huge volumes of messages are exchanged among millions of people at the same time. People around the globe can interact with each other within seconds as they send and respond to messages.

Indeed social media have brought together people from different cultures, age groups, religious, or non-religious backgrounds, and educational levels, creating a new form of adaptation. Social media contribute to one's sense of community. Media sites are convenient and efficient. Through online resources, people can stay socially connected to their friends, family, peers, and acquaintances. The social sites encourage learning through the exchanges of messages and the sharing of links, information, and resources. Chen and Zhang (2010) and Sawyer and Chen (2012, p. 151) summarize the contributions of these resources. They can be used to assist with intercultural adaptation to a host environment. People use social media to learn about their locale, establish and maintain relationships, and stay informed concerning events in their home countries. Social media contribute to one's sense of community, both in the host and home countries (Sawyer and Chen 2012, p. 162). They also open a context for assessing individual responsibility.

To determine the extent to which this can happen in the area of public health, researchers will have to explore the potential of various forms of social media, such as twitter, I-phone, YouTube, network sites, and Facebook. Within that communication context, information developed to help change behaviors and attitudes toward causes of health could come to satisfy basic needs in both urban and rural settlements in developing countries. Research shows numerous benefits in effective communication and health outcomes for patients and healthcare experts (Wanzer, Booth-Butterfield, and Gruber 2004). The connection patients feel with the clinician can ultimately improve their health through participation in their care, adherence to treatment, and patient self-management.

PERSPECTIVES ON GOOD PRACTICES IN THE ORGANIZATION

An accurate picture of good results from services provided by an organization cannot be given because of discrepancies in the tools used in the evaluation. Still, we can make the case that international development organizations do indeed bring some good results; otherwise, the government of the host country would expel them. It is impossible for an organization to invest technical and financial resources for decades without having visible results. It certainly cannot happen with UN agencies, whose funding comes from member countries with diplomatic ties. There is accountability for the quality of services, programs, and projects delivered and an audit of funds disbursed.

Reports on the organizations' Websites, as well as from private, commercial, and government-sponsored media show that, over the years, developing countries have experienced positive results through the communication of health information by development agencies. In Madagascar, the UNFPA collaborates with the Ministry of Health in organizing a health sensitization campaign that uses an audio/spot in the media for a week. The audience becomes more aware of the importance of using vitamins and vaccinating children. In the Comoros Islands, the UNFPA sponsors the training of journalists who report on maternal health and reproduction. Journalists accompany health workers from Association des Sages Femmes (Association of Midwives) into the field, interviewing the mothers and service providers to help the reporters tell the story accurately.

The UNFPA sponsors an annual award program to recognize the best coverage of health. This is one motivation for print and writers to produce and disseminate educational programs to targeted, affected audiences. The winner receives the award in a televised event organized by the agency. In the Democratic Republic of Congo (DRC), the state media reportedly waits for the date of a major event with potential national interest, such as World AIDS Day or Women's Day, to provide free broadcasts on health issues. According to the manager of a private television station in Kinshasa the number of programs and times to broadcast maternal health programs has increased since some media personnel participated in health reporting workshops sponsored by several intergovernmental organizations. This first in the station's twenty years of operation began after its journalist-candidate won the UNFPA award. This and other practices encourage the media to produce and print or air a greater number of quality messages. This form of education does initiate change in behaviors and good health and enhances the context for promoting and sustaining peaceful coexistence in the locale.

PERSPECTIVES ON POOR PRACTICES IN THE ORGANIZATION

A country's engagement in poor healthcare management practices can have a negative bearing on the international health organization that is in the host country to support actions in good health. Poor practices exist mostly at the level of service implementation and administration. This happens mostly at the level of coordination and collaboration among the involved partners implementing health programs, health services providers, and pharmaceutical agencies.

In terms of administration, many national governments do not have an effective control policy for importing medical supplies to pharmacies. As a result, there is little control over the disbursement of medicines to patients. Patients tend to trust medicines imported from Europe, Canada, and the United States, countries that have strict drug production and administration guidelines. Major complaints have been raised in Uganda, DRC, Niger, Kenya, and other countries over the quality of malaria treatment and prevention drugs imported from India, Nigeria, and China. A straw poll of patients in Kenya, DRC, and Niger concluded that L-Artem, a malaria treatment introduced to the African market in 2001, has not been quite as effective in destroying the virus that causes malaria. The drug is produced and distributed by Shalna Laboratories PVT. Ltd., and is described as containing 80 mg. of arthemether and 480 mg. of lumefantrine.[1] Conversely, patients found mefloquine hydrochloride tablets,[2] developed in the United States at Walter Reed Army Institute of Research in the 1970s, to be the most effective drug in the treatment of malaria patients. It also has milder side effects than other drugs in the same family.

While this is largely a programmatic rather than a communication issue, one must wonder if there is any level of coordination between the national health ministries and the international health organization in those countries, or a program set up to help the national government monitor the disturbing practice.

Other poor practices include quack pharmacies operating with no license or with undertrained technicians who administer drugs. Pharmacies operate in close proximity to each other, and patients often do not need prescription slips that often require extra expenditure and time to obtain. Patients also can negotiate prices among competing pharmacies. However, the absence of price control and the presence of pseudo-pharmacists complicate the problem of coordination for trained health practitioners in intergovernmental organizations such as the WHO, UNICEF, UNFPA, Doctors without borders, and other healthcare providers.

This problem also complicates the efforts of some international organizations to provide drugs to the population at affordable prices. More than 30 million malaria patients benefit from reduced price agreements through the Clinton Global Initiative (CGI), whose members have made 827 commitments in Africa in health, education, energy, environment, and economic empowerment with an estimated value of $28.9 billion. That is a drop of water in the ocean, however. Healthcare organizations and national governments have failed to implement preventive measures, or what the CGI founder, former U.S. president Bill Clinton, calls a "culture of creative experiment" (Clinton Global Initiative 2013).

The United Nations Economic Commission for Africa (UNECA) has added climate change to the agenda of high-level meetings with African health and interior affairs ministers over the last five years, and increasingly shared information with the media. The UNEC reports that African governments have been making feeble attempts to fight the effects of global warming. International health organizations and health-related agencies in charge of human movement, such as UN Habitat and the International Red Cross, seem to lack the resources to manage the presence of refugees or control their mass relocation. Any slow or inadequate response in tropical areas can lead to the massive spread of infectious, as well as air and water-borne diseases such as typhoid fever, tuberculosis, malaria, and cholera.

Some of the poor practices in communicating healthcare information are brought about by entities in the population being served. Take the case of DRC, a mineral-rich country in Central Africa with an annual GDP of $27.575 billion and $368 per capita income. The Democratic Republic of Congo (DRC) has been ravaged by corruption, human rights abuse, and military conflicts for over two decades. More than 100 international agencies, local NGOs, intergovernmental bodies and private enterprises have tackled the health and social problems in the country's cities and remote areas. Nevertheless, HIV/AIDS, malaria, polio, cholera, typhoid fever, yellow fever, the Ebola virus, and hemorrhagic fever continue to deplete the human capital. The maternal mortality rate per 100,000 births in the DRC in 2010 was 670, compared with 533.6 in 2008 and 550 in 1990. The under-five mortality rate was 199 per 1,000 births (Wikipedia 2013).

The data reflects an increase in mortality rates, despite campaigns jointly conducted by government and international agencies to sensitize the population. According to reports published by UNICEF, UNFPA, Doctors without Borders, UNHCR, and local media, the thirteen-year military conflict between the government and militia groups in the Eastern Region has increased sexual and gender-based violence and consequently the spread of HIV/AIDS among some 100,000 victims. Nevertheless, some donors and project implementing agencies claim that there has been measurable success.

COMMUNICATING DATA ON SEXUAL VIOLENCE

From a field performance standpoint, this author has observed a lack of coordination in the delivery of healthcare among intergovernmental organizations, health officials in national governments, and non-governmental health workers. A psychosocial clinician in DRC, working with victims of gender-based rape and sexual violence, revealed that many international NGOs and intergovernmental organizations implement sensitization campaigns against sexual violence and rape without first exchanging ideas with local social psychologists, heads of traditional groups, or government staff who work with the sex offenders and victims.[3] Even statistics on cases of sex offenders and treatment of victims are disseminated to international media, healthcare organizations and project financing sectors without consulting local experts. This is an age-old problem that development health communication experts find increasingly common. It needs to be addressed through a national dialogue involving all players in healthcare management and the communication of health messages in those developing areas.

Reports published on behalf of the agencies that implemented the Project for the Prevention and Response to Sexual and Gender-Based Violence in the DRC's North and South Kivu Provinces show that some 50,000 victims of sex-based crimes had received training, rehabilitation, and drugs. The report claims that data collection, sensitization, and advocacy efforts assisted 55,613 out of 64,082 affected persons in that region. This was from 2006 to when the project was dropped (UNFPA 2013). Despite this help, interviews conducted in the region with victims, offenders, health officials, and law enforcement officials, as well as press reports, show that daily violence continued after the effort was ended. Hence, even advocacy efforts have not been successful. The program had enabled 49,000 to have access to psychological care between 2006 and 2010. The report was published on the Websites of those agencies. Only 10 percent of $18 million (CAN) funded by the Canadian International Development Agency was spent on data collection; awareness and advocacy in the DRC; capacity monitoring and health and medical response; and in psycho-social, legal and judicial, and socio-economic improvement.

The report also reveals that 55,000 victims received technical assistance, while 8939 survivors and 2078 schoolchildren in the region received socio-economic reintegration assistance. Less than 10 percent of the amount funded by the Canadian Development agency ($18 million) was used in operations activities in the field. These statistics, however, do not reflect the massive impact of the health problems of the Congolese people, or their welfare and socio-economic interests.

Certainly, the development agencies have not played an integral role in curbing the problems that make the population vulnerable to violence and the spread of life-threatening disease. In 2013, despite the presence of the United Nations High Commissioner for Refugees (UNHCR) in the Eastern Region, peace-related UN initiatives, and peace keeping personnel based in the region, more than thirty armed groups in eastern DRC increased their activities. Local NGOs with more knowledge of the cultural factors that cause gender-based violence continued to receive less funding from international organizations and their own government. There was little data sharing. The Global Centre for the Responsibility to Protect, an international watchdog organization founded by supportive governments, human rights leaders, and aid organizations, has reported that inconsistency in the role of the UNHCR created a security vacuum when government troops redeployed to other areas. The Eastern Region faced M23, a militia group made of former government soldiers. The Global Centre contends that weak government structures are insufficient to protect civilians (Global Centre for the Responsibility to Protect 2013).

The violence and lack of control contribute to sexual violence in the Eastern Region. A former militia leader, currently the advisor for the Reconstruction and Stabilization Program for Outgoing Forces in Conflict in Eastern Democratic Republic of Congo, noted in an interview conducted with this author on September 4, 2013, in Goma, DRC, that if proper measures were taken by the national government to end conflicts between the national army and the armed groups, peace would be established. But so far authorities and organizations have not addressed that need.

Misunderstandings between the political groups, ignorance, drunkenness, unemployment, poverty, and sexual and gender-based violence perpetuated war in the Eastern Region. No region can advance politically, socially and economically without respecting and correctly applying the principles of peace (Ngwainmbi 2013). Therefore, a national comprehensive communication strategy would be needed that takes into account the principles of collaboration, coordination, advocacy, and fostering good relations between divergent groups and the people. If properly developed and fully implemented, such a strategy would contribute greatly to the development of the region.

UNDERSTANDING AND COMMUNICATING SEXUAL/GENDER-BASED VIOLENCE

Sexual violence and corruption relate to cultural beliefs and social standards, so one would have to rebuild the psychosocial structures that denigrate human beings to solve such problems fully. Studies on the epidemiology of rape and sexual violence are difficult to research because victims of a relatively younger age are reluctant to report to authorities or be identified. Meaningful statistics are elusive and may not reflect the extent of advocacy and communication activity invested in controlling the influence of the social disease on human life. That, of course, includes knowledge of levels of non-consensual and coerced sex. In a study of rape and the factors that have contributed to high numbers of rapes in South Africa, Jewkes and Abrahams (2002) cautioned that international comparison needs to be approached with caution because most developing countries lack the infrastructure to produce a substantial body of survey data.

Many organizations operate in the same environment and in some cases serve the same types of people, so it is often difficult to know how many people in an area need help. It is not uncommon to find USAID, the Gates Foundation, CARE, World Vision, Doctors without Borders, and a string of UN agencies all trying to address the same health problem in a single country. Like others, the Gates Foundation, the WHO, and the UNFPA have spent decades in Africa fighting the spread of malaria, tuberculosis, HIV/Aids, or polio. Each agency has its own data on the people treated or affected by the disease.

There is no coordination or collaboration among the agencies, partly because the governments are unable to monitor their work. Governments also may simply be unaware of the need for consistency in the health-related data being distributed. Numerous meetings have been held by government officials and representatives of the development agencies to set up plans for joint initiatives, efficient collaboration and result-geared development actions. Yet there is increasing discontent in the research community, community action groups, and financial donors over huge disparities in the data published by intergovernmental organizations, para-state agencies, and value-based international organizations, such as CARE and the Gates Foundation. The dissatisfaction is justified. Some organizations deliberately produce false data in order to solicit more funding to continue implementing activities without tangible results and to retain their jobs.[4]

MANAGING COMMUNICATION IN AID AGENCIES

The challenges in managing health messages exist at three levels: (1) implementation of tools and channels by the organization; (2) the absence of monitoring and evaluation communication outreach with target groups; and (3) public apathy toward the presence of international organizations.

Communication in intergovernmental agencies involves using machines and monitoring the movements of machines as well as observing the way people in the organization interact among themselves, with their partners, clients, and others. Obstacles are bound to prevail. Generally speaking, this happens because of misunderstandings, misinterpretations of initial exchanges between the corporate staff and the client or stakeholder, and incorrect use of information technology. The public may have a wrong assessment of the messages, either intentional or unintentional. Sometimes this is because the corporation has had prior conflicts with the public, or the information may simple be badly prepared.

Here we focus on other challenges faced by international development organizations that operate in developing countries as they manage communication:

- Evaluation and monitoring of communication products and program sources may be absent.
- Country Program Officers often face delays in organizing strategic meetings/working sessions or soliciting support/advocacy for implementation of results in the fields. They utilize face-to-face meetings with health officials in the national governments to exchange information. This in turn makes it difficult for communications officers to harness key messages to be disseminated. It also inhibits their ability to collect and prepare information for the various constituents, for example, the media, focus groups, and partners.

The problem is not entirely that of communication staff. There are persistent gaps in the agenda of Health and Population Welfare ministries and program sponsors. An interview with the technical specialist for reproductive and maternal health for the UNFPA office in Somalia revealed that senior health officials of the Ministry of Health do not use data for decision-making. They also seem unprepared to change their attitude toward using data to transform lives. According to Dr. Lordfred Achu, a technical adviser in reproductive health, some donors and government health officials have conflicting priorities when they come to negotiation meetings (Achu 2013). This less-than-supportive attitude has major implications in the selection of types of projects to be implemented. There is no assessment of the capacity for communication to change lifestyles and the overall results expected.

NGOs, parastate agencies in the field, and community leaders have complained that UN agencies abandon ongoing projects to fund new ones, without completing activities previously started. One program, for example, funded the construction of a police center and was expected to provide computers, furniture, and technical support to help the government of the DRC. The program, funded by the Canadian International Development Agency (CIDA) was terminated in 2013. Jointly implemented by the UNFPA, UNICEF, and another UN agency, the Project for the Prevention and Response to Sexual Violence in East DRC ended after just seven years. The project was dropped, even though data collected by different sources showed an increase in sexual assaults and gender-based violence.

One of the crucial challenges for communication teams is the growing criticism and negative public campaigns over the use of contraceptives to reduce the spread of diseases in highly populated areas. The opposition has been spearheaded by political parties opposed to governments in power. Research has also shown that public figures deliberately misinterpret the WHO and UNFPA campaigns against the spread of sexually transmitted diseases (STDs) and unplanned pregnancies in Nigeria, Uganda, and Cameroon, among other areas.

Local knowledge can also work against projects. A sense of suspicion permeates the community at the initial stages of knowledge sharing. When the AIDS epidemic first hit the northwest province in Cameroon in the mid-1980s, hawkers and small business owners quickly came up with an acronym for AIDS—American Intelligence to Discourage Sex. This soon led to public resistance against the distribution of condoms in the streets, education sensitization activities in schools, and messages on billboards. The local press reported that the anti-campaign quickly spread among young, educated adults and later among the uneducated, leading to greater ignorance and public nonchalance toward the deadly nature of disease. Within a few years, AIDS had become a pandemic. About 70 percent of pregnant women were diagnosed in the health clinics as being infected with the HIV virus. Although no meaningful data is available on the social consequences, the disease probably promoted prostitution and sexual violence, ultimately increasing transmission rates among married people in that region. The polygamous community has faced an increase in the number of cases of infidelity and adultery as well. The most widely published media reports of this ignorance concerned the president of South Africa, a married man, who, as South African media reported, considered himself cured by taking a shower after having sexual intercourse with an HIV-infected mistress.

Infected persons intent on avenging those responsible for their demise have knowingly infected unwitting partners through sexual intercourse. This was supported by results of a straw poll conducted by this author. Nurses and urban health staff in the Niger, the DRC, Johannesburg and Cape Town in South Africa, Cameroon, Kenya, and other African cities related that HIV-infected business owners, motorcyclists, cab drivers, and some professionals pay vulnerable women and men for sexual encounters. The commonest victims are sex workers without condoms, girls from poor families but also high school and college students, and wives released by their own husbands to prostitute themselves to support the family.

HIV infections may be increasing because infected people feel hopeless and become vindictive; they sleep with other people without using protection or revealing their health condition.

Another reality that is thwarting the efforts of health organizations in sensitizing populations against the spread of sexually transmitted diseases are questionable interpretations of human rights laws by civic organizations and human rights activists. Religious bodies, human rights groups, non-governmental organizations, and libertarians have publicly denounced disease-reduction measures being implemented by UNFPA and WHO. They regard this as an attempt to deprive people of their rights over their bodies or to control population growth. The Catholic Church is pro-life, holding a position that a fetus is a human being and deserves to have life, no matter what its health condition may be. If a woman and her unborn child have the HIV virus, advocates insist no one has the authority to decide the child's fate but its mother. While medical centers are required to document and report cases of infections to health authorities, no laws prohibit infected persons from spreading the disease through sexual contact. This is the common means of transmission in developing regions, especially Africa. A few African countries reportedly sequestered AIDS patients when the diseases starting taking lives. Since the early 2000s, however, the practice has been discontinued. Many governments lack the capacity to contain the alarmingly high number of cases being documented daily.

COMMUNICATION FOR BEHAVIOR CHANGE

The WHO, UNFPA, and similar organizations in developing countries have been disseminating messages for over four decades. However, an assessment of the extent to which those messages have helped people change behaviors or improve the quality of their lives shows a need to revamp health-based communication (Ngwainmbi 2013).

The problem may be beyond anyone's control, such as overpopulation and the inability of researchers to find treatments that control disease. Most issues are fabricated. Some are manmade. There may be a disconnect between healthcare experts and senior government officials. A lack of political will or good decision-making may exist with health ministers. Collaboration may be insufficient among healthcare providers, especially international development organizations. Funding has been limited to address life threatening diseases. Among other problems are weak program monitoring and evaluation, feeble advocacy and disease prevention campaigns, and uncoordinated and confusing messages disseminated by the development agencies.

STRATEGIES FOR EFFECTIVE INTERNAL COMMUNICATION

Organizations desiring to effectively share health messages with a fast growing and increasingly well-informed Third World population must first properly address communication among themselves and their partners. They must open internal communication channels. They must mobilize themselves, package their communication program and strategies into a unique format, and deliver the program as one entity.

Communication teams should evaluate and monitor the use of communication tools and channels and public feedback to determine the quality, reach, self-image, and sustainability of messages being delivered to target audiences. Those audiences include not only the affected population, but also donors, governments, development partners, the private sector, and educational and public research institutions.

Strengthening efficiency in internal communication requires having a forum (a conference or symposium) for communication officers, managers, and health program experts from all international agencies. They need to meet with senior national health officials, representatives of local health groups, traditional healers, and affected persons to come up with practical plans for implementing results-based health communication programs. The messages or knowledge needed to advise both the healthcare provider and the targeted population should come from all parties jointly. The participative approach, if undertaken with transparency and candor, can mean that everyone is behind the effort, instead of fighting it.

ORGANIZING MEETINGS THAT FOSTER COMMUNICATION

In organizing meetings, communications managers and meeting planners should understand the cultural diversity of participants. Meetings with representatives from different cultures may change the behaviors and understandings of those who lead and the participants. They should be aware that in some cultures, meeting times are not honored—people come late or sometimes not at all. Arrangements should be made to promptly share results and information on the meetings with those who have missed sessions. Implementing stringent rules on attendance may offend participants who have political influence or are high-level decision makers.

Officers should explore the practicality of communicating with senior health officials via email. Phones that display input for immediate information sharing may need to be provided. This might expedite decision-making and information exchange and curb delays in scheduling meetings.

Communication officers must build lasting partnership with media professionals through public interest and advocacy-based meetings. In-country staff should organize workshops on training journalists in the writing of stories that sell. Poorly trained local journalists and those reporting for foreign news agencies will continue to produce controversial and misinformed stories if the journalists are not considered to be building blocks of the nation. Journalists in Africa, particularly those from francophone regions, see journalism as a power negotiator, due to their own political formation. Training should aim to "civilize" their worldview in information dissemination, rather than reinforcing the dictatorial tone that often characterizes their information gathering and writing style.

Using teleconferencing technology to hold face-to-face meetings with partners and fellow staff across the globe invests less time and finances in meetings. In the current economic climate, in which most countries, even rich ones, face financial crises, teleconferencing should be used more often to reduce the cost of managing face-to-face meetings.

Some organizations must continue to hold face-to-face meetings because of the politically sensitive nature of some issues and legally binding agreements with governments. Geert Hofstede's (1998, 1996) position on being aware of cultural sensitivities or what can be called right and wrong doings in organizing business meetings should be followed. Organizers should handle activities before, during, and after the meetings, with working knowledge of the invitees, to ensure greater participation and buy-ins for their future messages and programs.

GETTING MORE VALUE DURING REGIONAL MEETINGS

More attention should be given to deciding whether a meeting is necessary and in producing pre-, during-, and after-meeting plans. Pre-meeting planning would include circulating information to those who will attend. Include objectives, agenda, time and place, and background material. Indicate that participants must arrive on time and have read the materials prepared. Assign roles to participants, such as note-taker and facilitator. Decide who sits where and ensure that the location will be in a physically pleasing and hospitable location with good acoustics, air conditioning, and other conveniences.

Generally speaking, make sure that adequate resources are available. Perhaps this means seeing that laptops work or preparing readable name tags.

During the meeting:

- Determine the decision-making process, if necessary.
- Make sure that discussions are not monopolized by only a few people.
- Summarize any major decisions or action plans resulting from the meeting.
- Insure that the level of confidentiality needed is understood by participants.

After the meeting:

- Prepare minutes and distribute as soon as possible.

- Follow-up on action items while engaging all persons involved with the meeting.
- Debrief management in terms of what made the meeting effective or ineffective and ask for feedback from participants.
- Regularly update voicemail systems and announcements on the corporate website.
- Create an online dashboard with employee login for center updates and information. This will require effort from webmasters, but it should make individuals more responsible and proactive. Webmasters are known for being territorial when it comes to making changes to the platform.
- Ask managers to meet with their staff to determine what is felt to be lacking in the communication structure. Learn the issues and design the corporate communication strategy around employee's needs.

Staff want to know that their senior management is approachable and understanding. Through monthly messages from the country representative or director, staff get most of their questions answered. The site also minimizes the spread of rumors. It promotes honesty and builds trust among staff, maintaining open lines of communication.

SUGGESTIONS FOR ENHANCING EXTERNAL COMMUNICATION

Websites increasingly reach into local communities, and they are vital to reaching out to the world. For that outside reach international organizations should have a "Search" menu with a form prepared in six of the largest language groups in the world in terms of population—Russian, English, French, Spanish, Arabic, and Chinese—to engage more stakeholders and member countries and provide the opportunity to gather knowledge about the work of the UNFPA, its partners and the UN system in general. Those working on websites should coordinate their efforts and decide on the frequency with which to populate their platforms and the types of messages needed by their stakeholders.

Webpages should focus on key thematic messages to inform the international academic and research community audience. These people have knowledge about and interests in the historical, economic, social, scientific, and cultural well-being of countries. Associations meetings, seminars, annual conferences are among events where knowledge of focal points can be shared.

Interactive social media are needed on Websites to engage the audience in dialogue over the issues of health and Africa's development. Facebook and Twitter can communicate with leaders between business trips and after key meetings.

Communication focal points from the agencies should organize an annual award ceremony on best practices in support of program/projects and best journalistic reporting. For example, choosing a "Reporter of the Year" could further publicize support by national health efforts of the government.

The Communication officers in development organizations such as the UN should collaborate with sports associations to reward journalists and media houses for carrying out the most intensive coverage of healthcare practices. An annual awards program jointly organized by an international organization, media association, health ministry, and the sports association may focus on disease prevention methods, or sexual violence reduction. The UN could also recognize countries that have made significant progress in fistula reduction rates and other life-threatening health conditions.

Social media can maximize internal communication within the agency or organization. Develop and post videos from country representative and post them on the Website.

BIBLIOGRAPHY

Arvey, R. (2013) "Why Face-to-Face Business Meetings Matter." *White Paper*. School of Business, National University of Singapore. (www.iacconline.org)

Chen, G. M., and Zhang, K. (2010). "New Media and Cultural Identity in the Global Society." In R. Taiwo, ed., *Handbook of Research on Discourse Behavior and Digital Communication: Language Structures and Social Interaction*. Hershey, PA: Idea Group, pp. 801–815.

Clinton Global Initiative (CGI) (2013). Report on CGI commitments in Africa, CGI Website. Available at www.clintonglobalinitiative.org/. Accessed 9 November 2013.

Global Centre for the Responsibility to Protect (2013). "Populations at Risk: Democratic Republic of the Congo," Global Centre Website. Available at http://www.globalr2p.org/regions/democratic_republic_of_the_congo_drc. Accessed 3 November 2013.

Hofstede, G. (1998). "Culture Consequences: International Differences in Work-Related Values." *In Cross Cultural Research and Methodology*. London: Sage Publications.

———. (1996). *Cultures and Organizations, Software of the Mind: Intercultural Cooperation and its Importance for Survival*. New York: McGraw Hill.

Huber, B.J. (2013). "Types of Corporate Communication." In "Money" section of eHow Website. Available at http://www.ehow.com/about 5422440 types-corporate-communication.html.

Jewkes, R., and Abrahams, N. (2002). "The Epidemiology of Rape and Sexual Coercion in South Africa: An Overview," *Social Science and Medicine*, 55 (7): pp. 1231–1244.

McDaniel, R. E. et al. (2012) "Using Intercultural Communication: The Building Blocks." In L. Samovar, R. Porter, and R.E McDaniel, eds., *Intercultural Communication: A Reader*, 13th Ed. Boston, MA: Wadsworth, pp. 4–18.

Milne, S. (2012). "The End of the New World Order," *The Guardian*, October 19, 2012.

Mowlana, H. (1997). *Global Information and World Communication: New Frontiers in International Relations*. Thousand Oaks, CA: Sage Publications.

———. (1996). *Global Communication in Transition: The End of Diversity?* Thousand Oaks, CA: Sage Publications.

Newbold, B. K., and Campos, S. (2011). "Media and Social Media." In *Public Health Messages: A Systematic Review*. Available at www.mcmaster.ca/mieh. Accessed 8 October 2013.

Ngwainmbi, E. K. (2013). "Communication Strategy for Prevention of Sexual and Gender-based Violence in Eastern Region, Democratic Republic of Congo." Unpublished paper.

———. (2005a). "Bridging the Digital Divide in Developing Regions: NEPAD Activities," *Columbia International Affairs Online Journal*, Columbia University.

———. (2005b). "NEPAD's Development Perspective: Bridging the Digital Divide with Good Governance," *Journal of Black Studies*, 35 (3): pp. 284–309.

———. (2004). "Globalization, Local Urban Culture and Change in West Africa: Toward Negotiating Socioeconomic Understanding with Foreign Companies and International Organizations," *Columbia International Affairs Online Journal*, March 2004. Available at www.ciaonet.org/wps/nge01.

———. (1997). "Review," *Information Infrastructure and Policy: An International Journal on the Development, Adoption, Use and Effects of Information Technology*, 5 (1). Tilburg, The Netherlands: IOS Press, pp. 71–72.

Sawyer, R., and Chen, G. M. (2012). "The Impact of New Social Media on Intercultural Adaptation," *Journal of Intercultural Communication Studies*, 21 (2): pp. 151–169.

Stein, L., and Sinha, N. (2012). "New Global Media and Communication Policy: The Role of the State in the Twenty-First Century." In L.A. Lievrouw and S. Livingston, eds., *Handbook of New Media*. Thousand Oaks, CA: Sage Publications, pp. 410–431.

Strauss, S.G., and McGrath, J.E. (1994). "Does the medium matter? The interaction of task type and technology on group performance and member reactions." *Journal of Applied Psychology*, 79, 87-97.

Uittenhout, H. (2012). "The Use and Effect of Social Media in Health Communication About Common Head Lice." Master's Thesis, School of Management and Governance, Department of Psychology, Health and Technology, University of Twente, Enschede, Netherlands.

United Nations Population Fund (UNFPA) (2013a). Unpublished memorandum from the office of the executive director, quoted on UNFPA Website. Available at www.unfpa.org.

———. (2013b). "Global Communication Strategy: Speaking with One Voice and Improving Fund-wide Communication," unpublished UNFPA report.

Wanzer, M.B., Booth-Butterfield, M., and Gruber, K. (2004). "Perceptions of Health Care Providers' Communication: Relationships Between Patient-centered Communication and Satisfaction," *Health Care Communication, 16* (3): 363–384.

Wikipedia (2013). "Health in the Democratic Republic of the Congo." Wikipedia Online Encyclopedia. Available at http://en.wikipedia.org/wiki/Health_in_the_Democratic_Republic_of_the_Congo#HIV.2FAIDS. Accessed 3 November, 2013.

NOTES

1. This information was found on the label of a package of the drug. This package had an expiration date of June 2015.

2. The drug is also known in pharmacies and health centers operated by international health organizations in Africa as mephaquine quinine, doxycycline, clindamycin, or plaqueril.

3. From an interview conducted August 19, 2013, in Butembo, DRC. The interview was part of a program of collecting data from healthcare providers, sex offenders, and victims of sexual violence aimed at informing national communication for prevention of gender–based violence.

4. This author interviewed health workers and NGOs in Goma, DRC, on August 2013. They raised the concern. The August 2013 interview was part of a communication strategy on the prevention of sexual and gender-based violence in the Eastern Region of the DRC.

III

Experiences in the Field: Resources and Practice

SEVEN

Persuasion Challenges in Local Communities

Polio Immunization's Failure in Northern Nigeria

Cosmos Ikechukwu Eze

THE STATUS OF POLIO IMMUNIZATION CAMPAIGNS IN NIGERIA

In 2003, Nigeria mounted a campaign to eradicate polio using such communication strategies as radio, television, information, and education. Communication materials came from health departments, caregivers, and other stakeholders, such as the World Health Organization (WHO), UNICEF, and opinion and religious leaders.

The campaign was launched after two northern Nigerian states (of Kano and Kaduna) unexpectedly suspended oral polio vaccinations. The suspicion that swept through these states was that the vaccines were contaminated and deliberately poisoned by Western countries, purportedly to induce infertility among Nigerians (WHO 2003). This led to a resurgence of polio cases, initially in Nigeria, but soon in parts of the world, such as India and Pakistan, where polio had been virtually eradicated. Even after vaccinations resumed in Nigeria in 2004 and in other re-infected countries, the goal of complete eradication was still not achievable (Renne 2006). Furthermore, Renne (2005) has noted that one of the reasons or difficulties encountered in eradicating polio was that some people believed that the vaccine was contaminated by anti-fertility substances. Babalola and Aina (2004) noted that significant misinformation about the causes of disease remains in northern Nigeria.

Four years later, in 2007, the Nigerian government rededicated itself to a program of complete eradication through intensive campaigning. Unfortunately fresh rumors and misinformation campaigns threatened the campaign's chance for success.

Another case that may have marred the polio immunization campaign involved Pfizer Pharmaceuticals. Prior to the polio immunization case in 2003, Pfizer, the giant U.S. drug manufacturer, obtained permission from the Nigerian government and the U.S. Food and Drug Administration (FDA) to test an experimental oral form of antibiotic for meningitis. After the drug was administered to volunteers, mostly children, health problems developed. This may have informed the action of Dr. Ahmad Datti, the physician who called on parents to avoid polio vaccine because it was tainted with anti-fertility drugs and substances that could lead to the death of children (Ayodele 2007).

POLIOMYELITIS: AN ANCIENT CONTROVERSY

Paralytic poliomyelitis has been known for over 3,000 years. An Egyptian stone carving portrays a priest with a withered leg, leaning on a staff, suggesting that he suffered from polio (John Paul 1971). Paralytic poliomyelitis has been known to occur, sometimes in epidemic proportions, far back in the past (Shehu 2004).

Polio is a highly contagious, incurable viral infection. At its peak, before Jonas Salk invented a vaccine for its prevention in 1955, polio paralyzed and killed up to half a million people every year. Once considered a global menace, polio is now mainly a disease of poverty. Spread through water or food contaminated with human waste, it is particularly devastating in crowded urban slums where sanitation is poor, children are malnourished, and there is a lack of access to basic health services (UNICEF 2007). Although the polio vaccination is the best way to prevent the polio disease, unfortunately, not everyone accepts this, as was the case in Nigeria where, in 2003, certain segments of the society decided to boycott polio immunization for their children.

Before 1988, more than 350,000 children were reported paralyzed annually by polio worldwide. However, since the launch of the Global Polio Eradication Initiative (GPEI) in 1988, the figure has been reduced drastically. By 1999, the GPEI had been largely responsible for reducing polio cases by 99 percent. For the first time, the possibility of complete eradication seemed achievable (WHO 2003). Unfortunately, in mid-2003, two northern states of Nigeria unexpectedly suspended oral polio vaccination, opening a battle that health initiatives have yet to win.

The furor began when some religious and community leaders declared that the vaccines were poisoned. Soon new polio cases increased in number in Nigeria and other countries where polio had nearly been eradicated. Some hold the view that it is simplistic to simply blame some religious and community leaders for the suspension of immunization in some northern states of Nigeria. There are other reasons, some connected to a tragic incident in 1996, when an outbreak of bacterial meningitis claimed many lives in parts of northern Nigeria.

During the meningitis health emergency of 1996, Pfizer, the American pharmaceutical giant, obtained permission from the Nigerian government and the U.S. Food and Drug Administration (FDA) to test an experimental oral antibiotic, troval floxacin, in Nigeria. American and Nigerian medical teams from Pfizer and Johns Hopkins University Medical School in Baltimore administered the drug to about 100 children, randomly selected from a population of sick children. An equal number of patients in the control group received a proven efficacious drug, ceftriaxone.

Families of the tested children filed suit in U.S. federal district court, asserting that eleven of the children in the study died, and others became paralyzed or deaf (Achebe 2004, p. 4). They accused Pfizer of using an experimental drug without fully informing the patients of the risks. The plaintiffs alleged that Pfizer researchers violated international law by failing to obtain informed consent from the families. The families further said that Pfizer increased the risk by failing to provide the proven treatment for patients who did not improve after taking the experimental drug and by giving control patients a weakened version of the standard therapy (Achebe 2004).

Pfizer rejected the statement, saying it was proud of the way the study was conducted. Clearly Pfizer believed that its actions were altruistic and utilitarian. However, the company eventually accepted responsibility and paid compensation. Some medical experts approve of the way the test was conducted. Others charge that Pfizer ignored several medical and ethical research codes, such as the Nuremberg Code of 1947 and the Declaration of Helsinki, written after medical experimentation on Jews during the Holocaust.

As a result of the Pfizer incident, many Nigerian parents were easily persuaded when their local leaders advised them not to immunize their children against polio.

NIGERIA'S HEALTH CARE INITIATIVES

Immunizations campaigns are not uncommon in Nigeria, where both governments and health agencies have been active in promoting better health for children and pregnant women through the National Program on Immunization (NPI). Nigeria embarked on a national program on immunization in 1980 with the aim of achieving 80 percent coverage of children up to four years old and pregnant mothers by 1990. The national coverage level increased from 15 percent in 1986 to 36 percent in 1988, far short of the 80 percent objective (Imoh 2007). In 1988, the mobilization strategy took the form of National Immunization Days (NIDs). These consisted of three-days per month of intensive immunization activities.

An evaluation of some of these programs revealed that they did not enjoy maximum acceptance, support, and patronage. As a result, many of them failed to achieve their targets (Imoh 1991). The ongoing transmission of wild polio virus (WPV) in some states in north central Nigeria, such as Sokoto, Kaduna, and Kano, is the result of the consistent failure to reach and immunize children in these states.

Besides the failure of communication strategies for polio immunization, inadequate engagement and accountability of state and local governments contributed to the failure of the entire campaign. Additional measures have been initiated by the federal government of Nigeria and the governments of the affected states. A national task force on polio eradication and routine immunization was established, along with state-level task forces or interagency coordinating committees in several endemic states. A national director was named for the National Primary Health Care Development Agency. At this writing, these measures have yet to yield the expected results. WPVs are still rampant in many states in northern Nigeria. Kano State alone has reported more than one-third of all the polio cases in Nigeria.

In states such as Kaduna, Sokoto, and Zamfara, encouraging signs have been emerging in the number of reported cases of polio infection. In those states the ownership and engagement of state and local government has improved, the task forces have better coordination with government and partner agencies, and community leaders have become more involved. Despite the outbreak of polio in neighboring states, Kebbi State has sustained a low rate of new polio cases and high immunization coverage of children under five years in 2011–2012. Other states, including Kano Katsina, Kaduna Bauchi, and Zamfara, have unacceptably low levels of polio immunization coverage of children (NPHCDA 2010).

In 2012, according to UNICEF (2012), Nigeria recorded forty-five cases of WPV infection. The cases occurred in the northern states of Niger, Jigawa, Kaduna, Kano, Katsina, Sokoto, Zamfara, Borno, Yobe, and Bauchi. During 2012, Nigeria contributed 90 percent to the polio burden in Africa, and more than 50 percent of this year's cases worldwide are from Nigeria (UNICEF 2012).

UNICEF (2012) observed that the number was lower than the twenty-five cases to six states for the same period in 2011 pointing out that in key infected states such as Borno, Kano, Sokoto, and Yobe, more than one in three children received fewer than four doses of oral WPV vaccine. Consequently, states such as Kaduna and Niger, which were listed as free from polio at the end of 2011, have been re-infected. In 2012, the proportion of missed children went down slightly (for example, 7.2 percent in

February, 7.4 percent in March, and 7.2 percent in May). Still, hundreds of thousands of children are missed in Nigeria (UNICEF 2012).

According to recent UNICEF social data statistics, Kano has the highest percentage of missed children (8.9 percent). Sokoto State had 8.1 percent. UNICEF, however, acknowledged that Nigeria's funding of polio eradication has increased from $17 million to $30 million. In 2012, the president of Nigeria declared that polio was a national emergency. Nigeria committed funds to the program because the Global Polio Initiative (GPEI) had funding difficulties. Billionaire Bill Gates, through the Bill and Melinda Gates Foundation, has given to Nigeria's eradication effort.

Due to the seriousness of the polio outbreaks in Nigeria, the thirty-six state governors, under the auspices of the Nigerian Governors' Forum, joined the crusade in 2009. They were determined to stop the spread of the virus and improve primary health care service delivery. They made a declaration of commitment at a special session on health convened by President Umaru Musa Yar'dua. The communiqué was signed by Minister of Health Professor Babatunde Osotimehin and Chairman Bukola Saraki of the Governors' Forum. The forum adopted five campaign strategies to stop the transmission of the polio virus. These include:

1. active leadership polio eradication activities, including routine immunization, and primary health care in general, directing that all children under five years be vaccinated as part of polio eradication activities;
2. improving the operational quality in states by meeting quarterly with leaders to review the planning, implementation, and results of polio eradication activities, routine immunization, primary health care, and identity remedies for poorly performing Local Government Areas;
3. allocating additional financial and human resources to strengthen primary health care so that it can sustain routine immunization services and better implement programs;
4. reporting quarterly to the president on the status of polio eradication efforts, including immunization; and
5. improving primary health care as a holistic way to address the issue of immunization through community health insurance (NPHCDA 2010).

Two years after these laudable initiatives, there appeared to be signs of improvement. First, a dramatic 90 percent reduction in the number of cases of paralytic polio was recorded. Also, in the global scene, Nigeria achieved more success than other polio endemic countries of Afghanistan, Pakistan, and India. Traditional leaders have also played a very important role in polio eradication since, the direct intervention of northern traditional leaders led by the sultan of Sokoto, Alhaji Sa'ad, most of the challenges were surmounted.

POLIO RETURNS IN SPITE OF EFFORTS

Recently, the disease has re-emerged in parts of northern Nigeria and in the other endemic countries of Pakistan, India, and Afghanistan. The WHO declared polio a world emergency. Already there a new cases of infection despite all the efforts to eradicate it.

The minister of health, Professor Onyebuchi Chukwu, admitted that mistakes were made in implementing the polio eradication strategies in 2012, which led to the upsurge. While addressing the head of Rotary International, Sakuji Tanaka, he reported that the government had devised new strategies to tackle the menace. One strategy has been to use Global Positioning System (GPS) devices to track the movements of migrants in areas of risk. Anyone involved in the campaign is held accountable for lapses. Dr. Chukwu reiterated that Nigeria would work with neighboring countries to ensure that there would be no cross-border transmission by those known to be infected. The Ministry of Health agreed to work with partner agencies.

Toward achieving this objective, the chairman of the Presidential Task Force on Polio, Dr. Mohammed Ali Pate, directed governors of the remaining polio affected states to work with the National Health Care Development Agency (NPHCDA) on immunization. Dr. Ado Mohammed said that all affected states would receive more attention and increased surveillance to stem further transmission of the virus. There is high hope that polio is one of a small number of diseases that can be eradicated:

- Polio only affects humans, so the virus cannot be transmitted by animals.
- The Oral Polio Vaccine (OPV) is effective and inexpensive.
- Immunity against polio is lifelong.
- The virus can survive for a very short time in the environment.

According to Onuekwe (2013), several years later, the Seeds of doubt about this assessment have been sown because a number of isolated cases of resistance and ignorance work against the elimination of the scourge, especially in the northern states. Between 2000 and 2010, a total of 4,748 children were paralyzed by polio in the northern states alone. The immunization campaigns in the northern states of Kano, Kaduna, Katsina, Zamfara, and Jigawa, are missing 40 percent of eligible children due to refusals. The incidence of the disease is four times higher than in 2006.

Some of the strategies used in polio immunization campaigns in northern Nigeria are advertisements, jingles, drama, documentary, and indigenous news through the mass media. Other strategies use house-to-house campaigning.

One of the strongest potential alliances is with is the traditional and religious leaders. They wield a lot of influence on their people. Leaders include the sultan of Sokoto, the emirs, the imams and other religious clerics. During Friday Jumat prayers, and at Koranic schools, village meetings, churches, and mosques, they preach and tell parents and guardians what they should do and how they should respond to such an issue as polio immunization. This avenue is in addition to what is broadcast on radio or television advertisements by the leaders.

For instance, Datti Ahmed, a physician, who headed the Supreme Council for Sharia in Nigeria and was a respected opinion leader, advised his people to boycott the polio vaccines (Ayodele 2007). This advice was heeded by many in northern Nigeria, leading to a massive boycott in 2003. On the other side is the sultan of Sokoto, Alhaji Abubakar Sa'ad, the goodwill ambassador for immunization in Nigeria. He has consistently campaigned on behalf of efforts at polio eradication. It was the sultan who hosted donors Bill and Melinda Gates when they arrived in Sokoto to share ideas on how to combat polio.

Despite the help that has come from traditional and religious leaders and other stakeholders, the desired result is yet to be achieved. Jegede (2007) posits that one reason for this is that the right message on polio immunization was not delivered. The messages were not properly couched to convince parents who are yet to come forward because of a misconception about oral polio vaccines. Evidently, these communication efforts yielded fragile results as the program recorded continuous rejection of vaccination by parents and consequently the transmission of polio virus among children under five, especially in northern Nigeria.

A Knowledge, Attitude and Practice (KAP) study sponsored by UNICEF to access the impact of social mobilization on polio eradication in Nigeria showed that, among the reasons for refusal, fear of side effects accounted for 52 percent. A lack of confidence in vaccination was responsible for 30 percent. The survey also found that, among possible barriers to immunization, lack of vital information accounted for 27 percent, while spouse disapproval accounted for 22 percent, according to the Quantitative Report, KAP Survey, for 2008. Again, Onuekwe (2013) notes that several communication and social mobilization strategies were adopted to convince adamant parents about the importance of polio vaccination, but little was achieved. These strategies included advocacy among leaders, community dialogues, showing a film to drive home the message of polio vaccination through entertainment, house-to-house sensitization, social mobilization, and program communication.

As rightly observed by Njelesani (1998), this information is not reaching the target audience because of weaknesses or gaps in the communication systems. The mass media also have been involved in polio campaigns. Radio, television, and the print media have been massively used to promote polio immunization.

The health situation in Nigeria is further aggravated by the lack of access to information that could help people avoid common and preventable diseases and health problems. It is with this in mind that the media need to give health matters their deserved priority, so that people can make rational decisions concerning their health.

Issues concerning polio have come up daily on radio and television, either as news or paid advertisements. Jingles and drama using celebrities have been on the increase. Yet the desired result is still a phantom. A multi-dimensional approach is needed to solve the problem of non-compliance. This can only be achieved through well designed, effective information and communication campaigns, with the assistance of stake holders, parents, and guardians, and traditional and religious leaders.

The urgent need is well recognized that new approaches and new policies are needed to ensure that all the people of Africa have access to relevant and timely health information. One new idea came out of the WHO Regional Office for Africa when the Information, Education and Communication (IEC) strategy was unveiled (WHO 1989). The strategy is to blanket the population with sensitizing information, education, and communication materials. The idea is that it will improve access to information that will bring about changes in behavior. In hospitals and clinics and through national immunization days, IEC materials on polio are made available to parents.

All of this information has failed to allay parents' fears, however. Adams and Dzokoto (2007) and Adams (2005) theorized that fears about enemies are the reason for the failure of immunization campaigns in northern Nigeria.

Even some northern leaders, mostly in rural areas, have attributed the polio epidemic to a spiritual attack (Renne 2005). As a result, rural people attribute polio to spiritual attack. Imoh (2007) found this view in focus group discussions in a rural area in northern Nigeria.

Communal resistance against public programs is not common in Nigeria, and the 2003 boycott of immunization was of historic importance because of the consequences of missing out on polio immunization. The resurgence of polio cases created a problem, not only for the government, health agencies, and the public in Nigeria, but also for other countries within and outside Africa.

PERSUASIVE COMMUNICATION CAMPAIGNS

The relevance of persuasive communication to health communicators lays ultimately in its proposed effect: change in an individual's attitude toward specific behaviors. (Simons 1976; Smith 1982). Attitudes are composed of evaluations of people, events, products, policies, institutions, or behaviors (Ajzen and Fishbein 1980; Audi 1974; Bagozzi 1978; Bagozzi et al. 1979; Breckler 1984; Lalljee, Brown, and Ginsburg 1984; O'Keefe, 1990).

According to O'Keeffe (1990), attitudes are learned, relatively enduring mental states that can exert influence on behavior. Attitudes are thought to predispose individuals to choose certain actions over others (Ajzen and Fishbein 1980; O'Keefe 1990). Persuasion can change an individual's attitudes, and consequently it can affect behavior.

Preexisting attitudes play a determining role in how people respond to health communications and other forms of social influence. Persuasion can be coercive or persuasive. Coercive forms of social influence can change behavior change more directly and immediately. Persuasive forms emphasize internalization of the new way of thinking, and behavior will follow (Kelman 1961; Smith 1982). Persuasion has distinct practical advantages over coercion, beyond its ethical advantages. Kelman (1961) notes that coercion is a less powerful form of social influencer in the long term because it relies on the presence of an authority figure to activate and reinforce behavior.

For health communication to be persuasive, it must be both transactional and response dependent. Communication is transactional when it allows for give and take (Smith 1982). Thus, to be persuasive, a communication must first motivate the receiver to pay attention to messages and interpret their content. Second, it must include interactive and transactional solicitation of feedback from audience members. Three, it must activate an understanding of message arguments and counterarguments (McGuire 1978, 1989; O'Keefe 1990; Smith 1982).

The persuasion process requires that individuals tune in to a message, attend to its content, comprehend its arguments, agree with what they hear, yield to the advocated positions, and apply the adopted attitudes to future decision making and action (McGuire 1978, 1989). A second, related dimension of persuasive communication is its response dependence. Persuasion must be viewed as a receiver-driven process that is dependent on a series of responses from the one being persuaded (Simons 1976; Smith 1982).

Because of the nature of all of this interaction, one could say that communicators do not persuade others at all. We provide the stimuli by which they persuade themselves (Simons 1971, p. 232). Simons (1976) argues that a communicator can send persuasive messages without intending to persuade, or the message can fail to persuade when the communicator wants it to. The recipient of a persuasive message is always free to participate or not participate in the process of persuasion.

PERSUASIVE COMMUNICATION IN THE POLIO ERADICATION CAMPAIGN

Many health communication campaigns involving a wide range of innovations and investments have been launched by successive governments in Nigeria with the intent of improving the quality of life of rural and urban dwellers. Programs such as the National Program on Immunization (NPI), Control of Diarrheal Diseases (CDD), Roll Back Malaria, Population and Family Planning, Reproductive Health, STD/HIV-AIDS, condom social marketing, and the polio immunization campaigns have been launched to implement the goals and objectives of the National Health Policy, which is based on the concept of health care for all.

An evaluation of some of these programs, which were proudly launched, reveals that they did not enjoy maximum acceptance, support, and use. Consequently, they did not achieve the targets set for them (Adeniyi 1972; Oti 1981; Imoh 1991). Even though public awareness of the existence and efficacy of many national health programs is relatively high, some people will not take advantage of the services, even if they are given free of charge. Several factors may be responsible for this anomaly. One major constraint to the effectiveness of these health communication campaigns at the national level is the lack of effective communication between the policy and decision makers and the users (Imoh 2007).

Health communication campaign strategies can foster positive health practices individually and institutionally and contribute to sustainable change towards healthy behavior. In northern Nigeria, for instance, the attitude of parents and guardians towards polio immunization campaigns has been lukewarm, despite the efforts of government, nongovernmental agencies, and other groups, such as Rotary International.

Used appropriately, health communication campaigns will help to identify the relationship that health workers have with the beneficiaries (patients and their families) because the individual approach will assist in making polio campaigns successful. As noted above, health workers in the vaccination programs have sometimes been driven away on the suspicion that they were agents of some multinational bodies that were spreading contaminated vaccines.

Communication is a persuasive tool that could be used purposely to alter the behavior of the recipients in the direction desired by the communication source. Health communication campaigns need not be restricted to the mass media. McCauley and Salter (1995), Kiragu (2001), and Mboho and Iwokhagh (2006) note the importance of churches, schools, opinion leaders, and parents in health campaigns. They observe that information obtained from the media is often incomplete, inaccurate, and perhaps not convincing. A good health communication campaign strategy can penetrate high resistance to polio immunization, even in northern Nigeria. Such a strategy could suggest targeted messages through other media to get the messages across to hard-to-reach, and the hard-to-convince parents and guardians.

EXAMPLES OF HEALTH COMMUNICATION CAMPAIGNS

Campaigns have traditionally relied on mass communication, with public services announcements on billboards, radio, and television and educational messages in pamphlets or other printed materials. Other campaigns integrate mass media with community-based programs. Still others use social marketing techniques. Increasingly, health improvement activities are taking advantage of digital technologies, such as CD-ROM and the World Wide Web. These can target audiences, tailor their messages, and engage people in interactive, ongoing exchanges about health. Health communication campaigns take many forms, and use many channels. Regardless of the forms and channels, they must adopt strategic planning methods. In this regard, they must involve some variations on these steps, which are common to most campaign methodologies:

1. Identify the problem and determine whether communication should be part of the intervention. The health problem may be polio infection.
2. Identify the audiences for the communication program and determine the best ways to reach them. The audience for the health communication program may be the parents, guardians, policy makers, and staff of agencies.
3. Develop and test communication concepts, messages, and materials with representatives of the target audiences. This could be done to determine the efficacy of the jingles, advertisements, and other communication content.
4. Implement the communication program based on results of testing. Having tested the communication program, for example, the Expanded Program on Immunization (EPI) or the polio immunization campaigns, proper implementing is very important. Many programs have collapsed because of poor implementation.
5. Assess how effectively the messages reached the target audience and modify the communication program, if necessary. A communication audit is important to determine how effective the messages have been (Schultz, Martin, and Brown 1984).

The use of the five-step strategic communication campaign planning process is illustrated in some exemplary health communication campaigns in Nigeria. National Food and Drug Administration Control (NAFDAC) is a well-packaged communication campaign against fake and adulterated drugs and other poor quality consumable items in Nigeria. The communication campaign has reduced the incidence of fake and adulterated drugs in Nigeria and has made Nigerians more aware about the drugs they take. The communication campaign was successful because the message was tailored to suit the society. Also, opinion leaders, traditional rulers, and religious leaders were involved in addition to the mass media in disseminating appropriate information.

Another successful communication campaign in Nigeria is the HIV/AIDS campaign. Since the first reported case in Nigeria in 1986, the HIV/AIDS epidemic has continued unabated, infecting millions (FMH Technical Report 2005). The government of Nigeria has put in place various programs aimed at controlling and mitigating the impact of diseases associated with AIDS. There are AIDS campaigns on radio and television, in print, and in such formal and informal settings as churches, schools, individual and families. The HIV/AIDS awareness campaign has permeated all segments of the society to such a magnitude that everybody has become well informed and more care is taken about it.

UNICEF has made concerted efforts aimed at improving the welfare of children worldwide. In Nigeria, the Accelerated Child Survival and Development Strategy is an intensive combination of life saving interventions, such as promotion of prenatal care, vaccination, and breastfeeding, and the distribution of insecticide treated mosquito nets. It is estimated that the entire program is preventing about 18,000 child deaths each year (UNICEF Annual Report 2006). The success of the approach is predicated on strengthening outreach, communication, and support to families and communities. The campaign has been translated into many local languages and broadcast on radio and television.

The WHO's global tuberculosis and AIDS campaign has received a lot of support. The campaign particularly puts a premium on follow-up at the national, regional, and global levels. Its priorities include ensuring that people, particularly young people, know what to do to avoid infection; providing treatment to all those infected; and promoting the search for vaccine and a cure (UNAIDS 2003).

The World Bank or UNEFPA-Women's Health Campaign is aimed at improving women's reproductive health. Campaigns fight fistula or female genital mutilation, and give access to good medical care, especially pre natal and postnatal. In Africa, especially Sub-Saharan Africa, campaigns have been mounted by several NGOs against violence against women and all sorts of practices that prevent women from improving their reproductive health. In Nigeria, UNEFPA campaigns are aimed at educating women on prenatal and postnatal care and on such issues as child spacing.

To these successful campaigns, one immunization effort can be added. As we have seen, the EPI campaign has made an impact. In Nigeria, EPI campaigns have been targeted at the eradication of polio, measles, and neonatal tetanus. The campaign, which began in 1980, has been exemplary in many ways. Worldwide, the immunization rate is high, with the exception of India, Afghanistan, and Nigeria, where many parents, guardians, opinion molders, and religious leaders mistrust vaccines. The strategies for achieving these goals have been to increase routine immunization coverage, to conduct supplemental immunization coverage and supplemental immunization campaigns; and to carry out effective disease surveillance (UNICEF 2000).

REVIEWING COMMUNICATION IN NIGERIA AND WEST AFRICA

Melanie et al. (2013) concluded that mass media campaigns can produce positive changes or prevent negative changes in health related behavior across large populations. Over the past few decades, media campaigns have been used in an attempt to affect various health behaviors. Such campaigns have mostly been aimed at tobacco use and heart disease prevention, but others have addressed alcohol and illicit drug use, cancer screening and prevention, and sex related health issues.

Polio communication reviews at international, national, and sub-national levels have supported improvements in the collection, analysis, and use of data for building consensus about communications and the inclusion of communication expertise in polio technical advisory groups. These reviews periodically study communications programs and develop recommendations to strengthen polio communication work.

Campaign messages can fall short and even backfire. Exposure of audiences to the messages might not meet expectations because of inadequate funding or the increasing fractured and clustered media environment. There also may be inappropriate or poorly researched messages that are boring or inappropriate for the target age group. Homogeneous messages might not be persuasive to heterogeneous audiences. Campaigns might address behaviors that the audience lacks the resources to change.

In response to apparent obstacles to communication in the three remaining polio endemic countries of Nigeria, India, and Pakistan, the Polio Eradication Initiative's (PEI's) Technical Consultative Group (TCG) met in April 2002 to raise questions about the nature, structure, conduct, and impact of polio eradication social mobilization and communication efforts. These questions are still valid because the polio eradication program is still bogged down in problems.

The group observed that mass media and mass distribution IEC materials have been well established in all three countries, involving . . .

- production of high-quality mass media communication, such as TV and radio spots;
- high-profile celebrities;
- production and improved distribution of high-quality print materials in India and Pakistan, but not Nigeria;
- mobilization of resources from international and local private partners in Pakistan;
- expanded use of regional local private sector partners in Pakistan;

- expanded use of regional/local broadcast channels and stations; and
- increased focus on evaluating media and products.

According to the report, communication between international agencies in polio partnership has improved in some cases dramatically. However, a persistent and potentially damaging ambiguity remains in the political and strategic prioritization of the Polio Eradication Initiative (PEI) and the Expanded Program on Immunization (EPI). Joint technical and social monitoring and evaluation is nonexistent (Taylor 2002).

The program remains fundamentally divided into "social and technical sides." The complementarity between the two program components has by no means been fully exploited. Poor data circulation, management and analysis can lead to social mobilization and communication activities that are not directly led by the findings of field-data. Therefore, activities cannot be evaluated unless their relation or contribution to the polio eradication goal of successful vaccine delivery can be directly attributed. Among other issues, they noted that the current epidemiological profile of polio is characterized by diverse reservoir-based patterns of relatively small-scale local circulation. Supplementary immunization activity (SIA) coverage averages are increasing. Data show a persistent coverage gap of up to 15 percent and, in some instances, more. It is this gap that supports continuing WPV transmission.

This is where social mobilization and communication should concentrate. Emphasis should shift from social mobilization and communication's intensive, mass awareness approach to a new intensive approach that addresses the specific conditions of the local groups in which children continue to be missed. Finally, the Technical Consultative Group (TCG) noted that poor oral polio vaccine coverage can be attributed to the refusal of households to accept vaccine. That refusal rises out of religious belief, fatigue, and ignorance. Furthermore, there is limited evidence that a repetitive communication strategy is effective.

THE FACTORS BY WHICH IMMUNIZATION SUCCEEDS OR FAILS

Social Circumstances

Social circumstances also play a lot of roles in immunization programs. Hanlon et al. (1988) conducted research on factors influencing vaccination compliance among peri-urban Gambian children. The vaccination status of 251 children aged twelve to eighteen months in two Gambian communities near cities was determined from their health cards. Two sub-groups were identified—children who were fully vaccinated and those who had received fewer than half of their vaccinations. The social and environmental circumstances of those children were investigated to detect factors associated with poor vaccination compliance. Mothers of poorly vaccinated children had less knowledge of the diseases against which their children should be protected.

Superstition

A lot of people attach superstitious beliefs to polio immunization. Some of the views have to do with disease causation and beliefs attached to the immunization. Ignorance and suspicion based primarily on rumors are known to hinder immunization. Babalola and Aina (2004) noted that this was more prevalent in the northern states of Nigeria.

According to Babalola and Aina, rumors peddled about immunization often led parents to avoid the practice. For example, there are rumors that certain vaccines, especially OPV, could cause paralysis in children. Not a single state was untouched by rumors about what some vaccines would or would not do (Babalola and Aina 2004).

The authors note that in Kano State, which is predominantly Muslim, and in some parts of Maiduguri, rumor had it that oral polio vaccine was intended to reduce fertility in Muslim communities. Hence, Muslim religious leaders and fathers are in the forefront of the battle against oral polio vaccine for infants. For example, during a national immunization day exercise in Zamfara State in January 2007, parents agreed to let their children receive drops of polio vaccine but refused to allow their children to be given Hepatitis B injections on the ground that the vaccine would cause paralysis (Renne 2006). In fact, in the northern States, Islamic scholars have questioned their use generally. As one scholar observed, "Immunization does not belong to Islam because Allah has given humans protections in their appropriate best form. We have been created in the best of forms, in the best of constitutions which is seen in the mental, spiritual and has endowed man with so many things. They are made of many systems, including immune system. Nature, is so kind, it has endowed man with so many things (Renne 2006)."

The superstitious belief attached to OPV in the northern states of Nigeria does not apply to all immunizations. The people seem to have singled out polio immunization for condemnation and avoidance.

Renne (2006) cited one Zaria resident, who observed:

> Anyone that says Zaria residents reject immunization is only saying something that is far from the truth. What we rejected was the polio immunization because we saw no reason why they were disturbing us with polio immunization when they did not effectively handle killer diseases like measles. Our point of contention is that it is only on rare occasions that one comes across death caused by polio or even a victim of it, then why the prominence. This is what we reject, not immunization generally.

Literacy Level

The literacy level of parents, guardians, and some stakeholders has a lot of impact on the success of polio immunization campaigns. In northern Nigeria, many parents lack basic education, which often causes them to have so much trust in what religious and traditional rulers say. Most traditional and religious leaders are also illiterate and mislead their followers, especially on issues such as imunization. Literate parents and guardians were much more likely to bring their children for immunization because they are aware of its benefits (Renne 2004).

Public Trust

Public trust is essential to success in promoting public health. Such trust plays an important role in public compliance with health interventions, especially vaccination programs that mainly target healthy people. Where public trust is eroded, rumors can spread (Ayodele 2007). Lack of trust was responsible for the failure of the polio immunization campaign in 2003. Negative rumors concerning the vaccine led many parents to avoid the practice.

Providing full immunization coverage and reducing infant and child mortality are high priority national public health objectives, not only in Nigeria, but also in Sub-Saharan Africa. Because children depend on their families to meet basic human needs, programs aimed at reducing child mortality could be improved by a better understanding of the home environments in which children are most at risk. The economic status of children is a major determinant of their health care. Children in relatively wealthy households are exposed to better health care (Gage et al. 1997).

Harsh economic conditions in families, whether rural or urban, were found by Babalola and Aina (2004) to be among the community and systemic factors affecting immunization in Nigeria. Five states were studied. According to the results, economic problems in Lagos State, resulting from unemployment, underemployment, and delayed payment of salaries, are major concerns. Virtually all study groups complained of their inability to meet basic needs for housing, food, and health care. Although immunization services are almost free, some parents said that children have to be fed and clothed before any money is spent for immunization. In many cases, widespread poverty makes it difficult for mothers to keep appointments while taking care of their personal needs.

In Enugu, fathers of non-immunized children said that they would rather be concerned with meeting family needs than be bothered with child immunization. One of them said that the "barrier is that I am hungry. I am always on the farm looking for what we are going to eat. So, if I don't immunize my children, it is because I am never around to make decision for them to be immunized."

Babalola and Aina concluded that the lack of funds may also hinder mothers, as well as fathers, in rural and urban areas from obtaining immunization for their children. Mothers from may not be able to travel to the urban areas where medical services are available.

Urban and Rural Issues

Urban campaigns have been stressful for many programs. Foege (1990) provides an overview of urban immunization. Frequently, lack of social cohesion makes it difficult to mobilize segments of a geographic area. Often urban areas have required such labor intensive efforts that the expenditure per person is prohibitive. In addition, the diseases themselves may put urban areas at a disadvantage.

Kathleen (1990) notes that in a Bangladesh campaign, the EPI was national and targets were set and vaccines ordered. Unfortunately, the implementation plan was based on the rural model, however, and cities were forgotten. The reason probably is due to the fact that disease is usually assumed to be a rural problem. Planners forgot that urban areas also have myriad problems.

Rural parents, especially farmers, are less likely than their urban counterparts to get such necessities as access to medical care and clothing. This certainly has an impact on their health.

Gender

Social and environmental factors such as gender have always been contentious whenever a polio immunization campaign in Nigeria is discussed. The issue of gender as it affects polio immunization cannot be swept under the carpet. In a study conducted by Aliede (2002) on media consumption patterns of selected urbanites and people in slums and rural areas, in Nigeria, 102 out of 150 respondents or 68 percent, agreed that such factors as gender, age, income level, and educational background influence the pattern of choice and consumption of media.

The study by Babalola and Aina (2004), "Community and Systemic Factors Affecting the Uptake of Immunisation in Nigeria," was a qualitative study of men and women of reproductive age. It was observed that, in the five states studied, women tended to know more about disease and vaccine than did men.

Kabir et al. (2005) conducted a cross-sectional descriptive study to examine attitudes and beliefs about childhood immunization among 200 mothers of children below the age of two years in the Kano village of Kumbotso. Seventy-five percent or 150 respondents were aware of the existence of routine immunization services in the village, while twenty-five percent, fifty respondents, were not. The majority of the respondents, 69 percent or 136 respondents, had poor knowledge of schedules of immunization services, while 31 percent or 64 respondents knew of services.

One hundred and sixty or 54 percent of the mothers were against their children being immunized, but up to 119 respondents or 59.5 percent believed vaccines do offer protection against diseases, and ninety-eight or 48.5 percent believed vaccines are safe. Mothers who had formal education were more likely to be aware of the existence of facilities for childhood immunization, compared to mothers who had no formal education. Mothers with formal education were also more likely to believe in the efficiency of vaccines.

The research concluded with an observation that, although the majority of the mothers were aware of immunization services, not as many knew the immunization schedule. In fact, Kabir et al. (2005) observed that the low level of knowledge among the mothers may be partly due to the lack of effective communication and counseling on health issues by health workers in the village.

The ability to make an informed decision without undue outside influence is a privilege that most individuals cherish. However, in many African societies, for cultural reasons, woman are not allowed to make important decisions without prior consultation and the approval of their husbands or significant members of the husband's family, such as the mother-in-law or older wives. Other underprivileged social groups also face problems taking part in services for cultural reasons.

Generally, men preside over household resources and make major decisions concerning the use of resources. Where women are relatively independent economically, the control of their resources may still be problematic in the case of immunization. If the ultimate decision maker does not see the need for immunization or lacks confidence in vaccines, the child is not likely to be immunized, even if the mother desires it. Babalola and Aina (2004) noted that in Enugu State many of the participants whose children were immunized made the decision on their own without seeking counsel or permission. In Jigawa State, male gender supremacy and authority in choices about domestic and matrimonial affairs was the main obstacle to health care. Women in many cases require the express permission of their husbands to attend health facilities, especially when this involves money. In urban and rural Borno and Kano states, fathers are responsible for making the final decision as to whether a child is immunized.

Also, in Lagos State in southern Nigeria, a focus group discussion (FGD) was conducted on childhood immunization practices among parents. Almost all the participants in the FGD groups reported that the final decision-maker regarding child immunization was the father, although a few reported that joint decisions are sometimes made, with the fathers merely endorsing a decision already made by the mothers. Even mothers of fully immunized children emphasized the need for a mother to inform and respect the father's decision regarding child immunization (Obadere 2005).

The gender of the provider is another factor. In all the communities studied by Babalola and Aina (2004) and Obadere (2005), there is a preference for female service providers. Preference for women providers is particularly strong in Kano, Jigawa, and in the predominantly Muslim rural community in Lagos. One service provider in rural Lagos explained, "We are all female. The only male has been transferred. . . . When the women in Purdah see a male they close their eyes and only open them after he leaves. This may discourage them from coming, and if the husband knows [the service provider was a man], they may not like it."

SUMMARY

In this study, polio immunization's failure in northern Nigeria was discussed. Despite all the communication strategies adopted, polio is still intractable and a lot of children are still at risk. Some of the communication strategies include information, education and communication materials, adverts, jingles, and advocacy. Results of focus group discussions on factors affecting the up-take of polio immunization in northern Nigeria reveals that fear, suspicion, spiritual, and sometimes gender issues are responsible for the failure. The resistance to polio immunization campaign in northern Nigeria has also been linked to religious politics, with some distrusting Western intervention on the belief that "Christian countries' concern to export biomedicine to all parts of Africa is not a charitable gesture, but self-interested and dangerous" (Last 2005, p. 561). The study recommends that further research be conducted to find a potent and viable communication strategy that will nip in the bud the threat of polio in northern Nigeria.

BIBLIOGRAPHY

Achebe, C.C. (2004). "The Polio Epidemic in Nigeria: A Public Health Emergency," p. 4. Available at http://www.nigerialinks.com/Articles/CCAchebe/2004/07/polio-epidemic-in-nigeria.html. Accessed 10 November 2013.

Adams, G., and Dzokoto, V.A. (2007). "Genital-shrinking Panic in Ghana: A Cultural-Psychological Analysis," *Culture and Psychology*, 13: pp. 83–104.

Adams, G. (2005). "The Cultural Grounding of Personal Relationship: Enemyship in North American and West African Worlds," *Journal of Personality and Social Psychology*, 88: pp. 948–968.

Ajzen, I., and Fishbein, M. (1980). *Belief, Attitude, Intention and Behaviour: An Introduction to Theory and Reasearch.* Reading, MA: Addison-Wesley.

Aliede, E. (2002). "Media Consumption Patterns of Selected Urbanites, Alumites and Ruralites in Nigeria," *Nigerian Journal of Communications*, 1 (2, August 2002).

Audi, R. (1974). "A cognitive-motivational Theory of Attitudes," *Southwestern Journal of Philosophy*, 5 (1): pp. 77–88.

Ayodele, S.J. (2007). "What Led to the Nigerian Boycott of the Polio Vaccination Campaign?" *Journal Pubmed*, 4 (3): p. 73.

Babalola, S., and Aina, O. (2004). "Community and Systemic Factors Affecting the Uptake of Immunisation in Nigeria: A Qualitative Study in Five States." Baltimore: Johns Hopkins University, Blorubag School of Public Health, Center for Communication Programs.

Bagozzi, R.P. (1978). "The Construct Validity of the Affective, Behavioral and Cognitive Components of Attitude by Analysis of Covariance Structures," *Multivariate Behavioral Research*, 13: pp. 9–31.

Bagozzi, R.P., et al. (1979). "The Construct Validity of the Tripartite Classification of Attitudes," *Journal of Marketing Research*, 16: pp. 88–95.

Breckler, S.J. (1984). "Empirical Validation of Affect, Behavior and Cognition as Distinct Components of Attitude," *Journal of Personality and Social Psychology*, 47: pp. 1191–1205.

David, M. (2001). *Science Now*. Washington, DC: American Association for the Advancement of Science.

Foege, W. (2000). *The Power of Immunization*. Atlanta: Rollins School of Public Health, Emory University.

Gage, A.J., Sommerfelt, A.E., and Piani, A.L. (1997). "Household Structure and Childhood Immunization in Niger and Nigeria," *Demography*, 34 (2): p. 295.

Global Polio Eradication Initiative (2012). "Global Polio Emergency Plan, 2012–2013: Getting Nigeria, Afghanistan, and Pakistan Back on Track." World Health Organization. Available at http://www.who.int/immunization/sage/meetings/2012/april/Working_draft_Global_PolioEmergencyActionPlan_04_April_v2.pdf. Accessed 13 February 2013.

———. (2008). "Immunization Plus—Eradicating Polio." World Health Organization. Available at www.polioeradication.org. Accessed 4 March 2008.

———. (2003). "A Global Race for a Global Victory: Facts, Figures and Highlights." World Health Organization. Available at http://reliefweb.int/sites/reliefweb.int/files/resources/43C340830FF33E65C1256D250049562A-who-pol-13may.pdf.

———. (2000). "Handbook for Polio Eradication," World Health Organization, p. 5. Available at http://www.polioeradication.org/content/publications/2002_comms-checklists.pdf.

Hanlon, P., et al. (1988): "Factors Influencing Vaccination Compliance In Peri-Urban Gambian Children," *Journal of Tropical Medicine Hygiene* 91 (1): pp. 29–33.

Imoh, G. (2007): "Communication Change in Health Behaviour: Determinants of Compliance at the Implementation Level." Paper presented the September 2007 conference of the African Council for Communication Education (ACCE) Conference, Zaria, Nigeria.

———. (2006). "Belief System and Receptivity to Messages of Rural Development: A Case Study of the National Programme on Immunization." In S. Ukala, ed., *Journal of African Arts and National Development*, Delta State University. Abraka, Ibadan: Prompt Books Ltd., pp. 190–204.

———. (1991). "Communication for Social Mobilization: An Evaluative Study of the Expanded Programme on Immunization in Nigeria." Doctoral thesis, University of Ibadan.

Information, Education and Communication (IEC) (2004). "Lessons from the Past: Perspective for the Future." World Health Organization.

Jegede, A.S. (2007). "What Led to the Nigerian Boycott of the Polio Vaccination Campaign?" PLoS Med 4 (3): p. 73. Available at doi:10.1371/journal.pmed.0040073.

Kabir, M., et al. (2005). "Knowledge, Perception and Beliefs of Mothers on Routine Childhood Immunization in a Northern Nigerian Village," *Annals of Nigeria Medicine*, 2 (1, January–June 2005): pp. 21–26.

Kabir, M., et al. (2004). "Immunization Coverage in Children Below Two Years of Age in Fanshekara, Kano State," *Nigeria Journal of Basic and Clinical Sciences*, 1 (1): pp. 10–13.

Kelman, H.C. (1961). "Processes of Opinion Change," *Public Opinion Quarterly*, 25: pp. 57–78.

Kiragu, K. (2001). "Youth and HIV/AIDS: Can We Avoid the Catastrophe?" Population Reports Series J, No. 41. Baltimore, MD: Johns Hopkins University School of Public Health, Population Information Program, p. 43.

Lalljee, M., Brown, L.B., and Ginsburg, G.P. (1984). "Attitudes: Disposition, Behaviour, or Evaluation?" *British Journal of Social Psychology*, 23: pp. 233–244.

Last, M. (2005). "Religion and Healing in Northern Nigeria." In T. Falola, ed., *African Religion and Social Change: Essays in Honor of John Peel.* Durham NC: North Carolina University Press, pp. 549–562.

Laulajainen, T. (2012). "Journalist Initiatives Against Polio, A UNICEF Nigeria News Note." Available at http://reliefweb.int/sites /reliefweb.int/files/resources/NEWSNOTE_Journalists_Against_Polio_Nigeria.pdf. Accessed 13 February 2013.

McCauley, A.P., and Salter, C. (1995). "Meeting the Needs of Young Adults," Population Reports Series J, No. 41. Baltimore, MD: Johns Hopkins University School of Public Health, Population Information Program, pp. 12–20.

McGuire, W.J. (1989). "Theoretical Foundations of Campaigns." In R.E. Rice and C.K. Atkin, eds., *Public Communication Campaigns*. Newbury Park, CA: Sage, p. 416.

———. (1978). "The Communication/Persuasion Matrix." In B. Lipstein and W. J. McGuire, eds., *Evaluating Advertising*. New York: Advertising Research Foundation, pp. xxvii–xxxv.

National Primary Health Care Development Agency (2010). "Report on Polio Immunization Plan." NPHCDA, Nigeria Federal Ministry of Health.

Nigeria Federal Ministry of Health (2006). "National Programme on Immunization," Federal Ministry of Health (FMH), Abuja, Nigeria.

Njelesani, E. (1998). "Broadcasting and Health Care Delivery in Africa." Paper presented at the 2d International Conference of African Broadcasters (AFRICAST), 2 October, 1998, Abuja, Nigeria.

Obadare, E. (2005). "A Crisis of Trust: History, Politics, Religion, and the Polio Controversy in Northern Nigeria," *Patterns of Prejudice*, 39: pp. 265–284.

O'Keefe, D.J. (1990). *Persuasion*. Newbury Park, CA: Sage.

Onuekwe, C.E. (2013). *Entertainment-Education and Behaviour Change: An Impact Assessment of a Polio Documentary Film in Northern Nigeria.* Ph.D. dissertation submitted to the Postgraduate School, Ahmadu Bello University, Zaria, Nigeria, pp. 3–7.

Renne, E.P. (2006). "Perspectives on Polio and Immunization in Northern Nigeria," *Social Science and Medicine*, 63 (7): pp. 1857–1869.

———. (2005). "Islam and Immunisation in Northern Nigeria." In *Promoting Polio and the Ethics of Eradication in Northern Nigeria.*" Unpublished.

Shehu, U. (2004). "Immunization as a Most Cost-Effective Public Health Measure." Paper presented at the annual meeting of the Barewa Old Boys' Association, Kaduna, Nigeria.

Schultz, D.E., Martin, D., and Brown, W.P. (1984). *Strategic Advertising Campaigns.* Chicago: NTC Business Books.

Simons, H.W. (1976). *Persuasion: Understanding, practice and analysis.* Reading, MA: Addison-Wesley, p. 232.

Smith, M.J. (1982). *Persuasion and Human Action: A Review and Critique of Social Influence Theories*. Belmont, CA: Wadsworth.

UNICEF (2006). "Annual Report, 1946–2006: Unite for Children." Available at www.unicef.org/unite for children.

UNICEF Nigeria (2011). "Polio Communication 2011 Summary Report: Addressing Communication Challenges." Available at http://www.poliofreenigeria.com/publication/2011%20Polio%20Communication%20Summary%20Report.pdf. Accessed 13 February 2013.

United Nations Development Programme (2004). "Human Development Report: Nigeria 2004 and AIDS: A Challenge to Sustainable Human Development," Human Development Report, UNDP, Abuja, Nigeria.

Wakefield, M.A., Loken, B., and Hornik, R.C. (2013). *Use of Mass Media Campaigns to Change Health Behaviour*. Carlton, Australia: Centre for Behavioural Research.

World Health Organization (2013). "Polio Case Count, 1996–2013." WHO. Available at http://apps.who.int/immunization_monitoring/en/diseases/poliomyelitis/case_count.cfm.

Wilkinson, R.G. (2005): *The Impact of Inequality: How to Make Sick Societies Healthier*. New York: New Press.

———. (1997). *Unhealthy Societies: The Afflictions of Inequality*. London: Rutledge.

World Bank (2006). "World Development Indicators: Population." Data from Center for International Earth Science Information Network (CIESIN), Columbia University, Chicago.

World Health Organization (2004). "Progress Towards Polio Eradication in Nigeria, January 2003 to March 2004." *Weekly Epidemiology Record*, 79 (17): p. 162.

EIGHT

Changing Food and Nutrition Priorities in the Public Health Agenda of India

A Historical Perspective

SubbaRao M. Gavaravarapu

The Indian constitution recognizes the right of the citizen to health. India, since its independence, has spent smaller proportions of its resources on public health than have many other countries (UNDP 2005). No wonder public health is considered to be "one of the most neglected aspects of development in India" (Dreze and Sen 2002).

Freedom from hunger and access to adequate food and nutrition is mandated by an extended interpretation of the Right to Life guaranteed by the Indian Constitution. In fact, Article 21 imposes upon the state the responsibility of protecting this right. Further constitutional commitments are articulated in Article 47, which mandates that "The State shall regard raising the level of nutrition and standard of living of its people, and improvement in public health among its primary duties" (Government of India 1960). Unfortunately, nutrition security has often been ignored and India today faces a strange paradox of being a home to teeming millions of undernourished people as well as a country with an emerging problem of obesity and associated chronic diseases (Shetty 2006; Griffiths and Bentley 2001; Popkin 2001). While accepting that the state-directed and internationally-supported public health and nutrition programs have contributed to the health and well-being of Indians, systematic and holistic weaknesses of India's public health system have acted as significant limiting factors (Amrith 2009). Within that framework, this chapter explores the inherent paradoxes in dealing with nutrition in the Indian public health discourse, policy, and practice in the colonial and post-colonial era.

PUBLIC HEALTH DEBATES IN COLONIAL INDIA

Initially, public health entered the public sphere from the elite circles of India's emergent colonial middle class. After the advent of the print technology in India and the evolution of newspapers in the latter half of eighteenth century, there were popular writings on health and illness, which were targeted to the middle-class reading public. These disseminated the Western ideas about the body, wellness, and treatment of diseases, covering such topics as vegetarianism, healthcare tips, beauty, nutrition, and care and feeding of infants (Amrith 2007). Even vernacular magazines in Hindi, Bengali, and Tamil were replete with articles on health, especially targeted at women (Lal 2003; Amrith 2009). Thus, health and nutrition debates about the general population remained only among the elite who, in their discussions about the poor, underpinned the colonial Malthusian discourse of over-population being responsible for recurrent famines and poor sanitation (Amrith 2007).

Public health became an important agenda item during India's struggle against colonial rule, a major part of which was the Swadeshi (self-sufficiency) movement of 1905 (Banerji 2004). The movement called for a boycott of British products and the revival of domestic products and production processes in all sectors. During this movement, there was an increasing interest to alleviate the problems of poverty while harnessing the indigenous products, culture, and economy (Visvanathan 1998). Initial discussions on poverty led to more serious discussions on health and hygiene, which prompted the engagement of elites in western medical ideas as the means to resolve public health problems of the poor (Arnold 1993). This was the time when nutrition research was born in India.

Sir Robert McCarrison, an Indian Medical Services (IMS) official from the British government, with his exposure to research in nutrition sciences in Europe, formed the opinion that there were problems with the customary native diet causing poor physical development, low resistance to diseases, and widespread ill health (Patwardhan 1961; SubbaRao and Sesikeran 2011).

On the policy front, the foundations for public health service in India were laid in 1864 with the appointment of Sanitary Commissioners for the three provinces of Bengal, Bombay, and Madras, but organized public health activity was halting in its progress over the two decades that followed (Gangulee 1938; Government of India 1941). There was an outbreak of plague in many parts of India in the late nineteenth century.

Being on the international trading route, there was immense pressure on the British Imperial Government of India to control this emergency. The government constituted the Plague Commission in 1896 under the chairmanship of T.R. Fraser, professor at the University of Edinburgh (Mushtaq 2009). The report of the Plague Commission, which was submitted in 1904 awoke the people and stirred the government to strengthen the existing public health administration. Since then, the State Public Health Services have been concerned with improving hygiene and sanitation and fighting epidemics of communicable diseases (Patwardhan 1961). Despite concerted efforts in scientific enquiry of deficiencies of Indian diets by McCarrsion and others and discussions on nutrition and well-being in the elitist domain, nutrition discussions did not enter the arena of public health administration.

THE NATIONALIST MOVEMENT AND PUBLIC HEALTH

Under the leadership of Mahatma Gandhi, the pre-eminent leader of Indian nationalism, the Indian freedom struggle became a national movement and got into its fold millions of Indians from all sections of society. By the 1920s, Gandhi's nationalist movement mobilized the Indian peasantry against colonial rule and socialists, conservatives, and communitarians turned their attention to the problems of the poor. There were small scale experiments to mobilize new ideas on public health. For instance, in the famine affected Bengal region, India's poet-reformist Rabindra Nath Tagore initiated the Sriniketan Rural Reconstruction Project, which promoted a holistic approach to rural development with focus on public health, sanitation, and agriculture (Amrith 2007). Ill health and starvation were found to be among the factors responsible for the prevailing economic scene, more important than such indicators as national income statistics and industrial development that have pre-occupied the works of pioneering such Indian thinkers and economists as Dadabhai Naoroji.

Amrith (2008) argues that the science of nutrition played an important role in lending new language to the discussion of economic change. He further states that discussions of India's poverty had, hitherto focused on the absence of industry on one hand and the incidence of famine, on the other. By the 1920s, the language of nutrition provided a more fine-grained analysis of deprivation and a new way of talking about well-being. In fact, Gandhi's writings on nutrition in his newspapers *Harijan* and *Young India* drew from the most advanced nutritional knowledge of that time. He also maintained public correspondence with Sir Robert McCarrison, a pioneer in modern nutrition research in India (SubbaRao and Sesikeran 2011).

Parallel to this on the policy front, the observations of the Royal Commission of Agriculture (1926) on the research of McCarrison made the British government nutrition conscious for the first time. This led to the recognition of Dr. McCarrison's Deficiency Disorders Enquiry Unit at Coonoor in South India as a full-fledged nutrition research laboratory.

In 1936, the League of Nations' Health Committee released "Physiological Bases of Human Nutrition." A summary of the report appeared in *Harijan* (as cited by Amrith 2008). Gandhi, who declared that he was not an opponent or foe of science (Kumar 2000a), turned to scientific knowledge in search of the diet that could build the vigor and vitality of an impoverished nation. His *ashrams* were a combination of hermitage and laboratory and were locations of scientific experiments (Visvanathan 1998). His experiments with food and hygiene were a critique of the public health commitment of colonial India. Gandhi referred to McCarrison's experiments feeding typical Indian diets to rats, textbooks on nutrition and balanced diets by H.V. Tilak. Apart from these, Gandhi corresponded with McCarrison and Dr. Wallace R. Aykroyd, successive directors of Nutrition Research Laboratories (Amrith 2008). Gandhi wrote extensively on his view that polished rice weakened the vitality of the Indian race (*Harijan* 26 [October 1936]). He also wrote on green leaves and other cheap foods for the health of villagers.

The modernist nationalists in the country identified public health and alleviation of hunger as important steps in building a healthy new nation. The Far Eastern Conference on Rural Hygiene at Bandung, Indonesia, impressed upon the participating governments that malnutrition was a public health problem and hence there was an immediate need to take steps to address it. This prompted the government to send personnel to Nutrition Research Lab in Coonoor for nutrition training. Trained nutrition personnel were to be officers in charge of public health nutrition in the provinces.

The nutrition sections that started during this period were confined to the three provincial states and took nearly two decades to expand to about a dozen centers. By late 1950s some of them were making scattered efforts to carry out nutrition surveys and didactic nutrition education programs (Patwardhan 1961).

The Indian National Congress, which was at the forefront of India's freedom struggle, tasted political power in the provincial elections of 1937. The National Planning Committee established by the Congress connected poverty with under nutrition and ill health in its reports on problem of population. Although the Planning Committee cited nutrition and sanitation as necessary elements in building a new India, it emphasized the use of legislation and latest technologies for birth control. Eugenics and other fad concepts were thought to be able to "relieve India from terrible waste of life and make India economically efficient." This was reiterative of the Malthusian discourse.

Historians identify the decade that followed as a "phase of transition" in science and technology. Ever increasing attention was being paid to development with science and technology as catalytic agents (Kumar 2000a). In 1944, A.V. Hill, the then biological secretary of the Royal Society was invited to report on the state of scientific research in India (Kumar 2000a, b). He pointed out multi-dimensional problems involving population, health, food, and natural resources. According to him, the complex problems of India were not physical, chemical, or technological but a complex of biological issues involving population, health, nutrition, and agriculture (Hill 1960; Kumar 2000b). The colonial British government soon took up plans for post-war reconstruction to make a display of their concern for the national welfare, and to pacify the Indian elite. In 1943, the first Health Survey and Development Committee, popularly known as the Bhore Committee, was constituted with conservative bureaucrats and international medical consultants who had discussions with the visiting international consultants. The Bhore Report, published in 1946, associated public health with plans for economic development. This report suggested that unemployment and poverty produce adverse effects on health through the operation of such factors as poor housing and clothing, lack of proper medical care and inadequate nutrition (Government of India 1946). The committee recommended setting up of a national health service and a modern health administration, in which the state makes itself responsible for providing the community with health protection (Ramachandran 2011). Although the recommendation to create a modern health administration did not materialize, owing to conflicting priorities, the terms set by the Bhore Committee left a lasting legacy.

CHANGING PRIORITIES IN THE POST-COLONIAL ERA

At the time British rule ended (1947), India was a veritable museum of nutrition deficiency diseases. For example, beriberi (both wet and dry) was prevalent along the eastern coast, pellagra was common in the Deccan Plateau, hard, pendulous goiters were a problem in the sub-Himalayan regions, and keratomalacia and kwashiorkar infected several thousands in the south and east (Ramachandran 2011). In post-colonial India, public health was well established in the political culture and within the thinking of the planners. Health was at once a human right, but the voices were a relative minority and could not compete with the needs at that time for industrialization and strengthening defense. There was, in the end, relative consensus that, in the Constitution, public health ought to be a directive "principle of governance," rather than a fundamental right.

In Nehruvian India, which believed in planned state intervention to tackle all kinds of social problems using modern technology (Visvanathan 1998), even public health, like agriculture and industry was amenable to technological transformation (Prasad 2007). At the same time, public health discourse in India was probably shaped by the international climate, especially after the establishment of the WHO of the United Nations in 1945. The WHO gave a symbolic legitimacy to public health with its founding declaration depicting health as a "fundamental human right" (Siddiqui 1995). The WHO also played a crucial role in the global circulation of a standard set of public health policies, along with the technology needed to implement them. India, as a sovereign nation, was entitled to the latest international technologies of health: DDT, antibiotics, and x-ray machines. In its quest to provide public health, the nation deployed external resources (Amrith 2007). In the two decades that followed, India, along with a number of Southeast Asian countries, used globally circulated new medical technologies to fight a number of infectious diseases, especially malaria (Jeffery 1988). Since then, nutrition would not explicitly figure in many health policy statements for years to come.

At that time, India faced a multitude of nutritional problems, such as chronic energy deficiency due to low dietary intake and a high prevalence of infection because of poor access to safe drinking water and sanitation. The threats of repeated famines and acute starvation due to low agriculture production and the lack of an appropriate public distribution system compounded the problem (Rajagopalan 2003a, b). The Indian policy makers saw malnutrition as a welfare problem and addressed it accordingly (Berg 1970). Naturally, the focus was on producing enough food at the national level to feed all people.

Nutrition, naturally, was considered to be primarily an issue of insufficient food quantity. The focus was on expanding agricultural output by bringing more land into cultivation and using modern technology and techniques of farming (Haddad and Geissler 2005). No wonder, the first three five-year plans assumed that economic growth and food production would themselves solve the problems of poverty and under nutrition (Planning Commission 2008). With the focus still on food production, by the 1960s the emphasis had shifted to crop yield or output. India embarked on a "Green Revolution," led by the newly formed Consultative Group on International Agricultural Research (CGIAR). The Green Revolution helped the country move from chronic shortages of food to an era of surplus. But the benefits did not seem to percolate to the grassroots level (Rajagopalan 2003b).

Around the same time, researchers around the world were pointing out that ill health in India, as elsewhere, was due as much to non-specific diseases caused by a lack of proper nutrition or sanitation as to the specific diseases against which concerted internationally attention was being paid (Scrimshaw et al. 1968; McDermott 1966). Soon, internationally, there was increased recognition that an integrated approach to improving nutrition was required. Applied Nutrition Programs were promoted by international agencies. As in many countries of Southeast Asia, there were broad-based community development programs designed to improve the quantity and quality of local food production and to raise incomes to make such foods affordable (Geissler 1993). However, in the Indian context in the early 1960s, the public health policy experienced a striking priority shift. Population control was seen as a panacea for all ills. Rao (1999) argued that the agenda of population control in India determined the directions of health policy.

Perhaps, the 1966–1967 Bihar famine dramatized the magnitude of malnutrition, with about 90 million people being affected. Policy makers realized that national development could not take place unless hundreds of millions of the poor experienced a better level of living and participated in the national development (Berg 1970). A Home Ministry report published in 1969 December, cited by Berg (1970) warned, "Failure to improve the lot of India's masses may lead to a situation where the discontented elements are compelled to organize themselves and extreme tensions building up with in a 'complex molecule' that is the Indian village."

The government accelerated efforts to produce grain. Introduction of high yielding seed varieties, fertilizers, and new technology were possible in the Green Revolution days.

Through the Mid-day Meal Program, which had operated since 1961 to attract more children to schools (Park 2000), a sizeable number of children were reached during the Bihar famine (Berg 1970). The findings around the same period suggested a link between malnutrition among children that affected mental development and physical growth. Good or bad development related to the potential productivity of adults (Gopalan 1974). In 1967, a Comprehensive Nutrition Plan was rolled out by the Ministry of Health. Berg wrote,

> Serious thought process for the first time is given to the developmental ramifications of malnutrition, to the economic dimensions of the problem, to vote getting appeal of nutrition in a democracy to national planning implications, and to evaluating alternate cost solutions. A first attempt to the latter was the Comprehensive Nutrition Plan.... It was to my knowledge the first attempt at an analytical systems approach to meeting the nutritional needs. (1970, p. 1408)

The same period also witnessed India's first venture into fortification of cereal foods with introduction of Modern Bread in 1968, through Government Modern Bakery plants that were set up with the help of Canada and Australia. During the drought years, the food ministry made an attempt to promote wheat consumption, as wheat unlike other cereals, was available in large quantities from abroad (Berg 1970). Although a significant proportion of the 1960s health budget was going toward malaria control and promoting family planning (Amrith 2007), these were the years during which the community development phase prevailed on the nutrition scene. The positive outcome of this phase, however, was the increased realization that combating the problems of nutrition required community involvement. It also was seen that the government needed a co-ordinated approach (FNB 1995b).

In the fourth five-year plan in 1970, specific nutrition intervention programs for improving nutrient status of vulnerable mothers and children were proposed (Planning Commission 2008). For the first time a section on the subject was introduced in the plan documents. The shift was obvious in the prime minister's message to the parliament during presentation of the budget for 1970–1971. The government had decided to give high priority to the problem of nutrition among children in the Fourth Plan (Berg 1970, p. 1396).

India's political and economic situation became a volatile issue in the early 1970s. Population growth from unplanned pregnancies was seen as the major cause for India's poverty. Between 1971 and 1976, population management became a political issue because of its proposed relationship to poverty, economy, widespread ill-health, and malnutrition. After campaigning on a platform of *"garibi hatao"* ("End poverty"), Indira Gandhi of the Indian National Congress Party became the prime minister (Turay 2007). These efforts to reduce poverty did not yield great results, as India was facing the Bangladesh War, poor harvests, and an oil crisis.

By 1974, inflation was rising. On June 26, 1975, Prime Minister Gandhi declared a state of political emergency on the premise of preventing economic deterioration, political disruption, social disturbance, and general chaos (Palmer 1977). Shortly after declaring the emergency, an anti-poverty Twenty Point Program was announced by the caretaker government (Turay 2007). Sanjay Gandhi, Indira Gandhi's son and a youth leader, was afforded political privileges, including permission to develop national policies. He proposed that unplanned population growth would pose a threat to the Twenty Point Program (Panandiker and Umashankar 1994). Using Malthusian reasoning, Sanjay spearheaded India's most controversial sterilization drive.

In 1976, with India's population, growing rapidly and the emergency extended for another year, the National Population Policy was announced. The Policy hoped to help ease the nation's economic hardship. It established incentives to be allocated to those who participated in population management efforts.

The sterilization drive lacked sustainability and was counterproductive to improving and protecting the nation's health. On one hand, it concentrated resources in one place when the country's health professionals were being used to reach sterilization goals rather than provide other services (Turay 2007). On the other hand, the compensations and incentives for sterilization operations rose to almost 10 percent of the total health budget (Jeffery 1988). These were some of the factors that led to the defeat of the Congress Party in the general elections that followed.

While continuing the spirit of *garibi hatao*, the policy makers were forced to look beyond population control. They turned to social and structural transformation to ensure food security for the populations. Schemes for poverty eradication also took shape. The fifth Five-year Plan implemented a cohesive minimum needs program, tying health to education, water supply, sanitation, and food. A string of nutrition programs directed towards specific nutritional deficiencies was initiated, including Crash Feeding Program and Supplementary Nutrition Program for preschool children, Prophylaxis Program on Nutritional Anaemia in Women and Prophylaxis Program of Vitamin A to combat nutritional blindness among children (Park 2000; FNB 1995a).

Launched October 2, 1975, in thirty-three "Community Development Blocks," the Integrated Child Development Scheme (ICDS), as of 2013, is one of the world's largest programs for early childhood development. ICDS was launched with the aim of breaking the vicious cycle of malnutrition, morbidity, reduced learning capacity, and mortality. It was designed to be an inter-sectoral program to reach out to children below six years of age, especially in vulnerable and remote areas. It was to give them a head start by providing an integrated program of early childhood education, health, and nutrition. The program planners soon realized that early childhood care and education would not succeed unless mothers were involved (MoWCD 2008). While the so called vulnerable groups have been reported to benefit most from these nutrition programs, there is a lack of area and population focus (Bajaj 1990). Despite all the government's efforts in the 1970s, population control still assumed greater policy attention and larger chunk of the healthcare budget. Even in public health debates and media space, issues such as malnutrition and chronic hunger received almost no attention (Sainath 1996).

By 1980s, public health achievements of India were being presented to the world: the elimination of diseases like smallpox and plague; decrease in mortality from cholera and successful malaria control. Despite, those efforts, the ever-growing population continued to be the reason for serious and urgent concern in the prevailing health picture. However, there was a realization that wholesale adoption of health policies and establishment of curative centers based on Western models was not effective in India. The introduction to the National Health Policy, 1983 said,

> In spite of such impressive progress, the demographic and health picture of the country still constitutes a cause for serious and urgent concern. The high rate of population growth continues to have an adverse effect on the health of our people and the quality of their lives. . . . The

> existing situation has been largely engendered by the almost wholesale adoption of health manpower development policies and the establishment of curative centres based on the Western models, which are inappropriate and irrelevant to the real needs of our people and the socio-economic conditions obtaining in the country. (MoHFW 1983)

The first National Health Policy in 1983 aimed to achieve the goal of health for all by 2000, through comprehensive primary healthcare services. It stressed the creation of an infrastructure for primary healthcare and close coordination with health-related services and activities. Nutrition, along with drinking water supply and sanitation, figured in the problems needing urgent attention (WHO 2008). However, the policy echoed the overwhelming position held by some observers that increased incomes would lead to increased consumption of nutritious food:

> National and regional strategies should be evolved and implemented, on a time-bound basis, to ensure adequate nutrition for all segments of the population through a well-developed distribution system, especially in the rural areas and urban slums. Food of acceptable quality must be available to every person in accordance with his physical needs. . . . The over-all strategy would necessarily involve organized efforts at improving the purchasing power of the poorer sections of the society. Schemes like employment guarantee scheme, to which the government is committed, could yield optimal results if these are suitably linked to the objective of providing adequate nutrition and health cover to the rural and the urban poor. (MoHFW 1983)

Simultaneously, an inter-sectoral planning approach, which the international development agencies implemented in the developed countries after the World Food Conference in Rome in 1974, was being promoted in developing countries. The international agencies even offered technical support for this activity (Haddard and Geissler 2005). Nutrition, as a separate section started appearing with the Sixth Five Year Plan (1980–1985). Needless to say, in subsequent documents, nutrition promotion has been described as an important objective in several sectoral plans and policies, introducing "multi-sectorality" in India's nutrition scene. Nutrition was to be promoted through developments in such sectors as agriculture, food production, health literacy, and poverty alleviation (FNB 1995a).

As regards the National Health Policy, the period after 1983 witnessed several major developments in the health sector, including adoption of the National Health Policy in 1983 and the seventy-third and seventy-fourth Constitutional Amendments in 1992 (for including promotion of health through the local bodies [Municipalities and *Panchayats*]). They have been assigned twenty-nine development activities that have a direct and indirect bearing on health. However, nutrition does not figure very prominently in these.

Adoption of the National Nutrition Policy (NNP) in 1993 and the International Conference on Nutrition (ICN), held in Rome in 1992, were landmark events in the battle to bring nutrition to the forefront of public health debates. The government soon considered malnutrition a national problem and not merely a sectoral problem and agreed that control of malnutrition was only possible through a national policy. With inputs, technical advice, and a framework from the international agencies, the National Plan of Action on Nutrition (NPAN) was developed as a sequel to the Nutrition Policy. The objective was to operationalize the multi-sectoral strategy (FNB 1995a, b).

In 2001, the People's Union of Civil Liberties (PUCL) filed a writ in the Supreme Court of India, demanding that the right to food be recognized as a legal right for every citizen in the country. The filing of the petition resulted in greater attention to the implementation of food safety net policies and programs. The Supreme Court passed significant interim orders to strengthen the country's food entitlement programs and schemes. The right to food is now very much a public interest issue. The successive governments have been taking specific steps in keeping with the interim orders of the court, to safeguard the right to food. The court has mandated that such constraints as insufficient resources cannot be cited as a reason for not safeguarding rights, stating that the problem should be addressed by reallocating budgets. As a result, budgets over the last decade have seen significantly increased allocations in resources for food entitlement and social security schemes, even though there have been reductions in overall sector allocations (Graham 2011).

The National Health Policy was revised in 2002. The revised policy encompassed strategies to achieve an acceptable standard of good health among the general population of the country. It set goals to be achieved by 2015. But in the public health scenario, HIV/AIDS, TB, and malaria prevention/eradication assumed great importance, due to growing international attention as well as support. Nutrition, despite making it to the national agenda, was viewed more as a welfare measure than a high health priority. The multi-sectorality of addressing the problem, as envisioned in NNP and NPAN, assumed lesser importance in the comparative priorities of each sector. In addition, there are constraints in the implementation of NNP, such as a lack of awareness at all levels, poor inter-sectoral involvement, poor coordination, and a low priority for nutrition in various sectors (WHO 2005).

The relegation of nutritional priorities to the closet in the gamut of public health issues is also obvious in that the National Nutrition Mission, which was formed under the chairmanship of the prime minister in 2001, has not met even once at this writing.

In recent years, nutrition and development transition has been taking place in India, due largely to demographic and epidemiological changes, the forces of internal migration, urbanization, the changes in food consumption patterns, and physical activity patterns. Increased consumption of calories, lack of dietary diversification, and decreasing physical activity are contributing to increased obesity and associated debilitating health conditions.

India today is facing a strange paradox of severe hunger and under nutrition on one side and increasing obesity on the other. The diet related non-communicable diseases are emerging as a disturbing trend, even among the less affluent communities (Shetty 2002). It becomes more important to recast focus on combating the double-edged problem of malnutrition (undernutrition and overweight/obesity).

SUMMARY AND CONCLUSIONS

Health and well-being initially emerged as important issues of public discussion among the emergent middle class of colonial India, which was exposed to western science and literature. Public health later became an integral part of the nationalist discourse in the colonial times. With underpinnings on alleviating poverty and uplifting rural development, the idea of public health under the nationalist agenda laid emphasis on sanitation as well as nutrition. For the country hit by terrible famines, the language of nutrition provided for a more fine-grained analysis of deprivation and a new way of talking about well-being. However, in the post-colonial era, nutrition dropped in policymaking consciousness. Discourse was about aligning with new medical technologies to fight a number of infectious diseases, such as malaria, cholera, and polio and subsequently to mitigate population growth.

However, the challenge of feeding millions of hungry people and ensuring public health nutrition emerged as important problems before the nation. The policy makers in independent India were guided by the notion that improving some social and economic determinants and increasing agriculture production would result in nutritional adequacy. Soon, India embarked on a string of welfare measures on one hand and green revolution on the other. While green revolution concentrated on increasing agricultural produce and augmenting food grain production, programs for nutrition improvement were generally considered to be welfare relief operations, rather than as aspects of the fulfillment of an essential precondition for social and economic development (Gopalan 1992).

The Indian experience has belied the easy assumption that improved nutrition will automatically result as a spin-off effect of improved food production, increased per-capita income, and programs promoting increased child survival.

As Peters et. al. (2003) suggest, the public health transition in the past five decades has not been smooth. Avoidable losses due to communicable and preventable diseases and, more importantly, due to malnutrition have been exceptionally high. In recent years, there has been increasing recognition of the importance of the nutrition factor in development, and several large-scale nutrition intervention programs have been attempted. A coherent, well-conceived national nutrition policy was in place for a long time, bringing about inter-sectoral involvement to tackle the problems of inadequate or over nutrition. This policy has not percolated to all the sectors, owing to low awareness, poor coordination, and low priority for nutrition.

Nutrition programs still do not enjoy high priority or adequate resource allocation in the development agenda. Nutrition improvement has always been perceived as a derived rather than a direct objective of the development process. As a result, there were hardly any attempts to ensure nutritional orientation of national food policies and to lay adequate focus on nutrition in primary healthcare.

BIBLIOGRAPHY

Amrith, S. (2007). "Political culture of health in India," *Economic and Political Weekly*, Vol. 42 (2): pp. 114–121.

———. (2008). "Food and Welfare in India, c. 1900–1950." *Comparative Studies in Society and History*, 50 (4): pp. 1010–1035.

———. (2009). "Health in India since Independence," BWPI Working Paper 79, Manchester, England: Brooks World Poverty Institute, University of Manchester. Available at: http://www.bwpi.manchester.ac.uk/resources/Working-Papers/bwpi-wp-7909.pdf. Accessed 18 November, 2009.

Arnold, D. (1993). *Colonizing the Body: State Medicine and Epidemic Disease in Nineteenth Century in India*. Berkeley, CA: University of California Press, p. 241.

Bajaj, S. (1990). "Nutrition Security System at Household Level—Policy Implications," *Women and Nutrition*, Nutrition Policy Discussion paper No. 6, Geneva: United Nations Administrative Committee on Coordination, Subcommittee on Nutrition. Available at http://www.unsystem.org/scn/archives/npp06/ch18.htm. Accessed 29 May 2008.

Banerji, D. (2004). "The people and health service development in India: A brief overview," *International Journal of Health Services*, 34 (1): pp. 123–142.

Berg, A.D. (1970). "Nutrition as a national priority—Lessons from the India experiment," *The American Journal of Clinical Nutrition*, 23 (1): pp. 1396–1408.

Dreze, J., and Sen, A. (2002). *India: Development and Participation*. New York: Oxford University Press.

Food and Nutrition Board (1995a). "National Plan of Action on Nutrition," New Delhi: Department of Women and Child Development Ministry of Human Resources, Government of India.

———. (1995b). "Need for an Integrated and Inter-sectoral Approach," *National Plan of Action on Nutrition*, New Delhi: Department of Women and Child Development Ministry of Human Resources, Government of India.

Gangulee, N. (1938). *Health and Nutrition in India*. London: Faber and Faber, pp. 144–161.

Geissler, C. (2003). "Stature and Other Economic Indicators of Development: Comparisons in Thailand and the Philippines, Korea and Iran." In Geissler, C. and Oddy, D.J., eds., *Food, Diet and Economic Change, Past and Present*. London: Leicester University Press.

Gopalan, C. (1974). "Nutrition and National Development," *Nutrition*, 8 (1): pp. 4–11.

Gopalan, C. (1992). "International Conference on Nutrition: An Overview and Commentary," *Food, Nutrition and Agriculture*, 5/6: pp. 50–55.

Government of India (1967). "Comprehensive Nutrition Plan, Working Document of the Ministry of Health," New Delhi: Ministry of Health.

———. (1960). *Constitution of India*. New Delhi: Government of India Press.

———. (1946). "Health Survey and Development (Bhore) Committee Report," Vol. 1, Delhi: Publications Division.

———. (1941). "Report of the Health Survey and Development Committee," Delhi: Manager of Publications.

Graham, E. M. (2011). "The Right to Food in India: From 'Parchment Victories' to Legal Enforcement Utilizing the Judicial System to Gain Social and Economic Rights," Doctoral dissertation, Haverford (Pennsylvania) College, Department of Political Science. Available at http://triceratops.brynmawr.edu/dspace/bitstream/handle/10066/7403/2011GrahamE_thesis.pdf?sequence=1. Accessed 12 April 2013.

Griffiths, P.L., and Bentley, M.E. (2001). "The Nutrition Transition Is Underway in India," *Journal of Nutrition*, 131 (10): pp. 2692–2700.

Haddard, L., and Geissler, C. (2005). "Food and Nutrition Policies and Interventions." In Greissler, C. and Powers, H., eds. *Human Nutrition*, 11th ed. Living Stone—imprint of Elsevier, pp. 634–639.

Hill, A.V. (1960). *Ethical Dilemma of Science and Other Essays*. New York: Rockefeller Institute Press, 375.

Jeffery, R. (1988). *The Politics of Health in India*. Berkeley: University of California Press.

Kumar, D. (2000a). "Reconstructing India: Disunity in the Science and Technology for Development Discourse, 1900–1947." In *Nature and Empire: Science and the Colonial Enterprise*. Osiris, 2d Series, 15: pp. 241–257.

———. (2000b). "Science and society in colonial India: Exploring an agenda," *Social Scientist*, 28 (5/6): pp. 24–46.

Lal, M. (2003). "Gender, Nationalism and Health Reform in Colonial North India." In Stuphen, M., and Andrews, B., eds. *Medicine and Colonial Identity*. New York: Routledge, pp. 14–40.

McDermott, W. (1966). "Modern Medicine and Demographic Disease Pattern of Overly Traditional Societies: A Technological Misfit," *Journal of Medical Education*, 41 (9): pp. 137–162.

Ministry of Women and Child Development, Government of India (2008). "Integrated Child Development Scheme." Available at http://wcd.nic.in/icds.htm. Accessed 17 May 2008.

Ministry of Health and Family Welfare, Government of India (1983). "National Health Policy, 1983."

Mushtaq, M.U. (2009). "Public Health in British India: A Brief Account of the History of Medical Services and Disease Prevention in Colonial India," *Indian Journal of Community Medicine*, 34 (1): pp. 6–14.

Palmer, N.D. (1977). "India in 1976: The Politics of Repoliticization. A Survey of Asia in 1976, Part Two," *Asian Survey*, 17 (2): pp. 160–180.

Panandiker, V.A., and Umashankar, P.K. (1994). "Fertility Control and Politics in India," *Population and Development Review*, 20: pp. 89–104.

Park, K. (2000). *Park's Textbook of Preventive and Social Medicine*, 16th ed. Jabalpur, India: Banarsidas Bhanot, pp. 447–451.

Patwardhan, V.N. (1961). *Nutrition in India*. Bombay: Indian Journal of Medical Sciences Press, pp. 1–2.

Planning Commission, Government of India (2008). "The First Three Five-Year Plan Documents." Available at http://planningcommission.nic.in/plans/planrel/fiveyr/welcome.html. Accessed 25 May 2008.

Popkin, B.M. (2001). "The Nutrition Transition and Obesity in the Developing World," *The Journal of Nutrition*, 131 (3): pp. 871S–873S.

Prasad, N.P. (2007). "Medicine, Power and Social Legitimacy," *Economic and Political Weekly*, 42 (34).

Rajagopalan, S. (2003a). "Nutrition: The challenges ahead," *Sunday Magazine, The Hindu* (2 March 2003), pp. 1–3.

———. (2003b). "Nutrition challenges in the next decade," *Food and Nutrition Bulletin,* 24 (3): pp. 275–280.

Ramachandran, P. (2011). "Nutrition Transition in India," *Bulletin of Nutrition Foundation of India,* 32 (2): pp. 1–8.

Rao, M. (1999). "The Structural Adjustment Program and the World Development Report 1993: Implications for Family Planning in India." In M. Rao, ed., *Disinvesting in Health: The World Bank's Prescriptions for Health.* New Delhi: Sage, pp. 82–108.

Sainath, P. (1996). *Everyone Loves a Good Drought.* New Delhi: Penguin, pp. 1–7.

Scrimshaw, N.S., Taylor, C.E., and Gordon, J.E. (1968). "Interactions of Nutrition and Infection," Geneva: WHO Monograph Series 57.

Shetty, P.S. (2002). "Nutrition transition in India," *Public Health Nutrition,* 5 (1A): pp. 175–182.

Siddiqui, J. (1995). "Creation of World Health Organization," *World Health and World Politics: The World Health Organization and the UN System.* Columbia, SC: University of South Carolina Press, pp. 56–60.

SubbaRao, G.M., and Sesikeran, B. (2011). *NIN: 1918–2011—Nine Decades of Leadership in Nutrition.* Hyderabad, India: National Institute of Nutrition.

Turay, K. (2007). "A Population Policy Transition: Human Rights and Population Politics in India During the Emergency and at the Present Moment." Paper presented in the Essays Workshop on Population Politics and Reproductive Rights: State Intervention and Fertility Control, 6th Berlin Roundtables on Transnationality, 14–19 February 2007. Available at http://www.irmgard-coninx-stiftung.de/fileadmin/user_upload/pdf/roundtable07/Turay.pdf. Accessed 20 August 2009.

United Nations Development Program (2005). *Human Development Report.* New York: UNDP, pp. 236–240.

Visvanathan, S. (1998). "A Celebration of Difference: Science and Democracy in India," *Science,* 280 (5360): pp. 42–43.

World Health Organization (2005). "Updating and Implementing Intersectoral Food and Nutrition Plans and Policies," *Report of an inter-country workshop, Hyderabad, India, 4–8 April 2005.* New Delhi: WHO Regional Office for South-East Asia.

———. (2008). "India: National Health System Profile," New Delhi: WHO, Southeast Asia Regional Office (WHOSEARO). Available at: http://www.searo.who.int/LinkFiles/India_CHP_india.pdf. Accessed 26 April, 2008.

IV

Implementation of Healthcare Programs: Case Studies and Practitioners' Experiences

NINE

Bridging Gaps in the Reproductive Health Agendas of Ministries of Health and International Financial Sponsors

UNFPA's Response in Madagascar and Somalia

Achu Lordfred

INTRODUCTION

Gaps exist in the agendas of ministries of health and international financial sponsors in the nations of Africa. We will look at those and highlight some existing mechanisms and innovative techniques designed and promoted by the United Nations Population Fund (UNFPA) to fill those gaps.

This chapter will look specifically at strategies for strengthening the ministries of health in Madagascar and Somalia as those governments deliver good reproductive, mother and child health, and nutrition programs to their people. We will make recommendations and plot the way forward for more effective aid delivery in fragile and conflict situations with a focus on reproductive and maternal health. Effective delivery is especially an issue in low-income countries. One emphasis will be on the health service delivery building block among the World Health Organization's (WHO) six building blocks for a health system.

Health systems have the potential to actually change health behaviors and improve health. Indeed, a resolution to this effect was passed at the 58th session of the Regional Committee of the World Health Organization Regional Office for Europe, September 2008 in Tbilisi, Georgia. This meeting resolved that the purpose of the organization was to "facilitate the exchange and sharing of experiences among Member States with regard to case studies and demonstration projects in the field of behavior change in the WHO European Region and beyond, in order to document the critical health system related factors that are at play, and to enable lessons to be learned and achievements to be replicated" (WHO Regional Committee for Europe 2008).

Strengthening health systems has become a priority in global and national health policy and practice because a gap remains between knowing what can make a difference in the health of individuals and populations and taking action to achieve results. The ministry of health is the government's arm that is responsible for advancing the health of the people. The ministry of health works through the adoption and implementation of health policies and programs that are achieved through stewardship and governance of health resources. A ministry of health's effectiveness however, is dependent on the level of institutional support it receives (Sheikh et al. 2013).

As senior health officials strive to fulfill their mandate, the role and capacity of ministries of health are often overlooked when plans are being made to strengthen health systems. Poorly performing health systems can be a barrier to healthcare and a critical social determinant of health (Sridhar 2010).

Socio-economic or geographical inequalities exist in the distribution of, and access to, health services. With the burden of ill health for those poorly served comes higher out-of-pocket expenses and so a high proportion of household income spent on health. Experience has shown that well-performing health systems can help tackle the social determinants to improve health equity. According to Francis Omaswa, the executive director of the African Centre for Global Health and Social Transformation and Jo Ivey Boufford, president of the New York Academy of Medicine (2010), the achievement of universal access to healthcare requires continuous support and concerted efforts from international organizations, governments, civil society organizations, and academia.

As health systems broaden their scope to cover non-communicable diseases and other priorities, health workers may face new, complex requests in the delivery of services. The challenge lies in addressing past and present gaps while simultaneously anticipating future directions toward strengthening the health workforce as an integral part of health systems.

STEWARDSHIP AND GOVERNANCE AS BUILDING BLOCKS OF AN EFFECTIVE HEALTH SYSTEM

Stewardship is a key foundation block for an effective health system, with governments as stewards or protectors of the public interest. Governments have the ultimate responsibility for assuring conditions that allow people to be as healthy as possible. Ministries of health and the ministers who lead them must be able to perform a set of core stewardship functions across the government (Omaswa and Boufford 2010).

Governance is also considered a core function of these ministries. It is the alignment of multiple actors and interests to promote collective action towards a goal—in this case, the best use of available resources for health. A number of non-governmental partners who bring important knowledge, expertise, and advocacy must be brought together to help them meet their responsibilities. These partners might include universities, professional associations, academies of medicine and science, and business and civil society organizations.

Ministers of health and their ministries play a central role in the process, but they are often overlooked by their governments when investments are made and initiatives designed to strengthen health systems. The health sector is often considered by such governments as one that only spends money, while other sectors produce and even save money. Hence, if resources are limited, health services are not a top priority. Health and education are often the first victims of budget cuts in times of limited funds and competing priorities. They are in the realm of "low politics," as opposed to security and military spending, which are seen as "high politics" (Sridhar 2010).

With the importance of health systems gaining increasing recognition in the international community, multiple definitions of health systems have emerged. Many have centered health systems on a framework to deliver effective personal healthcare services. Other initiatives have been less visible and often quite separate, focusing on the systems needed to deliver effective public health services, health research, and policy. In "Framework for Action: Strengthening Health Systems to Improve Health Outcomes," the WHO has defined six building blocks of a health system and strongly recommends their use by decision makers. These practices can be used to evaluate a community or national health system to determine where the greatest need for improvement lies and how to strengthen that aspect. These building blocks are:

1. Health services must be efficient, effective, and accessible.
2. Well-trained staff should be available.
3. Health information systems should generate useful data on health determinants and health system performance.

4. Access to medicines, vaccines, and medical technologies must be equitable.
5. Adequate funds must be raised for health, ensuring that people have affordable access to services.
6. Leaders must guarantee sufficient oversight, regulation, and accountability (Sheikh et al. 2013, p. 81).

THE AGENDAS OF MINISTRIES OF HEALTH, DONORS, AND INTERNATIONAL ORGANIZATIONS

An important challenge for the ministries of health in Madagascar and Somalia is that of gaining and keeping the support of donors while maintaining autonomy. Other ministries of health face rigid programming or prescriptive approaches that demand separate, vertical programs rather than an integration of activities. There may be low levels of cultural competency and the lack of knowledge regarding local conditions, disproportionate power, and inadequate resources.

Five core principles contained in both the Paris Declaration of 2005 and the Accra Agenda for Action in 2008: (1) ownership; (2) alignment; (3) harmonization; (4) results; and (5) mutual accountability. These principles have gained support across the development community, improving aid practice. It is becoming the norm for aid recipients to forge their own national development strategies with their parliaments and electorates (ownership). Donors support these strategies (alignment) and work to streamline their efforts in-country (harmonization). Development policies are directed to achieve clear goals and monitor progress towards these goals (results). Donors and recipients alike are jointly responsible for achieving these goals (mutual accountability).

The situations in Madagascar and Somalia fragmented and there is inefficient coordination. Donors emerge with diverse ideas for well-funded and well-meaning initiatives with good intentions. Many of these initiatives lack accountability, transparency, and evaluation. They tend to focus on short-term results, raising the question of sustainability. Also, there is frequently an overemphasis on creating parallel structures, rather than reforming and strengthening existing institutions (Sridhar 2010).

Sridhar observes that some critics call the present global health system a patchwork of donors, UN agencies, governments, civil society organizations, and the private sector. He speaks of donor influence on priority setting and the lack of accountability. The proliferation of initiatives brings other challenges for recipient governments, such as the lack of alignment of donors with the national approach, the lack of harmonization among donors, and excessive transaction costs that fall on recipient governments.

This author has observed that in Madagascar and Somalia, such donors as the European Commission and the World Bank have their own ways of implementing initiatives, that may incidentally weaken national health strategies and systems. Ministers of health from Tanzania, Kenya, and Uganda have reported that many ministries of health have become "donor dependent." As much as 40 percent to 60 percent of their health budgets come from outside funding sources. The priorities and services of donor-dependent national governments are vulnerable to the influence of donor priorities.

Qadeer (2000) noted that, although only about 1.6 percent to 2 percent of health sector financing in the in India came from external funds at that time, this small percentage still distorted national priorities. From 1990–1991 until 1998–1999, investments only increased for selected programs for Tuberculosis, Leprosy, and AIDS at the expense of the National Malaria Control and Diarrhoeal Diseases Control programs (pp. 25–32). Similarly, Deolalikar et al. (2008) asserted that external assistance constituted a sizable share of national disease control programs for TB, HIV/AIDS, and Malaria.

Donors tend to over-involve themselves through assistance that is more broadly aimed at strengthening local use of their funds. They impose technical assistance on recipient governments through consultants and training workshops. There is a chronic problem of hiring highly paid consultants from outside who do not know the country well. A lot of money goes back to those consultants. Many of the challenges outlined above stem from the lack of accountability of donors to recipient governments. Donors seldom report on their activities, and, while they monitor recipients according to good governance indicators, they themselves do not respect good governance. For example, there is a lack of transparency about the quantity of aid flowing into a country and how it has been used. This author observed in Madagascar from 2009 to 2012 that some donors were persistently reluctant to share with the Ministry of Health the exact amount in American dollars of the technical and financial contributions of their programs in support of the government of Madagascar.

Sridhar states that, since 2011, there has been a move towards funding non-state actors, especially by the newer institutions. For example, the Global Fund's use of country-coordinating mechanism (CCMs) gives a larger voice to civil society, as it is supposed to include a wide range of actors in a participatory process. The Global Fund's reliance on CCMs indicates that the focus of donors has changed from a state-centric approach to financing to a process aimed at increasing the role of non-state actors

The Global Alliance for Vaccines and Immunization GAVI and the Global Fund attach results from their grants when the money is committed based on expected impacts of vaccinations and bed net use. Similarly, both organizations claim improvements in delivering aid associated with their competitive grant processes. Donors eventually will demand to know how results on the ground correlate with these *ex ante* assumptions. They are concerned about the costs and risks involved with innovative financing mechanisms, which require evaluation as well. Do the benefits outweigh the costs? Could other options dominate when all costs are taken into account? (Brookings Global Economy and Development 2008).

Based on personal observation in Cameroon, Central African Republic, the Democratic Republic of Congo, to mention just these few, the capacity to absorb resources varies across different countries. Low country capacity to absorb funds from various sources could cause donors and financial organizations to think that they are contributing more through various pipelines than the country can use effectively.

New mechanisms and initiatives in health financing create new transactions costs for donors: Board meetings; a larger volume of daily business inquiries connected to the initiatives; an additional obligation to deal with affiliated civil society and business interests; and advocates for even more initiatives. Healthcare cost drivers are complex and interwoven, but the most problematic ones are inefficiencies, misaligned incentives, and fragmented care delivery in the current fee-for-service reimbursement system (Daschle et al. 2013). They also observe that organized systems of care emphasize the value of care delivered over the volume of care. These systems are often better able to meet patients' needs and desires and are able to effectively reimburse providers and practitioners for delivering high-quality care.

A MORE CRITICAL LOOK AT DONOR FUNDING

Different forms of aid initiatives entail numerous challenges for recipient governments. These include lack of alignment of donors with the national approach, lack of harmonization among donors, and excessive transaction costs on recipient governments. Too often donors have their own ways of implementing initiatives in a country, thereby weakening national health strategies and systems.

According to Sridhar (2010), the World Bank has been used to demonstrate why some governments choose not to take assistance. He quotes critics as saying that The World Bank offers loans, not grants. These loans are not aligned with national systems and priorities, and the World Bank is intrusive. He relates that critics say that, from assessment, only 40 percent of World Bank aid has tangible benefit. The other 60 percent is in the form of technical assistance that is more broadly aimed at strengthening local capacity. They impose technical assistance on recipient governments through consultants and training workshops. Making reference to consultants, Sridhar quotes critics from Nepal as saying that "there is a chronic problem of hiring highly paid consultants from outside, and a lot of money goes back to those consultants."

Much of the challenges outlined above stem from an underlying lack of accountability of donors.

According to Omaswa and Boufford (2010), donors seldom report on their activities, and, while they monitor recipients according to good governance indicators, they themselves do not respect the principles of good governance. They quote the health minister of Tanzania as saying that there is a lack of transparency about the quantity of aid flowing into a country and how it has been used. Part of the difficulty is that recent initiatives, such as The American President's Emergency Plan for AIDS Relief (PEPFAR) and the Gates Foundation, disburse funds directly to NGOs, making it difficult for ministries to plan their efforts.

REPRODUCTIVE AND MATERNAL HEALTH IN LOW- AND MIDDLE-INCOME COUNTRIES

In Low Income Countries (LICs) senior ministry of health staffs are overwhelmed with emergencies that overshadow basic operational responsibilities, including planning and strengthening health systems.

Concerning reproductive, maternal, neonatal, and child health, 70 percent to 90 percent of avoidable mortality is actually due to

- Risky behaviors, including a lack of basic sanitation infrastructure. Another behavioral factor is the lack of public awareness of healthy choices, or the conditions are such that healthy choices are not available.
- Factors in the human and natural environment.
- Genetic determinants of health.

In UNFPA's Organizational Priorities for 2013, the current executive director of the UNFPA, Babatunde, states that considerable progress has been made in women's sexual and reproductive health in low- and middle-income countries in the last two decades. Maternal mortality has fallen by half to 273,500 in 2011. Contraceptive use has increased. The rate of new HIV infection has plateaued or begun to decline in a number of countries. However, behind these positive trends lie significant differences among and within countries. At least 220 million women in low and middle-income countries who do not want to become pregnant are not using contraception. Every year, 80 million unintended births, and 40 million abortions, half of them illegal and unsafe, occur. Approximately half of all new sexually transmitted infections, not including HIV, occur in girls and women, the executive director noted.

The Program of Action of the International Conference on Population and Development (ICPD), held in Cairo in 1994, underlined the importance of providing an integrated set of sexual and reproductive health services through the public health system, rather than through vertical programs. These include family planning; safe abortion where legal; maternity care, including referrals to emergency obstetric care; prevention and treatment of STIs, including HIV. The Program of Action recognized that this approach best served women and girls. When well designed and implemented it has efficiencies that make such services cost effective. In terms of the UNFPA's Organization Priorities for the year 2013 strengthening the health system to provide good quality, integrated SRH services provides the foundation for action to prevent and treat other sexual and reproductive health (SRH) conditions in women, such as violence against women, Babatunde stated.

GOVERNANCE AND HEALTH CARE MANAGEMENT

Consistency or continuity of leadership of senior ministry of health staff is a big challenge. A significant challenge for leadership and management of health systems, especially across LICs in Africa is governmental decentralization. The capacities that need to be strengthened for effective implementation of decentralization are diverse and involve among others leadership, but also the adequacy of structural, organizational, and human resources.

Reproductive health experts and International donor agencies have, over the years, observed that there are often no clear cut boundaries in policy, strategic and normative roles of the ministries of health.

Because of their access to funding, donors and other financial partners retain greater power than the respective ministries of health. They often have competing social and fiscal priorities.

As a result of this power disparity between the donors and ministry staff, ministry officials face significant challenges in negotiating with donors and partners. These challenges are compounded by gaps in information necessary for identifying health service needs, developing appropriate plans, preparing evidence-based funding requests, and reporting to stakeholders. In Somalia, for example, some senior members of the Ministry of Health do not use data for decision making. They find it difficult to change the way they do business to meet the demands of technical experts and donors. Senior officers of the ministries of Human Development and Public Services of Madagascar and Somalia have to deal with various resources, competing priorities, and multiple models being imposed from outside as conditions for financial assistance. They are less able to make their own decisions about the elements in their health systems because of conflicting social and fiscal priorities of the European Union, the World Bank, and others.

Some decisions made by senior government health officials and other healthcare providers for the districts and health facilities do not conform to local customs and traditions. The Madagascar Ministry of Health decided to print education and communication materials with pictures and slogans that were adequate for one region. When they distributed these materials to the whole country, many found the slogans and pictures insulting and provocative, in violation of the customs and traditions.

Ministries of health have a complex set of responsibilities and challenges. Staffing, access to health and service needs, secure resources, identifying intervention strategies, development and implementation of and advocacy for health, promoting health and healthcare services, maintenance of the health infrastructure and communication and advocate for health.

In Madagascar, as you get below the regional health level, many organs of the Ministry of Health are either absent, or they tend to be chronically underfunded for of the various mandates. The problems are more visible in dealing with the underserved populations where there is high turnover in the political system and within the Madagascar ministries. There is very little institutional memory.

When this author asked several senior officials of the Ministry of Health to describe their agenda in the midst of so many competing demands, many of them described their central leadership challenge. With the high turnover, they must reestablish their identity as separate or new compared to their predecessors and identify priorities. This is difficult when they come into the job without relevant experience, training, or orientation.

Madagascar Ministry of Health officials decry the lack of epidemiologic and other reliable data on population health status. It is difficult for an incoming minister of health to understand the health priorities. A good "situation analysis" of the health system is regarded as critical by a number of senior ministry of health officials, but they often lack an understanding of public expectations and political commitment to health issues, tools, and levers that ministers need to change the system. In addition, the basic operational capabilities of ministries are often exacerbated by policies of decentralization.

Since 2009, civil society organizations in Madagascar tend to be either service providers or advocates, so they largely relate to the ministries on their own issues. A notable challenge is that of developing a national awareness that holds government accountable for delivering a comprehensive health agenda and for more general advocacy.

The governments of Madagascar (since 2006) and Somalia (since 2011) have structured and attempted to decentralize the health system into levels. The central, regional, district and health facility levels each have its own specific roles and responsibilities. The central level led by the minister of health, deals with policy and the development of norms and directives for the health of the Malagasy population. The regional office is in charge of coordinating several district health offices. The district office supervises several health facilities. Health facilities deliver service and care.

Health sector analysts and public health experts have noted that effective decentralization can only succeed when all actors—central and local governments, civil society, the private sector, and international development partners—have the same vision and commitment, as well as required capacities.

Within government, senior officials in the ministry of health need to convince presidents or prime ministers, ministries of finance, parliaments, and other national and local leaders of the importance of health-related funding (Omaswa and Boufford 2010). Underfunded planning and coordination, staff shortages, and low salaries for health workers overload the health facility. If it is forced to close, patients are left without care. In crisis situations like Madagascar and Somalia, healthcare providers and experts have observed a lack of appreciation for health needs within other branches of government. There is resistance to giving health activities a high priority, particularly when the government is not recognized by the international community.

The healthcare providers also realize the need for the ministries of health in Madagascar and Somalia to develop a persuasive argument to increase investment of the Gross Domestic Product (GDP) to attend to equity, quality, and financial protection as part of health reforms.

HEALTHCARE IN FRAGILE STATES

Effective and equitable health services can be a central contributor to state legitimacy (Rajar 2012). Very often, health interventions in fragile and conflict-affected states are limited to humanitarian relief, which does not advance either health system development or state legitimacy. Often very little information is available on the nature and extent of health inequities in fragile states and regions where populations are in conflict.

Health experts have successfully demonstrated that, to address health inequalities in conflict-affected fragile states, it is necessary to address the conflicts themselves. Experience in development of health systems in fragile and conflict-affected states has shown that someone must first address weaknesses in policy; leadership; management capacity; human resources for health, supplies; service delivery; and data collection and evaluation.

Further, conflict-affected states are significantly worse off in many key health indicators, such as births attended by skilled health personnel, under-five mortality rate, net primary school enrolment, and the proportion of undernourished in the total population. The worse the conflict, the worse the indicators become. This is precisely the situation of Madagascar and Somalia.

Health care and Political Crises in Madagascar and Somalia

Madagascar and Somalia have experienced significant crises. The most recent socio-political crisis in Madagascar dates back to 2009, while the chronic socio-political instability in Somalia has lasted for over two decades.

This author has observed that the staffs of the ministries of health are not motivated to be productive because they are not well paid. Some staffs resort to charging patients extra fees and carrying out other malpractices that discourage the local communities from using health services. In Madagascar some healthcare providers resorted to selling medication and supplies that were donated by UNFPA to the health facilities. These supplies were to be offered free of charge to encourage women to deliver in the hospitals and to improve access to lifesaving emergency obstetric and neonatal care to those pregnant women who developed complications and required cesarean sections.

Service providers also need continuing education and training in reproductive health and family planning, and some still need to be convinced of the benefits of family planning and reproductive health. In Somalia the lack of female physicians, especially in rural areas, prevents many women from seeking reproductive health services out of embarrassment over being examined by a male service provider.

Health experts have noted that the lack of collaboration and ineffective coordination among financial and technical partners in certain parts of Madagascar and Somalia creates problems in the planning and implementation of what is called the essential package of health services (EPHS). The central government ministries and the NGOs sometimes play donors against each other.

Those conditions damage the ability for such international organizations as UNFPA, financial donors, and the local government to deliver efficient reproductive, mother, child health, and nutrition programs. The good news is that UN agencies and country governments are making significant investments in capacity building programs for public sector officials that bring together multiple stakeholders.

Reproductive and Maternal Health in Somalia

Generally speaking, the use of healthcare services depends on the quality of those services. Countries with low levels of utilization of health services generally have low quality of services provided in health facilities. With respect to reproductive health, such countries as Somalia and Madagascar also have high levels of maternal and neonatal mortality and poor reproductive health in general. This is true for Somalia, which has very poor indicators, as stated above. According to the Multiple Indicator Cluster Survey (MICS), completed in 2006 by UNICEF, Somalia has some of the worst reproductive health indicators in the world

- Maternal mortality ratio of 1044/100 000 live births. Coupled with a high fertility rate, that translates into a one in ten life-time risk of dying due to a pregnancy-related cause for a woman. Only one in four pregnant women attends antenatal care.
- Skilled attendance at birth in the health facility is 9 percent, as opposed to 33 percent within the general population. Access to emergency obstetric and neonatal care services is limited, as reflected in a caesarean rate of less than 1 percent
- Despite the beneficial health effect on the whole family of adequate child spacing by at least two years, only 1 percent of Somali women use a modern method to space or limit children, although one fourth of women report having unmet needs in doing so,
- Over 97 percent of women have undergone some form of female genital mutilation or cutting (FGM/C), leading to increased risk of birth complications and a higher risk of death for their newborns,
- Sexual and gender-based violence in the form of rape is prevalent, especially in Internally Displaced Persons settings.

The Reproductive Health Strategy for Somalia for 2011–2015 identified three main priorities to be addressed by the government and her health partners and donors: (1) High maternal mortality ratios and the fact that most maternal deaths arise from complications during childbirth; (2) very high fertility and considerable unmet needs for family planning /birth spacing; (3) the high prevalence of traditional practices and the medical evidence that some of these practices, such as female genital mutilation/cutting seriously endanger reproductive health.

Further, from the health expert's perspective, collaboration between the Somalia Ministry of Health, donors and international organizations is a tedious task, but when they work well they are highly valued and productive for the people.

MULTISECTORAL RESPONSE TO THE REPRODUCTIVE, MATERNAL, AND CHILD HEALTH

Many health experts view health as a consequence of social and economic development. The importance of health can be discerned in the global drive to fulfill the Millennium Declaration and the Millennium Development Goals (MDGs), all of which are health related. The UN Secretary General has a personal interest in global health. Health was a key agenda item in recent Group of 8 (G8) assembly of world leaders who meet annually to discuss global issues and regional political summits.

The increasing attention to health is also demonstrated in the huge increase in resources allocated to countries through such agencies as the Global Fund, Global Alliance for Vaccines and Immunization (GAVI), and other new financing mechanisms. The growth of civil society injected with strong health advocacy interests driven internationally and locally, is another factor responsible for promoting the health of the population. Yet, historical paradigms have left ministries of health relatively under-resourced and "low-power" within governments. According to public health experts, a critical challenge in many LICs involves changing the powerlessness mindset of ministries of health for a can-do attitude in shaping health systems that reflect their priorities.

Major UN agencies involved with health and population management, including the WHO and UNFPA, have constantly been analyzing ways to improve the health of the world population.

The WHO, which has been leading the fight for better health, has proposed key actions:

- Deliver quality health services to all people, when and where they need them, with specific attention to vulnerable groups. Ensure increased outreach of national prepayment mechanisms that decrease out-of-pocket expenses for health. Floors Recommendation, 2012 (No. 202).
- Provide specifically designed health services and social protection measures for both socially disadvantaged and marginalized groups and the general population.
- Protect people with chronic illnesses from income loss.

The United Nations Population Fund (UNFPA) is a development agency. Its mission is to help nations reach a point at which every pregnancy is wanted, every birth is safe; and every young person's potential is fulfilled. UNFPA strongly believes in and promotes the ideology contained in the words "because everyone counts."

UNFPA partners with governments, other agencies, and civil society to advance this mission. Two frameworks guide its efforts—the Program of Action adopted at the 1994 International Conference on Population and Development and the Millennium Development Goals, eight targets to reduce extreme poverty by 2015. Since the date for achieving the MDG targets is fast approaching, work is being accelerated to analyze successes, galvanize support, and redouble efforts through celebrating achievements of the Cairo Consensus and highlighting the Urgency for Action ICPD at 15: Actions and Outcomes and the Millennium Development Goals report.

The goals of UNFPA are inextricably linked: Achieving universal access to sexual and reproductive health, including family planning; promoting reproductive rights; reducing maternal mortality; and accelerating progress on the ICPD agenda and the MDGs. UNFPA also focuses on improving the lives of youths and women by advocating for human rights and gender equality and by promoting the understanding of population dynamics. Population dynamics, including growth rates, age structure; fertility, mortality, and migration have an effect on every aspect of social and economic progress. Sexual and reproductive health and women's empowerment all powerfully affect, and are influenced by, population trends (UNFPA 2013).

Working with a range of partners, UNFPA assists governments in delivering sexual and reproductive healthcare, including:

- voluntary family planning;
- antenatal, safe delivery, and post-natal care;
- prevention of abortion and management of its complications and consequences;
- treatment of reproductive-tract infections;
- prevention, care, and treatment of those with sexually transmitted infections;
- information, education and counseling on human sexuality and reproductive health, as appropriate;
- prevention of violence against women, care for survivors of violence and other actions to eliminate traditional harmful practices; and
- appropriate referrals for further diagnosis and care management.

Improving maternal health is a key UNFPA priority and the results lag most behind its MDG target. Important UNFPA initiatives include the Maternal Health Thematic Fund, the Campaign to End Obstetric Fistula, and numerous partnerships. In 2005, the international community included universal access to reproductive health as one of its MDGs, underscoring its importance in improving health on a global level.

Access to reproductive healthcare also demands what UNFPA calls for reproductive health commodity security—the ability for all to obtain and use quality reproductive health supplies of their choice whenever they need them. UNFPA carries out relief and recovery work when necessary.

The WHO's recommended key actions to be undertaken in conflict affected and fragile contexts by UN agencies and donors:

- Develop health systems in fragile states and conflict-affected countries in order to contribute significantly to the preservation of life and the well-being of people in those countries. Global health funding programs should afford higher priority to fragile and conflict-affected states, based on their disproportionate morbidity and mortality rates for their stage of development and the recognized connection between an effective service system and long-term state legitimacy.

- Strengthen information systems in fragile states and countries in conflict through efforts to improve information systems, including health information systems. Such efforts are required to improve global understanding about health and the impact of conflicts, and to develop effective policy options.
- Strengthen the capacities of state policymaking functions and provider capacities to implement equity-focused healthcare interventions.
- Reduce exposure and vulnerability of children, women, and the elderly and displaced populations to communicable diseases during periods of conflict and fragility.

Madagascar and Somalia qualify for, and benefit at various degrees from, the various forms of aid and different concepts used to describe and encourage links between them. Some common forms of aid concepts according to Julia Steets (2011) include:

- Relief aid tasked with saving lives and mitigating suffering in targets populations affected by emergencies, is based on the humanitarian principles of humanity, independence, impartiality, and neutrality. This aid most often provides assistance through civil society.
- Recovery aid, which constitutes the grey area that aims at recreating pre- or non-emergency situations for target populations affected by emergencies. Development principles are followed as far as the humanitarian principles allow, and the preference is to work through local communities and local government.
- Development aid, aimed at improving the social and economic situation, targets societies as a whole. Aid follows the principles of ownership, alignment, results, and mutual accountability and usually works through national and local governments.

It is this writer's observation that donors are often challenged by their implementing partners. These partners often lack the expertise and capacity to operate across different forms of aid and do not coordinate their activities with other actors well.

An alternative is to strengthen intra-governmental coordination. Possible steps in that direction range from small, pragmatic measures to improve information exchange and joint planning to formal inter-ministerial committees, whole-of-government approaches or institutional integration. While efforts to enhance internal coordination are indispensable, they often encounter institutional barriers and have a limited effect.

"U.S. Maternal Health Donors: A Landscape Analysis," the 2011 report of the Global Health Visions Maternal Health Task Force, revealed ways that ministry of health funding could be better utilized and best address current funding gaps. One way is to plan a more horizontal, comprehensive approach to health by linking health sectors; addressing the root causes of maternal deaths; expanding and improving the health workforce through recruitment, training, and evaluation; increasing government accountability; investing in local NGOs; and focusing on implementing and scaling up interventions and technologies that have been proven effective.

In Madagascar, such financial sponsors as UNICEF, the WHO, UNFPA, World Bank, UNAIDS, USAID, JICA, and the French Embassy coordinate efforts in maternal and neonatal health within the framework of the H4+ (The H4+ is a joint effort by United Nations and related agencies and programs UNAIDS, UNFPA, UNICEF, UN Women, WHO, and the World Bank. Harnessing the collective power of each partner's strengths and capacities, the H4+ works to improve the health of women and children and accelerate progress towards achieving MDGs 4 and 5. The H4+ serves as lead technical partners for the United Nations Secretary-General's Global Strategy for Women's and Children's Health.[1]

The group's main objective is to encourage technical and financial partners to set maternal and neonatal health high on the agenda. Although the international community does not, at this writing, recognize the current government, yet the government in place has worked with senior officials of the Ministry of Health to engage the UN secretary general's Global Strategy for Women and Children's Health. With the help of senior officials of the Ministry of Health and coordination from the UNFPA, those financial partners transformed these engagements into a multi-year (2012–2015) operational plan to accelerate the achievement of MDGs pertaining to child health, maternal health, and HIV/AIDS. This operational plan is now the first referral document for interventions so that partners can work together to accelerate achievement of the MDGs.

These partners work with the Ministry of Health's central, regional, and district medical officers and NGOs. Partners working in the health sector, and especially on mother and child health, meet each December to review the past year's work plan, appreciate and analyze problems, determine and share lessons learned, set objectives, and determine the strategies to be adapted around regional and sometimes district particular needs.

The partners take into consideration the recommendations of this coordination and planning meeting as they set priorities with the Ministry of Health for their own work plans.

THE ROLE OF AID DONORS IN PROMOTING HEALTHCARE

In the case of Somalia, there is in 2013 a unique window of opportunity for more effective use of aid. After decades of short-term humanitarian efforts, a new United Nations Somali Assistance Strategy, the UNSAS (2011–2015), has identified health as a high priority in UN programs. There are few donors in health, and the United Kingdom's Department for International Development (DFID) is the lead bilateral donor. DFID's harmonization efforts have created an opportunity for the United Kingdom (UK), Swedish International Development Cooperation Agency (SIDA), the Australian Government Overseas Aid Program (Ausaid), USAID, and potentially the European Union, Italy, and Switzerland to align their support within one long-term program.

UNICEF, the WHO, and the UNFPA came together for the first time, resulting in a proposal for a Joint Health and Nutrition Program 2012–2016 (JHNP). This joint program is focused on reproductive, maternal health plus family planning, neonatal health and Nutrition. The objective is to rebuild the collapsed health system in Somalia by supporting an Essential Package of Health Services (EPHS) in nine regions.

The proposal marks a shift from decades of ad-hoc funding of small projects to a long-term health systems approach with sustainable impact. It highlights a flexible approach enabling transition between development and humanitarian help, where needed. They wish to create a resilient effort in health and nutrition that can respond to drought, floods, and conflict. Five NGOs of the Health Consortium for Somalia (HCS) have been piloting routine EPHS service delivery in defined areas within the three political regions of Somalia, Hargeisa, and Sahil Somaliland, Garowe and Karkaar regions of Puntland, and the Gedo region of South-Central Somalia. In 2013, the security situation permitted limited access of NGOs to these geographic areas. A new UN intervention enables UK support for reproductive, maternal, neonatal, child health (RMNCH), family planning (FP), and nutrition services to be implemented across Somalia, including areas known as emerging political entities, such as Galgadud, and Mogadishu.

Although the NGOs have demonstrated results and engaged with Somali counterparts, particularly on human resources, there is a limit to the extent that NGOs can progress in rebuilding the entire health system. Working through three agencies enables the UN to take the lead on health systems and support the Ministry of Health to build sustainable Somali capacity for the long term.

Service delivery is just one of the six building blocks of the Global WHO Health System Strengthening (HSS) model for improving the health system. This new intervention will scale up access to services, with a focus on RMNCH and FP, and it will support the other five blocks of a functioning health system: Leadership and governance; the health workforce; systems for health financing; ensured access to medical products, vaccines, and new technologies. It also improves the collection, quality, and use of information for health planning.

The EPHS framework sets out ten priority health interventions to be implemented at primary healthcare units in the community, health centers, and local and regional hospitals, with overarching support for nutrition. It was adopted by the three regional health authorities of Somaliland, Puntland, and the Transitional Federal Government (TFG) in 2009. The EPHS includes activities that increase demand, such as community meetings and radio and mobile phone messages to increase awareness about health issues. The benefits of family planning and safe delivery can be promoted, health clinics improved, family planning resources provided, and ante natal care and safe delivery taught. People learn about caring for newborns, administering vaccinations, and preventing and treating pneumonia, diarrhea, malaria, Tuberculosis (TB), and AIDS, as well as screening for and treating malnutrition.

The EPHS is a significant step forward, but it does not set out how the health authorities should prioritize, plan, fund, monitor, and report on the quality of care provided. Providing the EPHS interventions across Somalia requires support from a fully functioning health system.

The UN Joint Health and Nutrition Program enables strategic engagement with the private sector for scale up. It includes support to health authorities on innovative financing mechanisms for social franchising, maternity voucher schemes, and outsourcing through Public-Private-Partnerships (PPPs). Further work on accreditation of private sector facilities to ensure high quality of care will help reduce harmful practices, such as FGM/C. The health authorities have spoken of a strong desire to work with the private sector to monitor agreed standards of care and to increase affordable access to services.

THE CURRENT ENVIRONMENT IN SOMALIA

The role of health authorities within the new environment in Somalia has been defined, along with development of the Health Sector Strategic Plan in 2012 by the UN agencies, donors, NGOs in partnership with the health authorities. This process took into consideration the complex reality on the ground. The Directorate of Health within the Great Ministry of Human Development and Public Services has authority over a pluralistic, unruly, unstable healthcare arena, crowded with autonomous providers and entrepreneurs.

After a crisis as prolonged and severe as Somalia's the health authorities face too many demands, expectations, and proliferating priorities that cannot all be addressed at once. In 2013, efforts by UN agencies and the Somali government were concentrated on a few pressing, concrete, thoroughly researched measures that address local felt needs. Feasibility takes precedence over desirability.

Programs have been tested in the Somali capital. Understanding better the flaws affecting healthcare provision in the capital, and finding realistic ways to tackle them, might equip partners with valuable models to be applied elsewhere, once other regions open up.

In South-Central Somalia, emergency assistance absorbs a considerable proportion of donor assistance, and disease specific programs for polio, malaria and HIV/AIDS are receiving of the most existing funds. The World Bank affirms that, donor funding for public health in Somalia over the past decade could have been used more strategically.

Finally, there is increasing external assistance to the health sector from international health partnerships. Traditional bilateral donor agencies, especially DFID, SIDA, and AUSAID, are involved. So are some nearby countries, such as Turkey and Qatar. Consistent support is coming from the UN family. However, because external funding is not routed through, or reported to, the government, the amount of money spent in South-Central Somalia is not known.

According to consultants Goldsmith and Muhamad (January 2013), there is no accurate picture of the amounts of traditional and non-traditional, charity, and NGO funding of health services. External funding does not always align with the main causes of ill health. There is no consolidation of the funds spent on health in South-Central Somalia, by government, by donors or by the people.

CONCLUSIONS

Donor assistance for health-related activities in developing countries has grown rapidly. Unfortunately, aid is still far short of what is needed to achieve the MDGs. Additionally, shifting policy priorities and fluctuations in aid funding create ongoing challenges for donor agencies and aid recipients as they try to plan for global health needs.

Research has demonstrated that health outcomes cannot be achieved by action in the health sector alone; support from other sectors is critical. Further, improving health outcomes contributes to achieving goals in other sectors. A healthier population improves the overall level of productivity in the economy; increases employment reduces poverty, and improves school attendance of children. Healthy workers are fundamental for the productivity of businesses and livelihoods. Health is a contributor to, as well as an indicator of, development.

RECOMMENDATIONS

We have focused on Somalia, but the recommendations apply throughout Africa. Ideally, assistance should be free from political pressures. It should not detract from national plans. Funding should be in the form of grants that are properly aligned with national health systems, not loans. Donors should not intrude throughout the implementation of projects and programs.

All health stake holders should promote coordinated and accountable systems of healthcare delivery and payment, building on what has proven successful in the private and public sectors.

Politicians, policy makers, and the public need to be educated about the importance of stewardship and governance in strengthening health systems and the critical role of ministers and ministries of health. These are the backbone of successful and sustainable systems.

In Somalia, political and military developments have called for a reassessment of long-established patterns. Given that most healthcare is provided by private operators, the Directorate of Health's main role in the new context must be to interact with private providers, many of whom are well-established and wielding considerable power.

There is a need to build the technical capacity of ministry of health staff to move beyond planning and be able to collect and analyze data for policy analysis and decision making, define priorities and set standards, implement strategically using principles such as equality, quality and accountability, and measure results.

Better coordination among donors, local authorities, and implementers is needed to avoid the mistakes of the past and to ensure that priorities for future interventions are based more on evidence and results.

Somalia's ministries must do more than simply deliver care. The government must work effectively across all sectors of government to advocate for health in all policies.[2] The ministry of health must also work with ministries involved in decentralization of government and civil service reform. These important ministries include interior, public service, and state reforms, or ministries that might carry different names but have these spheres. Parliament's involvement is necessary to gain political support for health policies. Ministries of Health need to be well connected in the cabinet and know how to relate to colleagues, especially the prime minister and other officials who are key to getting the money and making decisions. The minister of health must know where and when decisions are being made and priorities set about resources and be present. She or he needs to understand domestic resources, foreign resources, and the relative value and advantages of each.

In order to provide the programs and services needed to promote the health of the Somali public, senior staff of the ministry of health must regularly advocate and negotiate for funding and other support from various partners and stakeholders.

To ensure reliable service delivery, attention must be paid to adequate remuneration of health staff in the public/not-for-profit sector.

Establish innovative and effective policy frameworks. These would allow coordination across sectors, enable and sustain equitable health system development, and present opportunities to engage civil society in health system decision-making and action, especially at the local level.

Improve universal health coverage by building on existing international commitments to ensure universal access to a nationally defined set of goods and services. The support is needed in such areas as maternity care. These goods and services would meet criteria of availability, accessibility, acceptability, and quality, as set out in the International Labour Organization's (ILO) Social Protection percent of all pregnancies.

Human resources demand special attention, strategic intelligence and action. Gaps in health worker distribution, competency, quality, motivation, and performance need to be addressed.

Ministries of health should strive in all health and development programs to implement policies that are inclusive and that take account of the needs of the entire population. Specific attention is due vulnerable groups,

Ministries of health, like all ministries, require certain critical kinds of staff expertise and infrastructure to perform their core policy, strategic and technical functions. In addition, ministries must be able to effectively work across sectors of government to advocate for health funding and promote health in all policies.

BIBLIOGRAPHY

Brookings Global Economy and Development (2008). "Innovative Health Financing: Donor Views on Progress, Problems, Opportunities and Strategy." Washington, DC: Global Health Financing Initiative working paper.

Chandler, C., et al. (2013). "Understanding the Factors Influencing Health-worker Employment Decisions in South Africa," *Human Resources for Health*, April 2013: pp. 11–15.

Capobianco, E., and Naidu, V. (2011). "A Decade of Aid to the Somali Health Sector, 2000 to 2009." World Bank paper. Available at http://www-wds.worldbank.org/external/default/WDSContentServer/WDSP/IB/2011/05/18/000333037_20110518004532/Rendered/PDF/618980WP0Aid0S000public00BOX358355B.pdf. Accessed June 2013.

Daschle, T., et al. (2013). "How to Build a Better Health-care System," *Washington Post*, 18 April 2013. Available at www.brookings.edu/research/.../2013/04/18-build-better-health-care-rivl... Accessed July 2013.

Global Health Visions (2011). "U.S. Maternal Health Donors: A Landscape Analysis." Global Health Visions for the Maternal Health Task Force. Available at maternalhealthtaskforce.org/buzzmeeting/background_mhtf.pdf. Accessed June 2013.

Goldsmith, C., and Muhamad, A. (2013). "Review of Compensation, Salaries, Incentives and Benefits for Health Personnel in Somalia." Mannion Daniels Ltd. Available at www.manniondaniels.com/.../review-of-compensation-salaries-incentives. Accessed August 2013.

Mubashar, S., et al. (2013). "Human Resources for Universal Health Coverage," *Bulletin of the World Health Organization*, 91: pp. 84–84A.

Omaswa, F., and Boufford, J. (2010). "Strong Ministries for Strong Health Systems Supporting Ministerial Health Leadership: A Strategy for Health Systems Strengthening." New York Academy of Medicine, pp. 1–32. Available at http://www.rockefellerfoundation.org/uploads/files/8819cca6-1738-4158-87fe-4d2c7b738932.pdf. Accessed August 2013.

Ravenscroft, J. (2013). "Access to Health Care in Mozambique: Health Financing, Human Resources," Global Health Check. Available at www.globalhealthcheck.org/?p=1359. Accessed September 2013.

Sridhar, D. (2010). "Seven Challenges in International Development Assistance for Health and Ways Forward: Innovative Solutions to Closing the Health Gap Between Rich and Poor," *Global Health Governance Journal of Law, Medicine and Ethics*: pp. 1–11.

Steets, J. (2011). "Donor Strategies for Addressing the Transition Gap and Linking Humanitarian and Development Assistance." Global Public Policy Institute report. Available at www.gppi.net/publications=reports/donor_strategies_linking_humanitarian_and_development_assistance. Accessed September 2013.

Taskforce on Innovative International Financing for Health Systems (2009). "More Money for Health and More Health for the Money." Available at www.ausaid.gov.au/publications/.../more_money_for_health.pdf. Accessed September 2013.

UN Secretary General Global Strategy Financing Working Group (2010). "Global Strategy for Women's and Children's Health: Financial Estimates in the Global Strategy." Available at www.who.int/entity/pmnch/activities/.../100922_1_financial_estimates.p. Accessed September 2013.

World Health Organization Regional Committee for Europe (2008). "Report of the 58th Session, Tbilisi, Georgia, 15–18 September 2008." Available at www.euro.who.int/__regional committee for Europe/...sessions/fifty-eighth. Accessed August 2013.

NOTES

1. See more at: http://www.everywomaneverychild.org/resources/h4#sthash.CAPNSdAe.dpuf.

2. Beyond the Ministry of Health, there is an interrelationship with ministries of finance for resources and education on health professions training and health education in schools. Ministries of economic development, agriculture, environment, housing, and transportation also have roles to play in the health system.

TEN

Controversies in Public Health

A Case for Prioritizing Integrated Communication in Public Health Interventions in Africa

Adebayo Fayoyin

INTRODUCTION

The primary goal of public health is to assure good and ultimately healthy living for the public. Public health strategies, policies, and services are intended to improve the overall health of the population through both disease prevention and health promotion. Unfortunately, many components of the work have been embroiled in public controversies and professional arguments in several parts of the world. In Africa, health programs and interventions have been affected by a plethora of disputes. Some of this unrest bodes serious consequences for the issues in question and the public at large. Nevertheless, public health controversies offer a major opportunity to understand the complexity of public health communication. Against this backdrop, this chapter examines dimensions of public health communication in the midst of controversies.

To contextualize the issues, this chapter will provide a brief review of the literature on the nature of some serious controversies in public health. We will examine two case studies, the boycott of polio immunization in northern Nigeria in 2003 and 2008, and Kenya's crisis over condom quality, shortages, and promotion. These cases demonstrate ramifications of public health controversies in regard to communications and affirm the significance of the ecological approach to public health communication. Based on lessons from the theoretical framework and findings from the cases, major convergence points for integrated public health communication will be identified. The study also recommends multi-disciplinary training in risk communication in the public health and mass communication institutions in Africa.

DEFINING PUBLIC HEALTH

Public health is a part of medicine intended to enhance the health of the community. The World Health Organization (WHO) defines health as "the state of complete physical, mental and social wellbeing and not merely absence of disease or infirmity" (Tarantola 2000, p. 2). Although the definition is rather utopian, it serves as the broad framework for understanding various dimensions of health, including public health. The Institute of Medicine (IOM) in the U.S. offers a condensed view of public health as actions that contribute to fulfilling society's interest in assuring conditions in which people can be healthy (IOM 2003). This view is consistent with the general idea that public health is concerned with community, the health of families, neighborhoods, and countries rather than on the health of individual members of the society (CDC Foundation 2013, p. 1). The notion of public health as the health of the community has evolved, however. There is a consensus that the field has suffered from an inability to properly articulate its focus and practice (Noland et al. 2004, p. 24).

CONTROVERSIES IN PUBLIC HEALTH

According to the *Chambers Dictionary of Etymology* (2008, p. 215), a controversy is a debate marked by an expression of opposing views. From both its Latin and French etymology, controversy means to be "turned against" or "turn opposite." Controversies have major implications for public health as risks that entangle programs. According to Johnson (2009, p. 1), achieving public health outcomes for the society involves a contentious process of blending "science, politics and activism," resulting in battles fought along both political and behavioral lines. This author agrees with Johnson's argument, based on field experience and insight from case studies. These suggest that some of the controversies in public health are associated with a lack of balance in the three elements. Therefore, effective communication is indispensable to mitigating such contention.

Patil (2011, p. 97) underscores the propensity of public health to become enmeshed in contention because of the multiple factors that comprise its nature and the divergent opinions of those deemed to be experts. Examples of areas in public health that have been affected by controversies are family planning, malaria treatment, and climate change. Chapman (2001, p. 1227) contends that controversies in public health are not over the goal of public health but are instead about strategy for achieving health outcomes. Divergent ideas, theories, and propositions on how to resolve public health issues are fundamental sources of controversy.

This is congruent with an investigation by Martin and Richards (1995, p. 1). They found that conflicting research approaches and scientific findings give rise to a plethora of scientific and technical controversies. Thus, there is significant evidence that health interventions and approaches are predisposed to encounter scientific, technical, and public disagreements. However, the communications dimensions of such controversies have been given little attention in the literature of public health communication.

In examining risk communication and public health in the United Kingdom (UK), Bennet et al. (2010, p. 3) concluded that controversies about risk to public health in such areas as food safety, environmental issues, medical interventions, and lifestyle practices result in bizarre consequences in terms of their management or how to regulate public reactions. A similar conclusion was reached nearly forty years ago on the public health situation in the United States by Haddon (1975, p. 1342). He posited that various public health measures and interventions against small pox, cholera, typhoid, and childbed fever suffered from public storm and professional turbulence. According to that author, public health strategies brought stormy debates over quarantines, inoculations, closing down contaminated wells, making obstetrics sanitary, pasteurization of milk, fluoridation of water, and control of auto accident injuries.

From the review of the literature on public health or scientific controversies, the following is an inventory of common causes of controversies in public health:

- Controversy centered on opposing views of experts, policy makers, or scientists. Science as a basis of public health promotes divergent views because there is divergence in interpreting objective and empirical research findings. The battle over conflicting ideas fuels controversies.
- Controversy concerning claims and counter-claims of solutions to public health issues by mainstream medical practitioners and pseudo-medical people. A prominent example is the controversy about the origin of the HIV virus or claims by pseudo-scientists, herbalists, and religious healers that they can cure HIV.
- Controversy based on antagonism to public health interventions (policy, strategy, program, project or service) from organizational, institutional, cultural, religious, ideological, or economic interests. Sex education for young people has been opposed in many parts of the world on moral, ethical, religious, and cultural grounds. Resistance may involve organized misinformation, propaganda, or even

disinformation. Such has come from anti-vaccination groups, anti-male circumcision networks, and other groups opposed to specific public health interventions or services.

- Controversy that emanates from bad medicine, spurious science, or medical errors in implementing public health programs. The problem might be unethical medical practices, outright lies, or inadvertent mishaps in public health services.
- Conflict over statistics or data, either among public health officials or between development agencies and government. Many times public health programs have generated inconsistent estimates, statistics, projections, trend data, and figures. Inconsistencies cause major arguments among development partners and the public.
- Conflict originating in media gaffes, misreporting, or misrepresentation of health issues. Poor reporting or sensationalization by the media fuels public debates or already heated controversies on certain public health issues.

In sum, controversies are common in the field of public health, but they manifest complex communication undertones and overtones. The undertones imply that a communication issue is at the root of the controversy, while the overtones suggest that, even if the source of the controversy is technical, it normally has implications for communication management.

This chapter argues that many controversies are rooted in problems associated with specific elements of the communication process. Disputes may arise over the source of information, the channels used for disseminating information, the nature or purpose of the message itself, how the message is presented, or the receiver's level of understanding. It is impossible to match exact domains of public health controversies with the various elements of the communication process. In general, though, communication is central to many public health controversies. This conclusion is shared by Bennett et al. (2010, p. 3), who note that poor public health communication is often a factor in allowing concerns to escalate and opposing groups to become polarized.

To provide additional conceptual underpinning for the following case studies, some of the central issues around vaccine and condom controversies need to be explored. Here we will highlight the global context of some of the issues and the associated local and international communication imperatives.

CONTROVERSIES ON THE USE OF VACCINES

Mass vaccination is one of the most important public health interventions in history. A report published by the Center for Disease Control and Prevention of the U.S. (CDC) observed that "it has saved millions of lives over the years and prevented hundreds of millions of cases of diseases

(2007, p. 9)." Vaccines are the most effective and inexpensive tools to control, prevent, and eliminate infectious diseases (Alonso et al. 2013; Baleta et al. 2012; Chatterjee and O'Keefe 2006).

Nevertheless, since they were discovered as a tool for public health, vaccines have encountered substantial opposition globally. Disputes over vaccine are grounded on multiple moral, ethical, safety, and efficacy issues (Burgess et al. 2006; Dittmann 2001; Blackford 2001; Gellin et al. 2000). In a study on the history of vaccines, Chatterjee (2013, p. 10) observes that vaccines have been at the center of contentious debates in professional, public, and media spheres. In a larger sense, however, the vaccine controversy originates from two sources, divergent scientific views (Friedlander 2010, p. 10) or pure anti-vaccination propaganda (Dugger and McNeil 2004, p. 2).

Controversies on vaccines are not peculiar to developing countries. The UK debate over pertussis and MMR (measles, mumps and rubella) vaccines from 1998 to 2005 has been described as a landmark case in the history of vaccination controversies (BBC 2002; Burgess et al. 2006; Leask and McIntyre 2003). The debate caused parents to avoid taking their children for vaccination, which, in turn, led to outbreaks of vaccine-preventable diseases (Baker 2003; Bellaby 2003, p. 725). Furthermore, Cassidy (2010, p. 139) reported that the controversy had several dimensions. There was professional miscommunication by scientists, organized activism against vaccination, weak public confidence in vaccine safety, the media's role in framing issues, and input from various interest groups.

Several studies have highlighted the primary role of communication in vaccine promotion. For example, Baleta et al. (2012) examined the influence of advocacy, social mobilization, and communication in the introduction of three child health vaccines in South Africa. These researchers concluded that varied communication channels were used to ensure positive public reception of the vaccines. The study noted that the mobilization of local, regional, and national media and specialized health media mitigated the impact of misinformation and negative reaction to the vaccines. They found that the integration of advocacy, social mobilization and effective communication contributed to success. The seventh report of the Independent Monitoring Board of the Global Polio Eradication Initiative (IMB 2013, p. 6) notes that polio vaccination has faced negativity and anti-vaccination campaigns, rumors, outright lies, and propaganda in many parts of the world. The report highlights the importance of communication and social mobilization for rapid refutation of unfounded and unsubstantiated claims. Continuous dialogue with communities and education communication of parents and communities on the advantages of vaccination effectively advocate for polio vaccinations among public and social decision makers.

We can see that vaccine controversy is not new, and it must overcome the coordinated machinery of misinformation and disinformation. There is evidence that anti-vaccination campaigns are not relenting. In fact, they are more consistent and coherent in their account than official sources of information (Reyna 2012, p. 3793). Nevertheless, vaccination has inherent risks that need to be understood. Therefore, risk communication strategies must be incorporated into preparations for public health interventions. As argued by IMB (2013, p, 26) and Waisbord and Larson (2005, p. 2), investing in communication for immunization is crucial in persuading various populations to accept vaccination. The impact of information on immunization behavior is mediated by social, cultural, and political influences, as well as by the global environment. There are certainly communications ramifications in vaccine controversies.

CONTROVERSIES ON THE USE OF CONDOMS

The word *condom* seems to have originated with the work of a Dr. Condom, a physician living during the reign of Charles II (1660–1685). He apparently sought to do his patriotic duty by creating and popularizing a device intended to protect members of the royalty. Long before Dr. Condom, contraceptives may have been used by civilizations, particularly in Egypt, Greece, and Rome, where pregnancy prevention was generally considered a woman's responsibility (Collier 2007). James (2002) explains that contraception methods were female-controlled devices. Before the fifteenth century in Asia, some Chinese condoms were made of oil silk paper, while the Japanese used lamb intestines or tortoise and animal horn (Collier 2007, p. 60). The effectiveness of these devices in preventing pregnancy and the spread of infectious diseases was not documented (Sparrow and Lavill 1994; Albert, Warner, Hatchett, Trussell, and Bennett 1995). The prophylactic sheath condom, also known as a rubber, raincoat, goalie, glove, hoodie or preservative, is made of latex rubber for protection against disease. Condoms have diverse uses in public health, but primarily utilized as a contraceptive or protective prophylactic device (Waugh 2010; Rutherford 2008; Maharaj and Cleland 2006). Despite the recognized role of condoms in public health, they are susceptible to a considerable amount of controversy. For instance, Stryker (quoted in Ramos 1996, p. 149) notes that "condoms seldom escape controversy. Their very mention can provoke an uproar." The statement captures the emotional power of condoms in various societies.

Part of the controversy stems from divergent views of condom efficacy. One interagency UN-WHO position statement on condoms describes male condoms as "the single most efficient, available technology to reduce the sexual transmission of HIV and other sexually transmitted infection" (UNAIDS/WHO/UNFPA 2009, p. 1). The statement also notes that the lack of information and limited access to condoms is a major contributor to the increasing number of young people infected with HIV. One other condom problem, according to Rutherford (2008, p. 276) and Winskell et al. (2011, p. 951) is that condoms prevent HIV only when used properly and consistently. The caution, "when used properly and consistently" suggests the central need for risk communication on condom use.

In addition to the disagreement on their efficacy and potency, questions have been raised about whether condom use is compatible with marriage or whether it promotes extramarital affairs (Chimbiri 2007; Williamson 2006). Other matters raised include whether condoms contain worms or break easily (Siegler 2012) and whether they are effective if the intention to use them is not followed by actual use (Baele et al. 2001; Bosompra 2001). There is the question of how they interfere with pleasure (Fontenberry 2010; Philpott et al. 2006) and over the potential of risk compensation due to poor risk perception (Richens et al. 2000). Following the research trend, this author suggests that public debates on condoms will receive more attention in public health research, but it is crucial to address the communication upshots of such disputes.

INTERNATIONAL DIMENSION OF CONDOM CONTROVERSY

The condom debate in public health has international dimensions that relate to trans-national communications. For instance, in 2009, Pope Benedict said condoms were not the solution to the problem of AIDS in Africa. While the Pope was merely restating the position of the Roman Catholic Church (Benagiano et al. 2011), many commentators contended that the controversy generated by the statement pushed the envelope on condom contentiousness (Israely 2009, p. 2). Although the Vatican defended the Pope's position, local, national, and international media and development agencies suggested that Pope Benedict distorted scientific evidence on the role of condoms in public health.

Certainly, the dispute with the Pope is the kind of issue that must be dealt with by communication if public health interventions are to succeed. First, the Pope's comments exemplify the divide between the scientific positions on condom efficacy and the old contentious moral debate on the use of condoms. Second, the situation illustrates the complexity of managing the media fall out from controversial statements of major sources of information in the society. Third, it underlines the impact of message source, in this case a high-level source, on public, political, and media agenda. These are major concerns with important communication dimensions.

This brief review of contention regarding vaccines and condoms shows that disagreements manifest themselves in various forms across the public health spectrum. Much of the controversy about vaccines and condoms emanate from contrary positions of policy and technical experts and from the risks associated with their use. This review prepares us to understand the communication imperatives and implications of the polio vaccine crisis in Northern Nigeria and the condom debate in Kenya.

CONTENTION OVER POLIO IMMUNIZATION IN NORTHERN NIGERIA

Nigeria is a polio endemic country, and vaccination is one of the foremost medical advances toward polio eradication. However, in 2003, many state governments, led by Kano State, boycotted the immunization drive by the WHO to immunize 15 million children. The backlash was based on rumors that the vaccines were laced with anti-fertility drugs intended to reduce the population of northern Nigeria (Chen 2004, p. 206).

The abandonment of polio immunization caused the exportation of polio from Nigeria to twenty countries across Africa, the Middle East, and South Asia. According to Agbeyede (2007, p. 40), by the end of 2003, Nigeria accounted for 45 percent of the world's polio cases and 70 percent of polio cases recorded in 2004. A number of advocacy strategies and communication activities implemented by the WHO, UNICEF, the CDC, bilateral governments, and others resolved the crisis and allowed the resumption of immunization in the country.

In 2008 some states in northern Nigeria rejected polio vaccination due to concerns raised by Islamic leaders on the likelihood that the vaccines were deliberately infected with HIV by Western countries to harm Muslims (Kaufmann and Feldbaum 2009, p. 1093). An Islamic leader and president of the Nigeria Supreme Council for Sharia, as well as a licensed medical doctor, stirred the hornet's nest. His pronouncement on vaccine safety and associated risks halted polio immunization in the country. His message was, "There were strong reasons to believe that the polio immunization vaccines were contaminated with anti-fertility drugs, contaminated with certain virus that cause HIV/AIDS, and contaminated with Simians virus that are likely to cause cancer" (BBC 2003).

The anti-vaccination campaign is sometimes traced to the broader divergence of opinion in the scientific community on polio vaccination. As a result, Nigeria became a distributor of polio nationally and a net exporter to many countries. Traces of wild polio virus from Nigeria were found in other parts of Africa and South Asia (Agbeyede 2007; Obadare 2005).

Studies have investigated the allegations raised by the Islamic leader, and the evidence is inconclusive. For example, the study "Contamination of Poliovirus Vaccines with Simian Virus 40 (1955–1963) and Subsequent Cancer Rates," published by the *Journal of the American Medical Association* in 1998 and 2010, found that "Simian virus 40 DNA has recently been detected in several rare human tumors." However, "after more than 30 years of follow up exposure to SD40-contaminated, polio virus vaccine was not associated with significantly increased rate of ependymomas and other brain cancers, osteosarcomas, or mesotheliomas in the United States" (Strickler et al. 2010, p. 292).

COMMUNICATION'S RAMIFICATIONS

Several lessons regarding communication can be drawn from Nigeria's controversy.

Rumors and Misconceptions Exist

Polio immunization proponents did not anticipate the existence of rumor, misconceptions, and anti-vaccination information. Religious and political leaders used numerous anti-vaccination arguments and propositions to influence the Islamic community (IMB 2013, p. 27). This included rumors that vaccinations were the West's revenge for the 9/11 attack.

The Importance of Risk Communication

Because of inadequate risk communication, the public failed to recognize the public health benefits of vaccination (Obadare 2005; Chen 2004). There are genuine concerns about vaccine safety since no vaccine is 100 percent safe. Moreover, there are additional potential risks from OPV vaccines, such as paralysis, cancer, and contamination (Strickler et al. 2010; Vernon 2003). Such risks call for making people aware through candid public education.

Mistrust of Western Outsiders

Mistrust of Western companies and their health interventions must be taken into account. Past mistakes have poisoned the well for some people. Nigeria, especially the Muslim areas, experienced medical calamity in the testing of new vaccines by the Pfizer Pharmaceutical Company in Kano State (Agbeyede 2007; Clements et al. 2006).

Weak Public Confidence

Public confidence was weak even in the population that had been vaccinated. There was no groundswell of proponents to consider the public health benefits of vaccination or consequences of rejection (WHO International Monitoring Board 2013, p. 28).

Trust in Leaders

People placed more trust in their political and Islamic leaders as sources of information. Parents tended to act on their messages, rather than on the information provided by experts and service providers, even with evidence that the vaccines were safe.

Media Coverage

In Nigeria, the media wrote and broadcast stories that only recycled rumors circulated by leaders. Anti-immunization messages were amplified through the mass media.

Unanswered Questions and Criticism

There was little robust rebuttal of anti-vaccination propaganda at all levels in Nigeria, especially at the community level. Vaccinators were not prepared to effectively handle the genuine questions posed by parents regarding vaccination risks.

After these problems came to light, a concerted attempt was carried out by various partners to resolve the crisis. Some of the specific actions were . . .

Advocacy to Influence Leaders

Several diplomatic advocacy activities were undertaken, including high-level face-to-face conversations of public health representatives with Nigerian authorities and UN agencies. An influential Nigerian in international affairs, Ibrahim Gambari, a senior adviser on African affairs to former UN Secretary General Kofi Anan, was appointed to facilitate dialogue with Islamic leaders. As an eminent Nigerian with substantial leverage within the Northern community, Gambari held consultations with various religious leaders to influence their position.

Involvement of International Organizations

International organizations such as the African Union (AU) and the Economic Community of West African States (ECOWAS) carried out advocacy and diplomatic activities to prevail on Nigerian authorities to negotiate with the Islamic group for a resuscitation of the polio campaign. High-level political discussions were also held with government officials to resolve the crisis.

Social Mobilization of Those with Local Influence

Targeted discussions and consultations were planned to educate and motivate local government leaders, social influencers, traditional rulers, and Islamic leaders. This involved thematic consultations, health promotion, and sensitization on polio eradication.

Use of Evidence

Various agencies used trend data, score cards, and impact assessment in their discussions with political and Islamic leaders. Efforts were made to make numbers tell the stories of children affected by polio to portray the impact of the boycott. Confidence building initiatives established credibility. For example, polio vaccines in Indonesia and India brought test results from outside Nigeria.

Media Advocacy

A host of media consultations, field projects, and sensitization efforts were conducted by development agencies to influence media agenda-setters and promote informed reporting on the issues. The public conversation was reshaped to accept resumption of the immunization program.

The combination of different communication activities at various levels of influence by agencies and stakeholders resulted in the resuscitation of the polio immunization program. Following the reimplementation of the program, the number of polio cases was reduced from 798 in 2008 to 397 in 2009 and only three in 2010. Nigeria has not had any major polio related controversies since the resolution of the crisis in 2008.

Nevertheless, a renewed approach to risk communication and social mobilization is needed for continuous engagement of local influencers, because there still exists a vibrant anti-vaccination propaganda machinery. It is also crucial to use adequate advocacy, social mobilization, and health education to deal with existing public concerns on existing polio vaccination programs and new ones that may emerge.

CONTENTION OVER CONDOM QUALITY, SHORTAGES, AND PROMOTION IN KENYA

In Kenya, condoms are recognized as critical to reproductive health interventions and HIV prevention. However, in the last few years, they have been at the center of heated debates that reveal a considerable need for communication. The contention stemmed from three issues, condom quality, condom supply, and condom promotion.

First, the mass media reported in 2009 that imported condoms lacked quality standards specified by the WHO. Samples of the condoms were subjected to quality tests and many were found to be of poor quality (*Kaiser Health News* 2002). Condoms that failed the test—"leaky condoms" as they were called—were displayed on national mass media and digital platforms. However, it was not clear whether the post-test process adhered to the WHO's policies for communicating results on quality testing standards.

Second, the country experienced a significant condom shortage in 2010. Among other reasons, the crisis was caused by communication breakdown among various agencies, poor internal communication within the procuring agency, and miscommunication in the clearing process. Following the shortage, media reported that some Kenyans were washing and re-using condoms while others were using polythene bags as alternatives (IRIN News Agency 2009).

Third, condom promotional campaigns caused considerable debate in 2013. A television advert promoting condom use within the context of extra-marital relationships was broadcast in May 2013. The one-minute TV advertisement led to a national uproar and was eventually pulled. Parents were reported to have found the it "embarrassing" while the religious leaders considered it "offensive" (*Daily Monitor* 2013). Although the Kenya National AIDS and STI Control Program defended the message as based on evidence and the HIV situation in the country, religious leaders said it depicted Kenya "as Sodom and Gomorra and not one that values the institution of marriage and family" (BBC 2013b).

Another condom promotion crisis was caused by a newspaper and billboard message purchased by the U.S.-based Catholics for Choice NGO in Nairobi. The sticking point was the message, "We believe in God. We believe that sex is sacred. We believe in caring for each other. We believe in using condoms. Good Catholics use condoms." Catholic leaders condemned the advertisement, saying it might plant a negative attitude that could destroy the moral fiber of the country (British Broadcasting Co. 2013a). They argued that the long-standing position of the Catholic Church on condoms had not changed. However, the sponsor of the campaign said the ad's message was based on evidence (Kibira 2013, p. 2). Catholics caught up in the controversy expressed differing views.

COMMUNICATION'S RAMIFICATIONS

Major communication imperatives and implications can be drawn from the condom campaign.

Weakened Public Confidence in Condom Quality

Public confidence in condoms sagged as a result of the poor quality and shortage crisis. Media reports suggest that the controversy over quality of condoms eroded public confidence in the comprehensive condom program agenda.

Unintended Effect of Public Health Message

The condom promotion activities revealed a disconnect between source and receiver in the communication process. While the source (government agencies in charge of HIV programs) held that the condom ads targeted married people with evidence-based information, some of the receivers (religions groups and many individuals) thought that they promoted immorality.

Media coverage

The mass media covered the controversy from various angles. Some of the headlines were:

- "Kenya Condom Advert Pulled After Religions Complaint" (British Broadcasting Co. 2013b),
- "Kenya Condom Ad Sparks Debate" (Global Health News and Commentary 2013),
- "Anger and Anxiety over Leaky Condoms" (IRIN News Agency 2009),
- "Kenyan Religious Leaders up in Arms over Condom Advert" (*Daily Monitor* 2013),
- "The Politics of Condoms" (*The Star* 2013),
- "Walking 26KM for a Condom (IRIN News Agency 2010), and
- Racy Condom Ad Sparks Controversy in Kenya (*Kaiser Health News* 2002).

Media coverage gave significant attention to various elements of the controversy. The coverage influenced the direction of public discussion on the issue.

Online Conversation

Social media were tools for public conversation, including messages making fun of the fact that Kenyans were washing and drying condoms or using polythene bags due to the shortage. However, a Facebook campaign against the controversial TV commercial was also established by an opposition group.

Reactions from Interest Groups

Interest groups reacted to the controversy in a variety of ways. The network of people living with HIV organized a demonstration to press their rights. The network of commercial sex workers advocated that government take responsibility for ensuring access to quality condoms. Young people largely turned to social media for ventilation on the issue.

International Dimensions

The controversy has a sub-regional impact. Rwanda banned condom imports from Kenya and Tanzania and said that condoms from Kenya would be tested further. This underscores the need for advocacy within such regional economic institutions as the East African Community (EAC) and the South African Development Council (SADC). There were reports that Kenyan condoms implicated in the quality saga were banned in Zambia.

Organizational Communication

The condom program in Kenya is supported by various agencies, including government, international development organizations and local NGOs. The condom shortage was attributed to inadequate internal communication that led to delays in procurement and poor forecasting by the procuring agent. To avoid a public relations backlash, some agencies were more interested in sustaining their image than in addressing the problem. Several organizational communication issues related to the WHO testing standards. The guidelines clearly specified that tests should be carried out in approved institutions under the same quality on which the condoms were produced. However, there were reports that different testing parameters were used, which point to the challenge of adhering to guiding principles.

Government estimates suggest that 85,000 Kenyans die of HIV every year, while 1.6 million are living with the virus (British Broadcasting Co. 2013a). New studies report that 44 percent of new infections occur among married people, and as many as 30 percent of couples had multiple sexual partners (Kibira 2013). The public debate generated by the condom advertisement and billboard campaign raised the profile of tricky issues in family health such as sex, which is not normally discussed in public. It also contributed to the wider public debate on social and behavior change on HIV prevention.

The condom debate in Kenya went on through July 2013. Overall, it demonstrates the need for integrated communication in promoting public health interventions.

LESSONS TO BE LEARNED FROM TWO CONTROVERSIES

From common threads in the theoretical framework and the major issues raised in the two case studies, five basic lessons can be learned. We will look at areas of convergence and divergence in relation to the communications ramifications.

1. Multi-level Influence

The case studies have confirmed that public health planners need to focus on different target groups or different levels of influence in health communication. This view is consistent with studies that highlight the ecological approach to health promotion and strategic levels of influence. Individual, interpersonal, institutional, community, and policy levels must be taken into account in trying to achieve public health outcomes (Glanz 2002; Mittelmark et al. 2008; McLeroy et al. 1988; Smedley and Smye 2000). The ability to address multiple levels of influence is fundamental to achieving individual and social outcomes. This is shown in the polio immunization case study, which illustrated the importance of engaging with individual parents who need to take their children to immunization centers, informal groups that influence the decision of parents, religious groups who are the gatekeepers for the Islamic community, service providers who have direct interactions with parents, the mass media that influence the public and political agenda through news-framing and agenda-setting function, and government policy makers who take part in decision making on the issue.

Engagement with religious institutions was found to be important in swaying their positions on immunization. Nevertheless, this should not be limited to the crisis situation alone. Engagement should be carried out on a continuous basis (Chen 2004; World Health Organization International Monitoring Board 2013; Obadare 2005). A similar pattern of engagement with those at various levels of influence is illustrated by the condom controversy case study. It was crucial to hold consultation with religious groups, government officials, and development partners. Media influences public discourse. Institutions who act to procure and promote need to be in the discussion.

In addition, both cases have significant international dimensions, raising the issue of transnational advocacy and communication. Due to global connectivity through information technology, the world is experiencing globalization of public health, including public health communication. Transnational public health advocacy and communication is a cardinal group of influencers to consider in communication.

2. Multi-strategic Communication

Various strategic communication approaches are needed to reach those at multiple levels of influence. This includes advocacy, social mobilization, community engagement, policy dialogue, and organizational communication. Influencing change during public health controversies involves engagement at various program levels (e.g., downstream, midstream, and upstream) and for diverse outcomes (e.g., policy, program, strategy, or service) levels. For both cases, advocacy was needed to influence key decision makers. Organizational communication helps multiple partners to communication with one voice. Social mobilization galvanizes momentum, while targeted client communication was needed for public health education. Concerning the condom shortage controversy, some agencies were concerned with protecting their image. During public health controversies, however, communication should not be seen as a public relations tool, but as a coordinated response towards risk reduction (Servaes and Malikhao 2010).

3. *Multi-media Mobilization*

Multi-media mobilization is a major element of strategic communication during public health controversies. Regardless of the nature of the dispute, the mass media usually becomes the central battleground. As shown in the two case studies, the mass media told people how to think about conflicting ideas, propositions, and theories. But it is pertinent to understand the dynamics of media coverage of science and public health controversies. Radford (2008) notes that journalism thrives on controversy. Hence, in covering science controversies, journalists are interested in the latest evidence or the latest twist. While there is truth in this view, media institutions are accountable in the task of ensuring responsible journalism, even in their coverage of health and scientific contentions.

Some studies on media effect in health controversies have indicated that the mass media contribute largely to the miscommunication of health issues (Bellaby 2010; Cassidy 2010). Seale's (2010, p. 865) position is that the mass media ignore findings that do not fit into the current media interest and launder data, which pass from one media institution to another. If, as Lutwick (2003) argued, media contribute to public misinformation of health issues, communication with media gatekeepers needs to be more effective.

Additionally, social media have become a major medium in broader health and social development. The case studies show that the internet was a major tool for private and public conversation during public health controversies. For instance, different social media platforms were used for private and public conversation on the condom crisis in Kenya, yet the Internet contains considerable anti-vaccination and anti-condom information. A study by Reyna (2012, p. 3794) gives evidence that the digital media amplify anti-vaccination information and other public health misinformation and disinformation, making the job of public health communicators more difficult. Therefore, public health communication practitioners should continually monitor the Internet to keep abreast of messages on public health issues, especially misinformation. This may be difficult to achieve in view of the freedom of expression on the Net, coupled with the absence of a global or central gatekeeper.

4. Multi-level Discourse

As previously noted, the nature of controversies results in arguments being "turned against" each other. Similarly, controversies lead to the discussion of multiple issues, generating different conversations and trying out different arguments. Opposition groups and coalitions challenge public health interventions through their strong lobbying or propaganda machinery (World Health Organization International Monitoring Board 2013; Friedlander 2010; Germain and Lifestrand 2009). Opposition to public health interventions is defended with diverse justifications and are grounded in a variety of intellectual standpoints. Hence, effective public health communication needs to prioritize which message to counter when dealing with opposition, whether in controversial or non-controversial contexts. Addressing opposition requires understanding the grounds of opposition, the robustness of evidence available, how the evidence is being deployed and how to manage the burden of proof in order to sway positions (Awodiya 2012; Rybacki and Rybacki, 2012; Toulmin et al. 1984). In order to neutralize opposition, this author proposes that public health communications practitioners develop several arguments for specific issues and audience groups, and for individual levels of influence. The information needs of different audience groups will be different, depending on the stage of the controversy.

5. Multi-risk Education

The case studies have demonstrated that controversies require good risk communication that reaches different target groups. Specifically for vaccine safety, Dittmann (2001, p. 2446) found that multiple levels of risk had to be addressed. These included the risk of vaccine preventable disease, risk reduction through immunization, benefits of immunization program compared to risk, and the risk of refusing or interrupting immunization. According to the WHO IMB (2013, p 23) and Obadare (2005), a major challenge in the Nigerian case study was the weak effort to communicate risk. However, communicating risks is difficult when the risks are unknown or when there is inadequate evidence (Bennett et al. 2010, p. 7; Calman 2002, p. 166).

CONCLUSIONS

Many conclusions can be drawn from this study. First, controversies in public health generate a mosaic of communication issues, imperatives, and implications. They also undermine the effectiveness of health policies, programs, or services. Second, examining health communication from the angle of health controversies provides public health practitioners with additional insights that can enrich program design and implementation. Based on this analysis, this study concludes that integrated public health communication that puts rights, risks, and responsibilities of key audience groups at the core of interventions is indispensable. Third, trust is a key feature of risk communication, but controversies undermine public trust and confidence in public health interventions. When trust is undermined, service is affected. Thus, public health communication needs to prioritize effective risk communication that enhances trust in the delivery of public health interventions. Finally, those planning communication interventions during controversies need to consider the challenges associated with communicating at various levels and structures in the society.

RECOMMENDATIONS AND SUGGESTIONS

The paper makes the following recommendations and suggestions for future research.

First, it is important to prioritize comprehensive, multidisciplinary courses in health communication for both schools of public health and mass communication institutions beyond tokenistic inclusion in their curriculum. Enhancing the competence of health professionals and mass communicators in Africa on the intricacies of public health dynamics and communication is fundamental to mitigating the impact of controversies in public health interventions.

Second, public health controversies emphasize why it is important to prioritize multi-agency communication in public health delivery. As Fischbacher-Smith (2010, p. 237) discovered, communicating across professional groups that use different languages is sometimes a major challenge in risk communication. Coordinated communication during public health controversies enhances the collective voice and message of partners.

Several risks need to be addressed during public health controversies. Some messages that those who promote condom use need to emphasize are consistent and correct use of condoms, risk compensation for noncompliance, and risk perception of the population. Further studies are needed to inform communication interventions around strategic risk communication and total market approach for demand generation. In addition, condom program advocates need to address the communication ramifications in the controversies, in order to generate an informed perspective on its promotion as a public health device.

In view of the avalanche of anti-vaccination campaigns, communication programs for polio eradication need to increase the focus on neutralizing misinformation. A multiagency approach is needed to achieve this result.

More interdisciplinary research is needed to investigate the communications ramifications of public health controversies and how best to practice health communication. Overall, this study maintains that the role of media during public health controversies deserves more attention in public health communication, in view of their capability for either communication or miscommunication regarding health issues.

BIBLIOGRAPHY

Agbeyede, L. (2007). "Risk Communication: the Overlooked Factor in the Nigeria Polio Immunisation Boycott Crisis," *Nigerian Medical Practitioner*, 51 (3): pp. 40–44.

Albert, A.E., et al. (1995). "Condom Use among Female Commercial Sex Workers in Nevada's Legal Brothels." *American Journal of Public Health* 85: pp. 1514–1520.

Alonzo, P.L., de Quadros, C.A., and Robert, A. (2013). "Editorial," *Vaccine* 315: pp. B3–B4.

Awodiya, D. (2012). *Human Communication: Principles, Processes and Context*, 2d Ed. New York: Springboard Communications.

Baele, J., Dusseldorp, E., and Maes, S. (2001). "Condom Use Self-efficacy: Effect on Intended and Actual Use in Adolescents," *Journal of Adolescent Health* 28: pp. 421–431.

Baleta, A.F., van den Heever, J., and Burnett, R. (2012). "Meeting the Need for Advocacy, Social Mobilization and Communication in the Introduction of Three New Vaccines in South Africa—Successes and Challenges," *Vaccine* 305: pp. C66–C71.

Baker, J.P. (2003). "The Pertussis Vaccine Controversy in Great Britain," *Vaccine* 21 (25–26): pp. 4003–4010.

Barnhart, R.K., ed. (1999). *Chambers Dictionary of Etymology*, Edinburgh: Chambers.

Bellaby, P. (2003). "Communication and Miscommunication of Risk: Understanding UK Parents' Attitude to Combined MMR Vaccination," *British Medical Journal* 327: pp. 725–728.

Benagiano, G., et al. (2011). "Condoms, HIV, and the Roman Catholic Church," *Reproductive BioMedicine Online* 22 (7): pp. 701–709.

Bennett, P., et al., eds. (2010). *Risk Communication and Public Health*. London: Oxford University Press, 229–243.

Blackford, J.K. (2001). "Immunization Controversy: Understanding and Addressing Public Misconceptions and Concerns," *The Journal of School Nursing* 1: pp. 32–37.

Bosompra, K. (2001). "Determinants of Condom Use Intention of University Students in Ghana: An Application of the Theory of Reasoned Action," *Social Science and Medicine* 52: pp. 1057–1069.

British Broadcasting Co. (2013a). "Kenya Condom Advert Opposed by Catholic Church," *BBC News*. Available at http://bbc.co.uk/news/world-africa-22449314. Accessed 23 July 2013.

———. (2013b). "Kenya condom advert pulled after religions complaint," BBC News, 20 March 2013. Available at http://www.bbc.co.uk/news/world-africa-21859665. Accessed 11 April 2013.

———. (2003). "Cleric Halts Nigeria Polio Drive," *BBC News*. Available at http://news.bbc.co.uk. Accessed 27 October 2003.

———. (2002). "Head to Head: MMR Controversy," *BBC News*. Available at http://news.bbc.co.uk.2/hi/uk_news/politics/1804079. Accessed 17 June 2013.

Brookings Institution (n.d.). *Innovative Health Financing: Donor Views on Progress, Problems, Opportunities and Strategy*. Washington, DC: Brookings Institution. Available at www.brookings.edu/~/media/projects/global%20health/donor_views.pdf.

Brunner, B.R., Larrisa, R., and Huber, B. (2010). "101 Ways to Improve Health Reporting: A Comparison of the Types and Quality of Health Information in Men's and Women's Magazines," *Public Relations Review* 25 (1): pp. 84–86.

Burgess, D.C., Burgess, M.A., and Leask, J. (2003). "The MMR Vaccination and Autism Controversy in the United Kingdom, 1998–2005: Inevitable Communication Outrage or a Failure of Risk Communication," *Vaccine* 24: pp. 3921–3928.

Calman, K. (2002). "Communication of Risk: Choice, Consent and Trust," *The Lancet* 360: pp.166–168.

Cassidy, R. (2010). "Risk Communication in the British Pertussis and MMR Vaccine Controversies." In Bennett, R.E., et al. eds. (2010). *Risk Communication and Public Health,* London: Oxford University Press.

CDC Foundation (2013). "What is Public Health?" Available at http://cdcfoundation.org.print/content/what-public-health. Accessed 12 June 2013.

Centers for Disease Control (2007). *Parents' Guide to Childhood Immunization.* Atlanta: Government Printing Office.

Chapman, S. (2001). "Advocacy in Public Health: Roles and Challenges," *International Journal of Epidemiology* 30: pp. 1226–1232.

Chatterjee, A., ed. (2013). *Vaccinophobia and Vaccine Controversies of the 21st Century.* New York: Springer.

Chatterjee, A., and O'Keefe, C. (2010). "Current Controversies in the USA Regarding Vaccine Safety," *Expert Review of vaccines* 9 (5): pp. 497–502.

Chen, C. (2004). "Rebellion Against Polio Vaccine in Nigeria: Implications for Humanitarian Policy," *African Health Sciences* 4 (3): pp. 205–207.

Chen, R.T., et al. (2001). "Challenges and Controversies in Immunization Safety," *Infectious Diseases Clinics of North America* 15 (1): pp. 21–39.

Chimbiri, A. (2007). "Condom Is an 'Intruder' in Marriage: Evidence from Rural Malawi," *Social Science and Medicine* 64: pp. 1102–1115.

Clemens, C.J., Greenough, P., and Shull, D. (2006). "How Vaccine Safety Can Become Political: The Example of Polio in Nigeria," *Current Drug Safety* 1: pp. 117–119.

Collier, A. (2007). *The Humble Little Condom: A History.* Amherst, NY: Prometheus Books.

Daily Monitor (2013). "Kenyan religious leaders up in arms over condom advert," 24 March 2013. Available at http://www.monitor.co.ug. Accessed 17 June 2013.

Dittmann, S. (2001). "Vaccine Safety: Risk Communication—a Global Perspective," *Vaccine* 19: pp. 2446–2456.

Dugger, C.W., and McNeil, D.G. (2004). "Rumor, Fear, Fatigue Hinder Final Push to End Polio." Health Systems Trust Website. Available at http://www.hst.org.za.

Finegan, J.R. Jr., and Viswanath, K. (2002). "Communication Theory and Health Behavior Change: The Media Studies Framework." In K. Glanz, B. Rimer, and F.M. Lewis, eds., *Health Behavior and Health Education: Theory, Research and Practice.* San Francisco, CA: Jossey-Bass, pp. 361–388.

Fischbacher-Smith, M. (2010). "Communicating Risk Among Publics and Between Organisations: The Case of Childhood Accidents." In R.E. Bennett et al., eds., *Risk Communication and Public Health.* London: Oxford University Press, pp. 229–243.

Fontenberry, J.D. (2010). "Fate, Desire and the Centrality of the Relationship to Adolescent Condom Use," *Journal of Adolescent Health* 47: pp. 219–220.

Friedlander, E. (2010). "The Anti-Immunization Activists: A Pattern of Deception," Available at http.www.pathguy.com/antiimmu.htm. Accessed 25 May 2013.

Gellin, B.G., Maibach, E.W., and Marcuse, E.K. (2000). "Do Parents Understand Immunizations: A National Telephone Survey," *Pediatrics* 106 (5): pp. 1097–1102.

Germain, A., and Lifestrand, J. (2009). "Women's Groups and Professional Organisations in Advocacy for Sexual and Reproductive Health and Rights," *International Journal of Gynecology and Obstetrics* 106 (2): pp. 185–187.

Glanz, K. (2002). "Perspectives on Groups, Organizations and Community Interventions." In Glanz, K.; Rimer, B.; and Lewis, F.M., eds., *Health Behavior and health Education: Theory, Research and Practice.* San Francisco, CA: Jossey-Bass, pp. 389–403.

Global Health News and Commentary (2013). "Kenya Condom Ad Sparks Debate." Available at htttp://blog.psiimpact.com/2013/03/Kenya-condom-ad-sparks.debate/. Accessed 7 June 2013.

Haddon, W., Jr. (1975). "Perspective on a Current Public Health Controversy," *American Journal of Public Health* 65 (12): pp. 1342–1344.

Institute of Medicine (2003). *The Future of Public's Health in the 21st Century*. Washington, DC: National Academy Press.

IRIN News Agency (2009). "Anger and Anxiety over Leaky Condoms." Available at http://www.plusnews.org. Accessed 11 April 2013.

Israely, J. (2009). "The Pope's Anti-condom Remarks: Candor over P.R," *Time* Magazine, March 19, 2009. Available at http://www.time.com. Accessed 7 June 2013.

James, S. (2002). "Of Lemons, Yams and Crocodile Dung: A Brief History of Birth Control," *University of Toronto Medical Journal* 79 (2): pp. 156–158.

Johnson, S.A. (2009). *Public Health Advocacy*. Edmonton, Alberta: Healthy Public Policy, Alberta Health Services.

Kaufmann, J.R., and Feldbaum, H. (2009). "Diplomacy and the Polio Immunization Boycott in Northern Nigeria." *Health Affairs* 28 (4): pp. 1091–1101.

Kaiser Health News (2002). "Racy Condom Ad Sparks Controversy in Kenya." Available at http://www.kaiserhealthnews.org/Daily-Report/2002/Marchdr00010098.aspx?=1. Accessed 10 April 2013.

Kibira, H. (2013). "The Politics of Condoms," *The Star* Website, 11 June 2013. Available at http://www.the-star.co.ke/news/article-123896/politics-condoms. Accessed: 17 June 2013.

Leask, J., and McIntyre, P. (2003). "Public Opponents of Vaccination: A Case Study," *Vaccine* 21: pp. 4700–4703.

Lutwick, S.M. (2000). "Pediatric Vaccine Compliance," *Pediatric Clinics of North America* 47: pp. 427–434.

Mcintyre, S. (2012). "Evidence in the Development of Health Policy," *Public Health* 126: pp. 217–219.

McLeroy, K.R., et al. (1988). "An Ecological Perspective on Health Promotion Programs," *Health Education Quarterly* 15 (4): pp. 351–377.

Maharaj, P., and Cleland, J. (2006). "Condoms Become a Norm in Sexual Culture of College Students in Durban, South Africa," *Reproductive Health Matters* 14 (28): pp. 104–112.

Martin, B., and Richards, E. (1995). "Scientific Knowledge, Controversy and Public Decision Making." In S. Jasanoff, et al., eds. *Handbook of Science and Technology Studies*. Newbury Park, CA: Sage, pp. 506–526.

Maticka-Tyndale, E., and Tenkrang, E. (2010). "A Multi-level Model of Condom Use Among Male and Female Upper Primary School Students in Nyanza, Kenya," *Social Science and Medicine* 71: pp. 616–625.

Mittelmark, M.B., et al. (2008). "Health Promotion." In K. Heggenhougen, ed. in chief; S. Quah, ed., *International Encyclopedia of Public Health*, 6 vols. Amsterdam: Elsevier.

Noland, V.J., Troxler, C., and Salemi, M.T. (2004). "School Health as Public Health," *Florida Public Health Review* 1: pp. 24–29.

Obadare, E. (2005). "A Crisis of Trust: History, Politics, Religion and the Polio Controversy in Northern Nigeria," *Patterns of Prejudice* 39 (3): pp. 265–284.

Omaswa, F., and Boufford, J. (2010). "Strong Ministries for Strong Health Systems Supporting Ministerial Health Leadership: A Strategy for Health Systems Strengthening." New York Academy of Medicine, pp. 1–32. Available at http://www.rockefellerfoundation.org/uploads/files/8819cca6-1738-4158-87fe-4d2c7b738932.pdf.

Patil, R.R. (2011). "Public Health Controversies: Common Characteristics," *Journal of Global Infectious Diseases* 3 (1): pp. 97–98.

Philpott, A.; Knerr, W.; and Boydell, V. (2006). "Pleasure and Prevention: When Good Sex is Safer Sex," *Reproductive Health Matters* 4 (28): pp. 23–31.

Qadeer, I. (2000). "Health Care Systems in Transition III. India, Part I: The Indian Experience," *Journal of Public Health Medicine*, 22 (1): p. 2532.

Radford, T. (2008). "Reporting on Controversies in Science." Available at http://www.scidev.net/en/practical-guides/reporting-on-controversies-in-science.html. Accessed 4 April 2013.

Ramos, P.S. (1996). "The Condom Controversy in the Public Schools: Respecting a Minor's Right to Privacy," *JSTOR: University of Pennsylvania Law Review* 145 (1): pp. 149–55.

Richens, J., Imrie, J., and Copas, A. (2000). "Condoms and Seat Belts: the Parallels and the Lessons," *The Lancet* 355 (January 2000): pp. 400–403.

Reyna, V.F. (2012). "Risk Perception and Communication in Vaccination Decisions: A Fuzzy-trace Theory Approach," *Vaccine* 30: pp. 3790–3797.

Rutherford, G.W. (2008). "Condoms in Concentrated and Generalised HIV Epidemics," *The Lancet* 372: pp. 275–276.

Rybacki, K., and Rybacki, D. (2012). *Advocacy and Argumentation: An Introduction to Argumentation*, 7th Ed. Boston: Allyn & Bacon.

Seale, C. (2010). "How the Mass Media Report Social Statistics: A Case Study Concerning Research on End-of-life Decisions," *Social Science and Medicine* 71: pp. 861–868.

Servaes, J., and Malikhao, P. (2010). "Advocacy Strategies for Health Communication," *Public Relations Review* 30 (1): pp. 42–49.

Siegler, A.J., et al. (2012). "Condoms 'Contain Worms' and 'Cause HIV' in Tanzania: Negative Condom Beliefs Scale Development and Implications for HIV Prevention," *Social Science and Medicine* 75: pp. 1685–1691.

Smedley, B.D., and Smye, S.L., eds. (2000). *Promoting Health: Interventions Strategies from Social and Behavioural Research*. Washington, DC: National Academy Press.

Sparrow, M.J., and Lavill, K. (1994). "Breakage and Slippage of Condoms in Family Planning Clients," *Contraception*, 50: pp. 117–129.

Strickler, H., et al. (2010). "Contamination of Poliovirus Vaccines with Simian Virus 40 (1955–1963) and Subsequent Cancer Rates," *Journal of the American Medical Association*, 279 (4): pp. 292–295.

Tarantola, D. (2000). "Presentation at the Economic, Social, Cultural Rights Committee, May 8 2000," Geneva: WHO.

Toulmin, S.; Rieke, R.; and Janik, A. (1984). *An Introduction to Reasoning*, 2d Ed. New York: Macmillan.

UNAIDS/WHO/UNFPA (2010). "Condoms and HIV Prevention: Position Statement Number 09." Geneva: UNAIDS.

Vernon, J.G. (2003). "Immunization Policy: from Compliance to Concordance?" *British Journal of General Practice*, 53: 399–404.

Waisbord, S. and Larson, H. (2005). "Why Invest in Communication for Immunization? Evidence and Lessons Learned." Publication of the Health Communication Partnership, Johns Hopkins Bloomberg School of Public Health/Center for Communication Programs and the United Nation Children's Fund.

Waugh, M. (2010). "The Role of Condom Use in Sexually Transmitted Disease Prevention: Facts and Controversies," *Clinics in Dermatology* 29 (5): pp. 549–552.

Williamson, N., et al. (2006). "A Qualitative Study of Condom Use Among Married Couples in Kampala, Uganda," *Reproductive Health Matters* 14 (28): pp. 89–98.

Winskell, K., Obyerodhyambo, O., and Stephensen, R. (2011). "Making Sense of Condoms: Social Representations in Young People's HIV-related Narratives from Six African Countries," *Social Science and Medicine* 72: pp. 953–961.

World Health Organization International Monitoring Board (2013). "International Monitoring Board Global Polio Program Eradication Initiative." Seventh Report. Geneva: WHO International Monitoring Board.

World Health Organization Regional Committee for Europe (2008). "Behaviour Change Strategies and Health: The Role of Health Systems." Resolution of the 58th session, Tbilisi, Georgia, 15–18 September 2008, 3. Available at http://www.euro.who.int/__data/assets/pdf_file/0016/70261/RC58_eres08.pdf.

V

Health Education: Cultural Factors and Funding

ELEVEN

HIV/AIDS in Africa

Contradictions, Controversies, and Containment

Charles C. Okigbo, Nan Yu, and Angella Napakol

INTRODUCTION

HIV/AIDS in Africa presents a very complicated picture because of its unique characteristics and the difficulty of fully understanding its etiology, courses, and impact on people and their communities. Persistent contradictions are evident in the conflicting views on circumcision, homosexuality, and sex education. Similarly, pervasive controversies are exemplified in different views of HIV/AIDS funding, the value of social media, and the new environment of complacency.

However, there is abundant hope on account of the significant positive results from effective uses of anti-retroviral (ARV) treatments that underline the unfolding expectations that the disease can now be checked. In the final analysis, the challenges of African HIV/AIDS healthcare are part of the global healthcare management system. Sustainable development of Africa is inextricably linked to the success of African healthcare management.

The pandemic poses challenges for effective healthcare management, with the attendant intercultural dissonance and its tripartite characteristics of contradictions, controversies, and containment. Globally, healthcare management is facing serious challenges of funding, public education, behavioral change, and resistant cultural practices, all of which are implicated in the global AIDS phenomenon and its containment. These apply with force and potency in Africa, where HIV/AIDS continues to be an ever-present danger to individuals, communities, and nation states. It is one of the greatest threats to the development of sustainable economies and one of the biggest drains on healthcare resources across the continent.

The full extent of its deleterious consequences extends beyond its toll as an incurable viral pandemic. It wreaks havoc through loss of trained personnel, strains the public health and education systems, reduces local productivity, and contributes to the continent's pervasive negative image. The pandemic continues to be a serious threat to the sustainable development of the continent and presents many difficulties in diverse areas for personal and national well-being. Prewitt (1988, p. ix) rightly noted that "even these many development-related difficulties do not exhaust the harm being visited on Africa by AIDS."

HIV/AIDS made its historic appearance in Africa in the early 1980s, when it was regarded as the "mysterious disease," with strange symptoms. Its mystique has never diminished, even after more than three decades of grappling with its etiology. Even when HIV/AIDS manifests differently in different regions of the continent, it is interculturally dissonant in the sense that awareness or knowledge of it does not accord with expected behavior. Higher levels of knowledge do not guarantee lower rates of infection. Although considerable progress has been made in HIV/AIDS healthcare management in Africa, much of what is known can best be characterized as contradictory because of conflicting views, and widespread disagreements about funding for its treatment. Healthcare planners cannot seem to agree on the best ways to manage the phenomenon. There are, however, some silver linings in the sky, arising from stabilization and containment measures that are yielding positive results in AIDS healthcare management. Largely, the good news has to do with treatment therapies and changing social values.

In this chapter, we describe the variegated nature of the pandemic and illustrate its contradictions and controversies, even when the situation holds good promise for containment. The disastrous effects of the pandemic in Africa are not in doubt, nor are its implications as a drain on healthcare resources.

HIV/AIDS IN AFRICA: TRIPLE DISASTER

The global HIV/AIDS phenomenon takes on a uniquely more sinister and pernicious garb in Africa than on any other continent, not only in its unparalleled ravaging nature but also in the way it catalyzes other health problems. The pandemic provides fodder for Africa's detractors who are ever so eager to find cause to castigate the continent for the disastrous consequences. Indeed, it is more than a simple disaster. Prewitt (1988, xi) referred to AIDS in Africa as a triple disaster which provides unwarranted justification for some of the continent's detractors:

> There is the tragedy of the disease itself, the human suffering, and death. There is [sic] the multiple ways in which AIDS complicates the already daunting development problems facing the continent and threatens to reverse hard-won advances. Finally, the special characteristics of AIDS—its mysterious origin, its resistance to biomedical treatment, its association with social deviance and its hint of exotic behavior—provide a ready justification for those who would just as soon not be bothered by Africa, its need for international aid, and its development difficulties.

HIV/AIDS in Africa is not only a triple disaster but also a very complicated healthcare and socio-cultural problem. The complexities are underscored by the dauntingly high prevalence of the infection; the full demographic impact on women, children, and young adults; the varying rates of infection in different countries and regions; and the different responses by national political leadership, among other groups involved. The healthcare impact of AIDS in Africa is tremendous and further complicated because the compromised immunity leads to greater incidence of other diseases such as malaria, tuberculosis, respiratory infections, diarrhea, pneumonia, and sexually transmitted diseases.

AFRICA AT RISK: PREVALENCE

The average adult HIV prevalence in Africa is 4.6 percent, which is significantly higher than the global prevalence of 0.8 percent (WHO 2013b). By 2011, an estimated 23.5 million people who were living with HIV resided in Sub-Saharan Africa, constituting over 69 percent of the global HIV burden. The continent also accounted for 92 percent of the pregnant women living with HIV and 90 percent of children who acquired HIV in 2011, according to UNAIDS (2012a).

Swaziland had the highest HIV prevalence, at 26 percent of the population, in the world as of 2011. That year, South Africa, which is in the same region with Swaziland, had the world's largest national population of people living with HIV (5.6 million) and a prevalence rate of 17.3 percent (UNAIDS 2012a, 2012b). Africa, especially the countries of the Sub-Saharan areas, have been at greatest risk on account of the high prevalence rate and the devastating demographic, social, and economic consequences of the pandemic. This large continent stands alone at the front of the global HIV battle (DeCock, Mbori-Ngacha, and Marum 2002; Rugalema 2000; Whiteside 2002). This unparalleled severity has led many to conclude that, but for Africa, the global HIV/AIDS pandemic "would still be tragic but substantially less important" (DeCock, Mbori-Ngacha, and Marum 2002, 68).

The situation of high prevalence is made worse by the tragic incidence of new cases, especially among children and other members of vulnerable groups. In such countries as Angola, DR Congo, Equatorial Guinea, and Guinea-Bissau, cases of new HIV infections increased between 2009 and 2011, according to UNAIDS (2012a). North Africa, which has fared better than other parts of the continent, reported a 17 percent increase in AIDS mortality and a 35 percent increase in the rate of new HIV infections.

Although new infections are no longer equated with a death sentence, on account of the effects of anti-retroviral (ARV) medications, the unavailability of these treatments among needy Africans heightens the risk for AIDS mortality. About 43 percent of people eligible for ARV medications in Sub-Saharan Africa had not received the proper treatment as of 2011 (UNAIDS 2012a, 2012b). Whereas ARVs are widely accepted in many parts of the world where they are readily available, in Africa, the challenges come from unavailability and also the social stigma associated with being identified as an ARV user and thus a HIV/AIDS case.

Negative social stigma in African communities impedes the effectiveness of ARV interventions and worsens the situation for better management of the HIV pandemic (Rankin, et al. 2005). The fear of social stigma is known to prevent some expectant women from getting HIV testing because a positive test result is tantamount to outright ostracism for themselves and their babies. Fear of social stigma is also responsible for nonuse of condoms among some married couples in Africa (Rankin et al. 2005). In many African communities, it is common for people identified as living with HIV to be isolated by their social networks and even their own families. In some African communities, the entire family may be shunned if one member is infected. There can be serious financial implications because others will not do business with a "HIV-tainted" person. Some families do not list HIV/AIDS as the cause of death in newspaper obituaries (Rankin et al. 2005). It is commonly believed that more than half of people living with HIV in Zambia, Rwanda, and Kenya have experienced verbal attacks by others because of their health status. In Cameroon, 13 percent of people living with HIV have encountered rejections at health services outlets as a result of their HIV status (UNAIDS 2012a). The high prevalence notwithstanding, it is not an entirely hopeless case.

HOPE RISING

Even though Africa still hosts more people living with HIV than any other continent, the intervention and education programs launched in the past decades have produced significant and positive results. UNAIDS (2012b) reported that AIDS-related deaths in Africa were successfully reduced by one-third between 2005 and 2011. The percentage of decline in AIDS-related deaths was observed in most African countries in this six-year period. Some countries dropped the death rate by more than half, as was the case in Botswana (71 percent), Rwanda (68 percent), Namibia (60 percent), Zambia (56 percent), Ethiopia (53 percent), and Cote d'lvoire (51 percent).

According to UNAIDS (2012b), an estimated 9 million lives have been saved by the more available and affordable ARV medications. The cost of standard ARV was dramatically reduced from U.S. $10,000 per person annually to about U.S. $100 in some countries (UNAIDS 2012b). From 2009 to 2011, about 2.3 million people have been added to the HIV treatment programs in Sub-Saharan Africa. Some African countries, particularly Botswana, Namibia, Rwanda, Swaziland, and Zambia, achieved over 80 percent treatment coverage in the targeted population. A significant increase of HIV treatment coverage has been observed in Zimbabwe (118 percent), South Africa (75 percent), and Kenya (59 percent) in recent years (UNAIDS 2012b). This change dramatically ended the HIV-epidemic peak of the late 1990s and significantly improved the quality of life for people living with HIV. Many of them can return to their regular life routines, continue to work, and take care of their families.

New HIV infections in Sub-Saharan Africa reportedly decreased from 2.4 million in 2001 to 1.8 million in 2011, a 25 percent decline. Over this ten-year period, many African countries experienced a sharp decrease in the rate of new infections. For example, the newly infected cases dropped by 90 percent in Ethiopia, 72 percent in Malawi, 71 percent in Botswana, 68 percent in Namibia, 66 percent in Ghana, and 60 percent in Burkina Faso. The rate of new HIV infections dropped by 50 percent to 58 percent in Zimbawe, Gabon, Rwanda, Togo, Zambia, Djibouti, and the Central Africa Republic. Between 2001 and 2011, a relatively slower pace in reducing new infections has been observed in some other countries, particularly Kenya (32 percent), Mozambique (31 percent), Niger (29 percent), Swaziland (37 percent), and Sierra Leone (37 percent) (UNAIDS 2012a, 2012b).

Other encouraging news on the African HIV/AIDS situation includes the widespread success in reducing the number of children who are newly infected with HIV. In more than twenty African countries, there is a decline in the number of children newly acquiring HIV. In such countries as Burundi, Kenya, Namibia, South African, Togo, and Zambia, the rate of new infections among children has been successfully reduced by as much as 40 percent to 59 percent. This success is largely attributed to the increasing strategic initiatives and healthcare services designed to prevent mother-to-child transmissions (PMTCT). In twenty-one African countries, PMTCT has been extensively integrated into maternal and child healthcare. For example, in Botswana, Ghana, Namibia, South Africa, Swaziland, and Zambia, the PMTCT covered up to 75 percent of the targeted population by 2011 (UNAIDS 2012a, 2012b). The signs of hope in HIV/AIDS treatment in Africa come, not only from the expanded public education, increasing ARV treatment, and better services to prevent mother-to-child transmissions, but also from increasing investments by individual African countries.

In the past, almost every African country relied nearly exclusively on international donors, but recently, many countries are becoming more self-reliant. South Africa, which has made the largest domestic funding for AIDS in Africa, invested U.S. $1.9 billion in 2011, a five-fold surge from 2006. Other countries, such as Kenya, Togo, and Zambia, have significantly increased their domestic investment for HIV/AIDS prevention. Most of the expenses covered are for programs in basic HIV prevention and treatment; promoting male circumcision and condom use; enhancing treatment, care, and support for people living with HIV; preventing mother-to-child transmission; and enhancing behavioral changes.

There is no doubt that HIV/AIDS is an ever serious and present danger in Africa. However, there are silver linings in the clouds, which are now leading many to see the situation as reflecting a mixed picture.

THE MIXED PICTURE: HALF-FULL OR HALF-EMPTY

Globally, HIV/AIDS remains an evolving mystery in spite of the significant advances in understanding its etiology and seemingly overcoming it, albeit temporarily, with effective ARV treatments. In Africa, it is still wrapped in abundant contradictions and endless controversies, which are punctuated with modest containment. There is no doubt that as ARV programs become more common and affordable, the disease once regarded as always fatal, is increasingly being commonly perceived as a chronic illness, leading many to argue that HIV/AIDS is no longer as readily stigmatized by the society as it used to be.

People living with HIV can live relatively long and stable lives by receiving proper medications, thereby lessening the social stigma associated with the condition. This is true in countries like Brazil (Abadia-Barrero and Castro 2006), but not necessarily in Africa. In Rwanda, for instance, the visible change of body appearance, a side effect of taking ARV medications, can generate social stigma and inhibit medical adherence (Mutimura, Stewart, and Crowther 2007). A longitudinal study that investigated over 1,400 people living with HIV in Lesotho, Malawi, South Africa, Swaziland, and Tanzania revealed that although social stigma declined over time for affected individuals surprisingly, those following the treatment experienced more social stigma over time than people who did not. Thus, as valuable as ARVs may be as containment instruments, they can lead to contradictory and controversial results with regard to stigma. Thus they demand careful attention from healthcare professionals, especially in treating new patients.

The African HIV/AIDS glass is both half-empty and half-full, as the picture is both disheartening and hopeful and promising. Contradictions are evident in the changing prevalence, the increasing and declining number of cases of new infections, and perceptions of stigma, but especially in the roles of circumcision, homosexuality, and sex education in the African situation. Not to be underrated are the controversies associated with funding, especially the President's Emergency Plan for AIDS Relief (PEPFAR), social media, and complacency. The irony in the contradictions and controversies is made more poignant by the prospects for containment, which find expression in the putative value of ARVs, decreasing incidence of new cases, and Africa's changing social values. The reductions of HIV mortality and new infections definitely provide rising hope. Yet the lags in HIV prevention services and the rise in new HIV cases in some countries lead many to agree that the crisis of HIV/AIDS is not over. It is at best only contained in the face of contradictions and controversies.

AFRICAN HIV/AIDS AND CONTRADICTIONS

HIV/AIDS in Africa presents a perplexing picture that is wrapped in perennial contradictions, some of which have proved impervious to resolution and correction. Some of the earliest untruths and misinformation about its true origin, nature, causes, manifestations, and consequences have persisted after over three decades of purposeful public enlightenment by local and international organizations. Some of the issues surrounding HIV infection stand at the confluence of culture, tradition, personal beliefs, religion, morality, and biological or sexual drives. The contradictions associated with HIV/AIDS in Africa are bound to change from time to time and from one region to another.

At this writing, three of the most noteworthy contradictions relate to circumcision, homosexuality, and sex education.

Circumcision

It is not surprising that circumcision is a contradictory subject in HIV/AIDS discourse in Africa because, whereas it is wholly accepted among some ethnic groups, it is abhorred and derided among others. The situation has become more confusing with recent campaigns against female circumcision while other campaigns are, at the same time, calling for stepping up the practice among all male members in the belief that it can contribute to fewer new HIV infections. Some studies show that, when provided by well trained professionals in safe settings, medical male circumcision (MMC) potentially reduces sexually transmitted diseases and specifically reduces the risk of contracting HIV in heterosexual men by 60 percent (AVERT 2013). Based on successful randomized studies in Kenya, South Africa, and Uganda, which attested that MMC reduced the rate of HIV contraction by 60 percent, 53 percent, and 51 percent respectively (WHO 2013), the World Health Organization (WHO) and the Joint United Nations Program on HIV/AIDS (UNAIDS) encouraged the scale up of MMC as a preventative strategy against the spread of HIV. Indeed voluntary MMC was encouraged in thirteen African countries, including Uganda, South Africa, Tanzania, Namibia, and Malawi (Hankins, Forsythe, and Njeuhmeli 2011).

However, the seemingly beneficial prevention tool is surrounded by contradictions, and thus has been challenged by scientists, health practitioners, and government officials, among others. Cultural beliefs among some African groups make MMC less attractive, especially in those societies where the practice was traditionally nonexistent. For example, in the Kenyan Luo community in Nyanza province, the region in which the epidemic is most serious (15.3 percent), people who opt for circumcision are ridiculed by their peers. The fear of appearing to be too eager for foreign values has made some elders less supportive, even when they do not oppose it (IRIN News 2012). Respect for traditional values intersects with local politics, ethnic practices, and religion to compound the contradictions associated with circumcision, as is the case in Malawi (Parkhurst, Chilongozi, and Hutchinson 2013). Due to such contradictions, many African countries are reluctant to adopt the practice wholesale.

Nevertheless, such countries as Uganda, Kenya, and Botswana have adopted the practice. The Ugandan National HIV/AIDS Strategic Plan 2011/2012 revealed that 380,000 men had been circumcised by March 2012. The government was determined to circumcise 1 million men every year for the next three years to achieve the target of 4.2 million men (IRIN News 2012).

One contradiction about circumcision is based on the observation that it provides some ill-informed men with a false sense of protection, as they wrongly believe circumcision makes them immune to infection after their operation. The true value of circumcision in the fight against HIV/AIDS is likely to remain contradictory and controversial. For example, Sub-Saharan Africa, where circumcision is common, still has the highest HIV/AIDS prevalence rate in the world, with some countries having prevalence rates as high as 24 percent (AVERT 2013), while Europe, with its lower incidence of circumcision, has lower rates of HIV/AIDS. If circumcision presents a contradictory picture in Africa, so does homosexuality, which is often clothed in a religious and moral fashion.

Homosexuality

There are few issues on which different African countries have more agreement among themselves than the issue of homosexuality. It is massively disapproved of by governments, religious groups, and traditional leaders. Not even civil society and human rights organizations in Africa have risen enthusiastically and potently to the defense of gays and lesbians on the continent. According to Naurath (2007), Africa has the lowest acceptance level of gays and lesbians. When asked if the place they live is good or bad for homosexuals only 8 percent of African respondents answered in the affirmative, while 77 percent said it was not good. In thirty-eight out of fifty-two African countries, homosexuality is illegal (Afro-News 2009), and it is closely associated with immorality and sexually transmitted infections. In such countries as Nigeria and Uganda, the legislative bodies have promulgated stringent laws against homosexuality.

Even though there is no significant association between homosexuality, or men having sex with men, and HIV/AIDS, a combination of opposition from legislators and politicians, disapproval by Christian and Muslim religious leaders, and condemnation by traditional leaders has resulted in an unsafe social environment for gay people in Africa. The pervasive and prevalent negative attitude towards homosexuality in Africa does not necessarily result from fears of HIV transmission. Rather it reflects the people's unwillingness to get in line with the global trend of increasing acceptance of gays, lesbians, bi-sexual, and transgender lifestyles. The situation in Africa requires strategic education and advocacy campaigns, which will not be easy to accomplish because sex education in Africa presents its own contradictions.

Sex Education

In many Western countries, sex education is freely discussed between parents and their young primary school-age children. Many such children are also formally educated on human sexuality as part of the school curriculum.

The situation in Africa is quite different. Parents and teachers seem to believe that what their wards don't know cannot hurt them, and thus parents are averse to providing children with the enlightenment they need about human sexuality. Even into their teen years, many African youths are denied ready access to sex education. According to Biddlecom et al. (2007), about half of fifteen to nineteen year olds in Malawi, Kenya, Burkina Faso, Ghana, and Uganda did not receive sex education. The instruction was not available at home or offered at school, especially for students who dropped out of school before reaching the higher grades. The result is a high level of ignorance about sexually transmitted diseases. UNICEF (2009) reported that in many African countries, although more than 90 percent of fifteen to nineteen year olds have heard of HIV/AIDS, less than 40 percent know how to prevent it or how it is transmitted. Many African youths also are reportedly ignorant of other sexually transmitted infections, with Botswana and Ghana having the lowest level of knowledge. In the absence of a cure for HIV/AIDS, the best defense is effective sex education, which is best initiated before harm is done by ignorance.

Unfortunately, in many African countries and communities, talking to young people about sex and sexually transmitted infections is still taboo. Considerable progress is being made in the education of girls. However, work must continue to break the cycle of ignorant children growing up and continuing the tradition of not talking about sex with their children.

Sex education, when properly planned and successfully implemented, can be an effective tool in checking unhealthy sexual conduct among various community members of all demographic groups. Comprehensive sex education is effective in improving knowledge and reducing risky sexual behaviors. It does not necessarily increase sexual activity of which the community disapproves. Adolescents and young people are less likely to be vulnerable to HIV when they are offered relevant, gender-sensitive prevention information, skills and services in an enabling, protective environment.

Education, especially sex education, is the primary tool that can directly address the increasing incidence of new HIV/AIDS infections among the youth. The value of sex education is not limited to young people and can be one of the best approaches to addressing the increasing incidence of discordant couples. The traditional silent approach contradicts scientific knowledge and popular belief in the power of knowledge to redress problems. These contradictions are all part of the mystique surrounding HIV/AIDS in Africa. They are made even more mysterious by insidious controversies.

AFRICAN AIDS AND CONTROVERSIES

If there are contradictions in our approach to the HIV/AIDS pandemic in Africa, there are also controversies in the way HIV/AIDS is discussed. This contributes in no small way to some current challenges. The very nature of the affliction is controversial, and there is less than unanimous agreement about its origin. Views change from time to time, and at this writing, funding, new social media, and complacence appear to be driving the controversies. These shall have far-reaching consequences on how the pandemic is contained in Africa. Of the three controversial elements, funding appears to be the most critical, as it could have significant impacts on how the new social media are used as well as the effects of the broader mass media.

Funding

In a sense, there is a feeling of euphoria about HIV/AIDS in many parts of Africa because of the increased availability of local and external funding. It is now possible to extend ARVs to many HIV/AIDS patients in need. The Global Fund to Fight AIDS, Tuberculosis, and Malaria and PEPFAR are two of the most popular current funding sources. These two alone have radically changed the public perception of HIV/AIDS from an irreversible death sentence to a life-long health condition. Both provide financial resources to support treatment and care for people living with HIV, tuberculosis, and malaria. PEPFAR, which was established in 2003, during the George W. Bush presidency in the U.S., is one of the best legacies of the Bush administration and has endeared the U.S. to the African focal countries that have benefitted from this unusual generosity. The Global Fund was established in 2002 and has provided a dramatic increase in resources for the fight against the three pandemics.

Both Global Fund and PEPFAR have been very successful. In 2012 alone, 11 million pregnant women received HIV/AIDS testing and counseling due to PEPFAR. As a result, 230,000 children were born HIV free. Worldwide, approximately 9.7 million people were receiving compassionate care by 2008 and almost 2 million Africans had access to ARVs (PEPFAR 2012).

These achievements have not prevented rampant criticism and incipient controversies to follow the funds through parts of Africa. Among other things, receiving outside money might establish a culture of begging and dependency. Unilateral conditions unfavorable to African groups might also lead aided countries down the slippery road of perpetual indebtedness, laziness, poverty, higher inflation, and continuing dependency.

Some aspects of foreign funding are said to be responsible for the significant improvements in keeping more HIV/AIDS patients alive and looking healthier than would have been the case. By giving them a life line, literally in some situations, a false impression is created in some quarters that HIV/AIDS is no longer a mortal danger. Some are led to be less risk averse and to engage in more dangerous sexual conduct. In Uganda, abstinence-only campaigns as a result of PEPFAR have been blamed for HIV/AIDS infections, which had been reduced from 15 percent down to 5 percent by 2001. They had inched up to 7.3 percent a little over a decade later (Uganda Ministry of Health and ICF International 2012).

Yet another controversy is based on the unpredictable nature of foreign aid, which often depends on the internal financial and economic policies of donor countries. The outlook for increased foreign aid, including funding for global health programs, will be affected adversely by the challenges of balancing the U.S. federal budget. When the U.S. Congress enacted the Leadership Act (for PEPFAR) in 2003, the mood regarding foreign assistance was different from the national mood in 2013, when the emphasis appeared to be more on budget cuts, sequestration, and foreign debt reduction.

No doubt, some of these controversies are based on half-truths and incomplete information that need open, aggressive, and strategic communication to correct. Both Global Funds and PEPFAR are engaging in robust public enlightenment through the mass media to make their stakeholders more appreciative of their work. Both traditional and new media have critical roles to play in HIV/AIDS healthcare management in Africa. Interestingly, the new social media are becoming more commonplace throughout the continent and should contribute to the improved public enlightenment about HIV/AIDS. Unfortunately, some of the new social media have become controversial.

Social Media

Mass communication in Africa today is a far cry from William Hachten's (1971, p. xiii) characterization of it as diverse and astonishing. He saw it then as ". . . a Sudanese camel driver jogging along listening to Radio Cairo on a small transistor radio; a Ghanaian civil servant reading the *Daily Graphic* while drinking a shandy at Accra's Ambassador Hotel; a Wolof man sitting with a group of his fellow Senegalese watching an experimental television program in Dakar." Today, the Sudanese is more likely to be watching Aljazeera by satellite from Doha, Qatar. The Ghanaian may be reading *Newsweek* Magazine online at home, and the Senegalese may be listening to Radio France International on his mobile phone. Even in Africa, it is a brave new world of new media.

Such is the pervasiveness of the global media, that there is no true distinction between national (local) and international (foreign) communication. Similarly, the new social media can be both local and global at the same time. Whatever social media tools and methods are available today in Western industrialized countries are also available and useable in the industrializing countries of Africa. Blogs, Facebook, Pinterest, and YouTube, among the many social media options, are veritable tools for HIV/AIDS prevention. They are ideal for mobilizing, engaging with, educating, and empowering young people (Sidibe et al. 2012). As Cameron et al. (2013) found, social media can be effective tools for addressing a variety of public health related problems in which communication and awareness are crucial objectives. It is in this regard that a new Facebook application has been designed to help people in need of organ transplants to raise awareness about their condition and to ask for possible donors (O'Reilly 2013).

Although the many benefits of using social media in strategic HIV/AIDS communication are undeniable (Moore 2012; UNAIDS 2011), controversies swirl around the practice. In some of Africa's big cities, adventurous men and women now use social media to arrange and engage in high risk sexual escapades that portend grave consequences for HIV/AIDS and other sexually transmitted infections. One such forum is "No Strings Attached.com" (NSA), which has operations in Kenya, South Africa, and Uganda, with plans for further expansion to other African countries. Its modus operandi is to use a social media outlet to facilitate engagement in casual sex among strangers, who make no commitment or intend to ever meet again. The new social media in Africa, on their face, may appear to be the same as what has happened with new media in other parts of the world. In reality, the media in Africa are part of the continent's social landscape, and thus are taking on uniquely African cultural colorations. Only time will tell whether the new wine of social media can keep well in the old wine skins of traditional African culture. For now, the controversies that accompany use of the new social media as tools for HIV/AIDS communication in Africa are persistent and enduring. By their innovative and flippant nature, the new media in Africa tend to create a lackadaisical mood. For right or wrong reasons, they are accused of contributing to the perception, which is gaining ground in many areas, that AIDS and the diseases associated with it are no longer so deadly.

Complacence

Part of the mystique surrounding HIV/AIDS in Africa is how easily seemingly good developments, such as a positive funding climate or the availability of new social media, can become negative forces or turn into controversies. Such is the case with the current situation of reduced death from HIV/AIDS due to the successes of ARV treatments and public health education campaigns. In many African countries, cardio-vascular disorders (CVDs) are on the rise and are seen to be more dangerous than HIV/AIDS. The perception of HIV/AIDS has changed from an "instant killer" disease to a manageable health condition.

Ironically, because of the efficacy of Highly Active Antiretroviral Therapy (HAART), HIV/AIDS complacence is on the rise (Mackellar et al. 2011). Complacency is not peculiar to Africa. A recent United Nations annual AIDS epidemic update has shown that the increase in new infections is expected to rise to 5.3 million worldwide (Moulson 2012).

Complacence is partly responsible for the variegated nature of new infections in Africa, where some countries are still in grave danger while others have stabilized. According to the Uganda Ministry of Health and ICF International (2012), new infection rates had risen in that country from 124,000 in 2009 to 128,000 in 2010 and 145,000 in 2011. Rising infections despite ongoing prevention efforts demand the search for vigorous and dynamic prevention strategies that address complacence.

Treatment may be available, with a possibility to live longer, but people living with HIV/AIDS generally experience a low quality of life. HIV/AIDS causes significant life changes, many of which are not easy to adapt to. Among other effects are anemia, diarrhea, nausea and weight loss, resistance to medication despite good treatment options, and the risk of contracting different strains of the virus (AVERT 2013).

Information on HIV/AIDS is readily available, but much of it may not be wholesome. The Internet and the other new social media tools are good platforms for prevention messages, but as noted above, they can contribute to complacence especially where there are no authoritative gate-keeping checks and controls. The best medicine against complacence is persistent communication to reiterate and reinforce the message that the battle with HIV/AIDS is not over. It is only contained for now. The preceding sections have shown that the problems of HIV/AIDS in Africa are compounded by contradictions and controversies. Now we will show that all hope is not lost, as the situation increasingly reflects our ability to contain the syndrome of diseases.

HIV/AIDS IN AFRICA: CONTAINMENT

The enormous amount of resources expended on HIV/AIDS treatment and education in Africa has resulted in significant progress in the fight against the disease and has led to a state of containment of the pandemic. Talk of a cure for the HIV virus is premature and the hope for a vaccine has not materialized, yet the achievements in containment are undeniable. Referring to the progress made in the last decade worldwide, including in Africa, Simon Bland and Mphu Ramatlapeng (2013, p. 5), as board chair and board vice chair of the Global Fund, noted that "few would have imagined back in 2002 that we would have been able to successfully save millions of lives and prevent millions of infections and that we would bend the curve by halting and reversing the spread of each of these diseases" (i.e. AIDS, tuberculosis, and malaria).

The outlook for successful management of HIV/AIDS in Africa is better now than at any time in the history of the pandemic because of a combination of positive forces that include local and international results-based funding, effective partnerships among program planners and implementers, involvement of local constituents, constant learning, and local/national public leadership.

Caldwell and Caldwell (1994, p. 214) referred to the Sub-Saharan HIV/AIDS epidemic as "an extraordinary phenomenon" because, "apart from some continued infection through blood transfusions, the epidemic is sustained almost wholly by heterosexual vaginal intercourse, . . . [and] an AIDS epidemic unsupported by intravenous drug injection or homosexual, bisexual, or heterosexual anal sex is itself unique." This unique blessing has contributed in no small measure to the prevailing state of containment. The known causes of HIV/AIDS in Africa make it easier for preventive actions and strategies to be promoted among the populations at greatest risk, thereby enhancing the opportunities for better containment. HIV/AIDS containment has also benefitted from the ongoing social changes in African societies. Africa is a continent on the move, and at the same time is experiencing rapid changes in obvious and indiscernible ways. The changes are in areas ranging from government and politics to the acceptance of new values and ideas. As Berman (2013, p. 9) noted in his book, *Success in Africa*, in spite of the news media's penchant for reporting about famines and hunger in Africa while the entertainment industry builds "a fortune depicting Africa as a place for happy animals and miserable people," there is a new Africa of positive social change.

CHANGING SOCIAL VALUES

African social values and belief systems are changing fast because of the historical and ongoing encounters with Western culture. As Caldwell, Orubuloye, and Caldwell (1994, p. 233) explained, "African society and its belief systems have probably been changing more rapidly than is the case for any other major society."

These changes do not mean wholesale jettisoning of African tradition and past. In many cases, the traditional is situated side by side the modern in a creatively integrative manner. In a large number of African communities today, many erstwhile dangerous and risky behaviors and practices are being modified; some of these have implications for HIV/AIDS management and containment. Among these are early marriages for girls, wife or widow inheritance, female circumcision, and the non-education of the girl child. Family sizes, child spacing, polygamous marriages, and gender relations are some of the areas where globalization and new ideas from international development agencies have made a significant impact on African traditional values and practices. Advances in these areas are leading to improved empowerment of women, human rights, and gender equity. Many of these changes are leveraged by international organizations through their universalistic development programs, such as variegated support for the Millennium Development Goals (MDGs).

The health and education MDGs are especially providing a new sense of urgency and greater impetus for development in health and education all across Africa, even if some of the goals may not be realized in many countries by the deadline of 2015. Across the continent, new values and practices congruent with expectations for societal improvements and economic development are increasingly being adopted. Improvements have come in such areas as reduced infant and child mortality, declining family size aspirations, and renewed momentum towards better health practices. These improvements indicate a brighter future for healthcare management in Africa and are contributing in no small way to better health for all in general and better containment of HIV/AIDS in particular. These achievements notwithstanding, there are still serious challenges for healthcare in Africa.

HEALTHCARE MANAGEMENT CHALLENGES

HIV/AIDS in Africa is necessarily part of the global public healthcare management challenges. The survival of human civilization is completely dependent on our ability to successfully manage conditions in the international community. Africa is an important part of that community on account of its size, population, and proclivity for health hazards. HIV/AIDS healthcare in Africa is a necessary part of global public health, which Stone (2012, p. xxi) has explained in terms of collaborative efforts of strategic analyses and responses or interventions that transcend boundaries and address "public health problems confronting all the people of the world." AIDS in Africa cannot be isolated from global public health.

In Africa, the pandemic presents unique challenges that are compounded by the peculiar nature of the disease, the difficulty in determining how extensive it is, and the probable socio-economic and political impact. Even with the combined funding support of local and international partners, it is impossible to determine what levels are adequate to meet the needs for prevention and successful treatment.

Much progress has been made in learning about HIV/AIDS in Africa. However, the true incidence and nature of the illness still elude researchers and healthcare managers because of how sexual matters and private healthcare issues are treated in many traditional communities. Thus, over thirty years after the first cases of HIV were reported in Africa as "Slim's Disease," we still face conspicuous ignorance, conflicting points of view, unresolved controversies, and exaggerated or underestimated prevalence rates.

Poverty and political leadership complicate AIDS healthcare management. Although Africa is experiencing rapid growth in many areas, poverty is still endemic. The continent has some of the poorest countries in the world and poor people are at greatest risk for HIV/AIDS. Poverty is worse because bureaucratic political leadership in Africa serves as a catalyst for corruption, civil strife, and other social crises.

Fortunately, there are evident signs of political, economic, and social development that provide rays of hope. Many African countries are beginning to pay more attention to healthcare issues, realizing that, without good health, a society cannot develop. It is becoming clearer to many that the continent's future is inextricably linked to its healthcare management, especially containment of HIV/AIDS.

CONCLUSION

News about the discovery of "cures" for AIDS have served as a beacon of hope for combating the deadly complex of diseases, that has taunted the science community for over three decades. In July of 2013, two male AIDS patients in the U.S. were reported to be HIV-free after receiving bone marrow transplants. The virus didn't return, even after they stopped receiving treatment for a few weeks (Herper 2013). Early in the same year, an American infant was reported to be functionally cured of HIV by immediate and intensive treatment after birth. The baby had stayed free of HIV ever since (Pollack and McNeil 2013). Based on a UNAIDS report (2012b), in 2011, more than half a million fewer people died of AIDS than in 2005. This is largely due to the more affordable ARV treatment for people living with HIV.

Anecdotes and preliminary reports like these can easily raise people's hope that this may be the end of the incurable-HIV era. Besides, the decreasing incidence of new infections worldwide and the rapid growth in ARV coverage strengthens expectations for an AIDS-free generation. However, some experts are quick to caution: Not so fast—AIDS is not over (Sidibe, Piot, and Dybul 2012, p. 2058).

Globally, HIV/AIDS is still a big health burden to many countries. An estimated 34 million adults and children worldwide were living with HIV in 2011. Worldwide, the death toll was 1.9 million in 2001 and 1.7 million in 2011 (WHO 2013a). Africa, especially Sub-Saharan Africa, is significantly affected (UNAIDS 2012a). In the past decade, HIV intervention programs have achieved notable improvement in reducing mortality and diminishing new infections, yet many countries still face severe threats. Without a cure or a vaccine, HIV/AIDS will continue to cause serious setbacks in global healthcare management.

The situation in Africa is not helped by contradictions and controversies about the pandemic. The final picture that emerges combines conflicting views with controversies, in the face of a healthy dose of containment. These challenges for healthcare management suggest that, in the next several decades, the path to successfully combating HIV/AIDS in Africa will remain convoluted, complex, tasking, and tortuous. Africa, which is home to about 1.03 billion people, will remain unique in the global battle against HIV/AIDS.

BIBLIOGRAPHY

Abadía-Barrero, C. E., and Castro, A. (2006). "Experiences of Stigma and Access to HAART in Children and Adolescents Living with HIV/AIDS in Brazil," *Social Science & Medicine*, 62: pp. 1219–1228.

Afro-News (2005). *Legal Status of Homosexuality in Africa.* Available at http://www.afrol.com/categories/gay_lesbian. Accessed 22 August 2013.

AVERT (2013). "Global Fund to Fight HIV/AIDS, Tuberclosis, and Malaria (GFATM)." Avert.org. Available at http://www.avert.org/global-fund.htm. Accessed 22 August, 2013.

Baker, R. (2000). "Controversy over Male Circumcision and HIV Transmission in Developing World." Circumcision Information.com. Available at http://www.circumcisioninformation.com/baker_hiv.htm. Accessed 26 August 2013.

Berman, J. (2013). *Success in Africa: CEO Insights from a Continent on the Rise.* Brookline, MA: Bibliomotion.

Biddlecom, A.E., et al. (2007). "Protecting the Next Generation in Sub-Saharan Africa: Learning from Adolescents to Prevent HIV and Unintended Pregnancy." A paper for the Guttmacher Institute. Available at www.guttmacher.org.

Bland, S., and Ramatlapeng, M. (2013). *The Global Fund Annual Report, 2012.* Global Fund.org., released 24 July 2013. Available at http://www.theglobalfund.org/en/publications/2013-07-24_Annual_Report_2012/.

Caldwell, J.C., and Caldwell, P. (1994). "The Nature and Limits of the Sub-Saharan African AIDS Epidemic: Evidence from Geographic and Other Patterns." In Orubuloye, I.O., et al., *Sexual Networking and AIDS in Sub-Saharan Africa: Behavioural Research and the Social Context.* Canberra, Australia: Australian National University.

Caldwell, J. C., Orubuloye, I. O., and Caldwell, P. (1994). "Underreaction to AIDS in Sub-Saharan Africa." In Orubuloye, I.O., et al., *Sexual Networking and AIDS in Sub-Saharan Africa: Behavioural Research and the Social Context.* Canberra, Australia: Australian National University.

Cameron, A.M., et al. (2013). "Social Media and Organ Donor Registration: The Facebook Effect," *American Journal of Transplantation,* 13 (8), pp. 2059–2065.

DeCock, K.M., Mbori-Ngacha, D., and Marum, E. (2002). "Shadow on the Continent: Public Health and HIV/AIDS in Africa in the 21st Century," *The Lancet*, 360: pp. 67–72.

Hachten, W.A. (1971). *Muffled Drums: The News Media in Africa.* Ames, IA: Iowa State University Press.

Hankins, C., Forsythe, S., and Njeuhmeli, E. (2011). "Voluntary Medical Male Circumcision: An Introduction to the Cost, Impact, and Challenges of Accelerated Scaling up," *PLoS Medicine* 8 (11): e1001127.

Herper, M. (2013). "Hint to a Cure? Two Men Remain HIV Free After Bone Marrow Transplants," *Forbes*, July 3, 2013. Available at http://www.forbes.com/sites/matthewherper/2013/07/03/two-patients-remain-hiv-free-after-bone-marrow-transplants/. Accessed 21 August 2013.

IRIN News (2012). "Uganda: Mixed Progress in Male Circumcision Campaign," Integrated Regional Information News (IRIN), November 6, 2012. Available at http://www.irinnews.org/report/96725/uganda-mixed-progress-in-male-circumcision-campaign. Accessed 19 August, 2013.

Kaiser Family Foundation. (2013). "The U.S President's Emergency Plan for AIDS Relief (PEPFAR)," Kaiser Family Foundation Website, http://kff.org/global-health-policy/fact-sheet/the-u-s-presidents-emergency-plan-for/

Mackellar, D.A., et al. (2011). "HIV/AIDS Complacency and HIV Infection Among Young Men Who Have Sex with Men and the Race-specific Influence of Underlying HAART Beliefs," *Sexually Transmitted Diseases* 38 (8, August 2011): pp. 755–763.

Moore, A. (2012). "Making a New Media Declaration a Reality," AIDS.gov., October 23, 2012. Available at http://blog.aids.gov/2012/10/making-the-new-media-declaration-a-reality.html. Accessed 18 August, 2013.

Moulson, G. (2012). "UN: Growing AIDS Complacence Dangerous," ABC News, November 28, 2012. Available at http://abcnews.go.com/Health/story?id=116647&page=1. Accessed 22 August 2013.

Mutimura, E., Stewart, A., and Crowther, N. J. (2007). "Assessment of Quality of Life in HAART-treated HIV-positive Subjects with Body Fat Redistribution in Rwanda," *AIDS Research and Therapy*, 4: pp. 1–8.

Naurath, N. (2007). "Perceived Acceptance of Homosexuals Differs Around Globe," *Gallup World*, November 2, 2007. Available at http://www.gallup.com/poll/102478/perceived-acceptance-homosexuals-differs-around-globe.aspx#2. Accessed 19 August, 2013.

O'Reilly, K.B. (2013). "Facebook Grapples with Rules for Patients Seeking Organ Donors," *American Medical News*, July 1, 2013. Available at http://www.amednews.com/article/20130701/profession/130709967/6/?utm_campaign=20130701&utm_medium=&utm_source=rss. Accessed 19 August, 2013.

Orubuloye, I.O., et al. (1994). *Sexual Networking and AIDS in Sub-Saharan Africa: Behavioural Research and the Social Context*. Canberra, Australia: The Australian National University.

Parkhurst, J., Chilongozi, D., and Hutchinson, E. (2013). "Doubt, Defiance and Identity: Resistance to Male Circumcision Policy in Africa," a paper presented at the Social Sciences and Humanities in HIV/AIDS Conference, Paris. Available at http://www.asshhconference.org/presentations/monday/01_CS26.pdf. Accessed 27 August 2013.

Pollack, A., and McNeil, D.G. (2013). "In Medical First, a Baby with HIV Is Deemed Cured," *The New York Times*, March 3, 2013. Available at http://www.nytimes.com/2013/03/04/health/for-first-time-baby-cured-of-hiv-doctors-say.html?ref=opinion. Accessed 21 August 2013.

Prewitt, K. (1988). "Foreword: AIDS in Africa: The Triple Disaster." In N. Miller and R.C. Rockwell (1988). *AIDS in Africa: The Social and Policy Impact*. New York: Edwin Mellen Press.

Rankin, W.W., et al. (2005). "The Stigma of Being HIV-positive in Africa," *PLoS Medication*, 2: e247. At doi:10.1371/journal.pmed.0020247.

Rivers, B. (2007). "Global Fund Terminates Two Grants to Uganda," *Global Fund Observer Newsletter*, 73. Available at http://www.aidspan.org/gfo_article/global-fund-terminates-two-grants-uganda. Accessed 28 August 2013.

Rugalema, G. (2000). "Coping or Struggling? A Journey into the Impact of HIV/AIDS in Southern Africa," *Review of African Political Economy*, 27: pp. 537–545.

Sidibe, M., Piot, P., and Dybul, M. (2012). "AIDS Is Not Over," *The Lancet*, 380: pp. 2058–2060.

Stone, D.H. (2012). *The Growing Global Public Health Crisis and How to Address It*. New York: Radcliffe Publishing.

Supulveda, J., et al. (2007). *PEPFAR Implementation: Progress and Promise*, Institute of Medicine of the National Institutes. Washington, DC: National Academies Press.

Uganda Ministry of Health and ICF International (2012). "2011 Uganda AIDS Indicator Survey: Key Findings." Calverton, MD: ICF International.

UNAIDS. (2012a). "Regional Fact Sheet 2012." Available at http://www.unaids.org/en/media/unaids/contentassets/documents/epidemiology/2012/gr2012/2012_FS_regional_ssa_en.pdf. Accessed 27 August 2013.

———. (2012b). "Results 2012," World AIDS Day Report. Available at http://www.unaids.org/en/media/unaids/contentassets/documents/epidemiology/2012/gr2012/jc2434_worldaidsday_results_en.pdf. Accessed 28 August 2013.

———. (2011). "Preventing HIV with Social Media and Mobile Phones." Posted 2 May 2011. Available at http://www.unaids.org/en/resources/presscentre/featurestories/2011/may/20110502sm/. Accessed 28 August 2013.

United States President's Emergency Plan for Aids Relief (2012). "Working Together for an AIDS-free Generation: Latest PEPFAR Results." PEPFAR, World AIDS Day

2012 Update, December 2012. Available at http://www.pepfar.gov/funding/results/index.htm. Accessed 28 August 2013.

Valdiserri, R.O. (2004). "Mapping the Roots of HIV/AIDS Complacency: Implications for Program and Policy Development," *All AIDS Education and Prevention, 16* (5): pp. 426–439.

Whiteside, A. (2002). "Poverty and HIV/AIDS in Africa," *Third World Quarterly*, 23: pp. 313–332.

World Health Organization (2013a). "HIV/AIDS Fact Sheet 360." WHO Media Centre. Available at http://www.who.int/mediacentre/factsheets/fs360/en/. Accessed 28 August 2013.

———. (2013b). "HIV/AIDS Data and Statistics." WHO.org. 2013 Global Treatment Report. Available at http://www.who.int/hiv/data/en/. Accessed 28 August 2013.

Index

About the Contributors

Andy O. Alali is Professor of Communication in the Department of Communications, California State University, Bakersfield. A Fulbright Scholar at the University of Abuja, Nigeria, Alali received his Ph.D. from Howard University. His books include *Health Communication in Africa; Media Coverage of Terrorism; Mass Media Sex and Adolescent Values;* and *HIV/AIDS in Public Schools: A Primer for Policymakers.* Alali is editor of *The Journal of African Communications* and Associate Editor of the *Journal of African Social Sciences and Humanities Studies.*

Mario J. Azevedo is Interim Chair of the Department of History and Philosophy at Jackson State University. He previously served as Dean of the College of Public Service, Associate Dean of the School of Health Sciences, and Chair of the Department of Epidemiology and Biostatistics at Jackson State University, and Chair of the Department of Africana Studies at the University of North Carolina at Charlotte. Dr. Azevedo has published and edited at least a dozen books in history and health in Africa and the developing world. His peer-reviewed articles and book chapters appear in over ten referred journals.

Francis M. Bwambale is professor of health in the School of Public Health at Makerere University, Kampala, Uganda. He has received the BDS, MCs, CEB, and UMAPs. He has authored several articles on public health in Africa and has received a number of grants in health and fellowships from the USAID, CDC, and U.S. universities. Dr. Bwambale is widely known in East and Central Africa for his academic and humanitarian work, particularly in Uganda, Sudan, Kenya, and the Democratic Republic of Congo.

Cosmos Ikechukwu Eze is Senior Lecturer at Ahmadu Bello University, Zaria, Nigeria, where he joined the Department of Mass Communication in 1992. He has published conference proceedings and several book chapters, including ICTs and Language Development in Northern Nigeria: Problems and Prospects in Health Communication, Gender Violence and ICTs in Nigeria, published by Ibadan University Press.

Adebayo Fayoyin serves as Regional Communications Adviser with UNFPA in its regional office in Johannesburg, South Africa. He has assisted various development organizations in designing, implementing, and monitoring advocacy, health communication, and corporate communication projects. With a Ph.D. in communication and language arts from the University of Ibadan, Nigeria, he has over twenty years of field experience in communication for development and social and behavior change. Dr. Fayoyin oversees more than twenty-five media and communication centers.

SubbaRao M. Gavaravrapu serves as a senior scientist at India's National Institute of Nutrition. He has been the ICMR International Fellow at the Johns Hopkins Bloomberg School of Public Health, Baltimore. His Ph.D. in health communication is from the University of Hyderabad, India. His research interests are in nutrition and food safety communication, with special emphasis on social, behavioral, and cultural aspects of the communicative processes. He is Asian editor for the *American Journal of Health Behavior*.

Tom S. Kiiza is Interim Director of the Public Health Program and Academic Registrar at the Mountains of the Moon University, Fort Portal, Uganda. He is building a health center in Kasese District in Western Uganda. He holds degrees in Philosophy and Religious Studies. His research interests are in religion, philosophy, globalization, public health, and animal kingdom conservation.

Achu Lordfred, a specialist in obstetrics and gynecology, serves as Senior Reproductive and Maternal Health Adviser for the United Nations Fund for Population in Somalia. He received the MD from the Faculté de Médecine et des Sciences Biomédicales de Yaoundé, Cameroon, and Geneva University. His research interests are in reproductive and maternal health, adolescent and youth sexual and reproductive health and rights, gender issues related to sexual and reproductive health and rights.

Srinivas Melkote has taught in the fields of telecommunications, journalism, and mass communication for over thirty years. He is Professor of Communication in the School of Media and Communication Studies at Bowling Green (Ohio) State University. Dr. Melkote holds degrees in Journalism and Sociology from the University of Iowa and the University of Osmania India, respectively. He has published extensively in books and journal writings on the role of communication and mass communication in directed social change, participatory communication, health communication, strategies for HIV/AIDS prevention, and related areas.

Angella Napakol holds a master's degree in Mass Communication and serves as a lecturer in the Department of Mass Communication at Uganda Christian University, Mukono. Her research interests are health communication, risk and crisis communication and public relations, and intercultural communication.

Emmanuel Ngwainmbi is graduate professor of communication and chair of the Department of Mass Communication at Jackson State University in Jackson, Mississippi. He is on the editorial board of the *Journal Intercultural Disciplines* and *Journal of Development and Communication Studies.* He is the author of twelve books and numerous other writings on the black experience, Africa's development, international communication, and globalization. Ngwainmbi lectures widely in the United States, Europe, Asia, and Africa on culture, mediation, and the new world order.

Charles Okigbo holds Ph.D.s in Education and Journalism from Southern Illinois University, an MPA in Public Policy and Administration from Harvard's Kennedy School of Government, and graduate degrees from the University of Ohio, University of Leicester (UK), and University of Nigeria, Nsukka. He was pioneer registrar of the Advertising Practitioners Council of Nigeria (APCON) and executive coordinator of the African Council for Communication Education (ACCE). Okigbo has consulted for governments and UN agencies and edited books in mass communication. His publications have appeared in *Action Research, Journalism Quarterly, Journalism and Mass Communication Educator, Journal of Development Communication,* and *Qualitative Market Research: An International Journal,* among others. He teaches Advertising/PR Principles and Practices, Communication Analysis, Health Communication, and Strategic Communication Research at North Dakota State University, Fargo, and coordinates the Global Mass Media Project.

Ravindra Kumar Vemula holds a doctorate in communication from the University of Hyderabad, India. An Assistant Professor of Mass Communication and Journalism, School of Communication, at the English and Foreign Languages University, Hyderabad, India, his research interests are health, development, and international communication and new media theories. Dr. Vemula is co-chair of the HIV/AIDS and Communication Working Group of the International Association for Media and Communication Research (IAMCR). He has published in such journals as the *Journal of Creative communications; Media Asia; Journal of Global Communications;* and the *International journal of Development Communication.*

Nan Yu holds a doctorate in Mass Communication and serves as an assistant professor in the Department of Communication at North Dakota State University, Fargo. Her research focuses on understanding cultural influences in health practices and the use of new technologies to improve health education and health behavior. Her research has appeared in many journals, including Health Communication, International Public Health Journal, Visual Communication Quarterly, Electronic News, and *International Journal of Human-Computer Studies.*

ABOUT THE EDITOR

Emmanuel Ngwainmbi is graduate professor of communication and chair of the Department of Mass Communication at Jackson State University in Jackson, Mississippi. He serves as a senior communication consultant to various United Nations agencies and has served on the editorial board of the *Journal Intercultural Disciplines, Journal of Black Studies,* and the *Journal of Development and Communication Studies.* A reviewer for the

International Journal of Communication, among others, and the author of numerous articles, book chapters, and monographs on black experiences, Africa's development, international communication, and globalization, Professor Ngwainmbi has authored thirteen books and numerous book chapters and scholarly articles. Some of his writings appear in the Columbia University International Affairs online journal, *Sage*, and Greenwood Press.

Among other works, Professor Ngwainmbi is the author of *The Unpaid Dowry*, *Exporting Communication to Developing Countries*, *A Bush of Voices*, and *Shackles on a Ghost's Skull*. He has contributed to Encyclopedias of African Religions and anthologies and has received awards in journalism and the social sciences from the Chinese Academy for Social Sciences, Who's Who among America's Teachers, among many others.

www.ingramcontent.com/pod-product-compliance
Lightning Source LLC
LaVergne TN
LVHW101446200926
848483LV00001B/61